THE LIBRARY OF
PHILOSOPHY AND THEOLOGY

Edited by
JOHN MCINTYRE AND IAN T. RAMSEY

THE LOGIC OF SELF-INVOLVEMENT

THE LOGIC OF SELF-INVOLVEMENT

*A Philosophical Study of Everyday Language
with Special Reference to the Christian Use
of Language about God as Creator*

DONALD D. EVANS

*Assistant Professor of Philosophy of Religion
McGill University*

SCM PRESS LTD
BLOOMSBURY STREET LONDON

FIRST PUBLISHED 1963
© SCM PRESS LTD 1963
PRINTED IN GREAT BRITAIN BY
THE CAMELOT PRESS LTD
LONDON AND SOUTHAMPTON

CONTENTS

II · SELF-INVOLVING ELEMENTS IN THE BIBLICAL CONCEPTION OF CREATION

PREFACE

THIS BOOK has involved both philosophical analysis and theological study. The philosophical analysis is the result not only of private reading and reflection but also of many discussions with other philosophers. I cannot mention all of these, but I should like specially to acknowledge the help which I have received from Mr J. O. Urmson and Professor I. T. Ramsey, and also from Professor Gilbert Ryle, Mr R. M. Hare, Mr Graeme de Graaff and Lady Oppenheimer. During three Oxford terms I worked under the late Professor J. L. Austin. In chapter 1, I shall acknowledge my use of his original work concerning performative language, which forms the starting-point for the rest of the book. Here I wish to pay tribute to him as a teacher of philosophical method: he was exacting and stimulating and kind.

In the general field of biblical theology, I am greatly indebted to Professor James Barr for his warm encouragement and his vigorous criticisms. I have also consulted Professor Barr, Dr G. B. Caird and Professor S. B. Frost concerning some details of biblical scholarship. I am very grateful to the Reverend W. A. Whitehouse; when I was struggling with an early draft of the book, he reassured me that my new venture in philosophy of religion was really worth pursuing.

My wife deserves a special tribute. Not only has she helped me to clarify various obscurities in the text; she has lived with this creation on Creation for four long years.

The Canada Council and McGill University provided grants which helped to make it financially possible to write this book.

Naturally no one except myself is responsible for the views which have been presented or the mistakes which may have been made.

Note that all biblical quotations are from the Revised Standard Version (R.S.V.) unless another translation is indicated. For the Authorized (King James) Version I have used the abbreviation 'A.V.'; for the New English Bible, 'N.E.B.'. The abbreviation '*op. cit.*' is used only when the work has been cited, with full title, within the previous three pages of the book.

INTRODUCTION

1. *Self-involving language and Creation*

IN WHAT ways is language self-involving? That is, what are the logical connections between a man's utterances and his practical commitments, attitudes and feelings?

In this book we shall consider self-involvement in everyday language and in religious language. In the latter case, we shall focus our attention on one complex example: Christian language concerning Creation. In saying, 'The Creator made the world', does a man commit himself to any future conduct, or imply that he has a particular attitude or intention, or express a feeling or attitude? Or is the utterance a neutral, impersonal statement of fact, like saying, 'Jones built the house'? Rudolph Bultmann, the biblical theologian, claims that an affirmation concerning God as Creator '*cannot* be made as a neutral statement, but only as thanksgiving and surrender.'[1] Bultmann would admit that some people do in fact treat such utterances as neutral statements, but he would deny that such people have a properly *biblical* or *existential* conception of Creation; their language is not the 'language of faith'.[2] Like other biblical theologians, however, he does not provide an adequate account of how any language can involve a speaker logically in something more than a mere assent to a fact.

Modern philosophical analysis has provided the beginnings of such an account. R. M. Hare,[3] P. Nowell-Smith[4] and others have explored the language of morals in such a way that the whole area of logically-self-involving language has been opened up. And, as we shall see, J. L. Austin's discovery of 'performative' language gives us a fundamental insight concerning linguistic or logical self-involvement. But it seems to me that an

---

[1] *Jesus Christ and Mythology*, London, 1960, p. 69, my italics.
[2] *Ibid.*, p. 67.   [3] *The Language of Morals*, Oxford, 1952.
[4] *Ethics*, London, 1954.

adequate and accurate map of the whole territory has not yet
been given. In Part I of this book I shall try to provide such a
'map'. In Part II, I shall make use of this map as I give a
detailed analysis of the biblical conception of divine Creation.

Part I is an analysis of 'self-involving' elements in everyday
language. The meaning of this technical term will not become
fully clear until the analysis is completed, but I can at least
indicate the meaning by giving some examples here:

(1a)   In saying, 'I submit to your authority', I *commit* myself to
       various future *actions*.
(1b)   In saying, 'Thank you for your kindness', I *imply* that I have
       an *attitude* of gratitude.
(2)   In saying, 'Glorious!', I *express* my *feelings*.
(3)   In saying, 'I look on life as a game', I *express* my *attitude*
       towards life.

These examples of self-involving language are taken from the
three chapters of Part I. Chapter 1 deals with commitments to
action and implications of attitude or intention; chapter 2 deals
with expressions of feeling; and chapter 3 deals with expressions
of attitude.

What would be an example of an utterance which is *not* self-
involving? Consider, 'Jones built the house'. In saying this, I
do not commit myself to future conduct (except to such purely
verbal conduct as not asserting something which contradicts
this statement). In saying this, I do not imply that I have any
particular attitude or intention (though I do imply that I
believe what I say). In saying this, I do not express any particular feeling. And in saying this, I do not express any particular attitude. Since the utterance, 'The Creator made the
world' seems to be rather like, 'Jones built the house', we might
expect to find that it too is not self-involving. But in Part II we
shall see that, when it occurs in the biblical context, it *is* self-
involving. (The relation between context and linguistic self-
involvement in everyday language will be considered in Part I.)

The self-involving elements in everyday language are often
connected with correlative human *actions*. If the Queen appoints
me as her steward, and I acknowledge this new status and role
by saying, 'The Queen has appointed me as her steward,' I
commit myself to future conduct in accordance with the status
and role. This is an example of an *institutional* action (appointing)

for which a self-involving utterance is a correlative response. There are also *impressive* and *expressive* actions for which a self-involving utterance is a correlative response. For example, a pianist's concert may move me to express my feelings as I exclaim, 'Magnificent!' In Part II we shall see that, according to the biblical conception of Creation, God's action is an appointing of creatures to a status and role, and an impressive-expressive revelation of His glory. A man acknowledges his status and role, and he expresses his feeling of reverent exaltation, when he says, 'The Creator made the world'—if he says this in the biblical context.

Since I will use the analysis of everyday language and everyday actions to shed light on biblical language and divine actions, I may arouse various suspicions. On the one hand, philosophers may wonder whether a religious bias will lead to a misuse of secular materials. On the other hand, theologians may fear a distortion of distinctive biblical conceptions as these are forced to fit into yet another philosopher's procrustean bed of alien, non-biblical categories. Contemporary analytic philosophy and contemporary biblical theology have become so settled in their divorce, and so sure of their mutual irrelevance or antagonism, that any attempt to combine both fields in a single book runs the risk of not receiving a fair hearing from either side. So here I should assure both sorts of reader that I have at least been aware of hazards in my enterprise.

Readers whose interests are mainly philosophical may be encouraged to read Part I when they come to see that it is not merely a prolegomenon to Part II, but an autonomous study of self-involving elements in everyday language. By itself, Part I is very relevant to important issues in the philosophy of mind (for example, the nature of intentions, opinions and feelings), and in moral philosophy (for example, the 'autonomy of value': no statement of fact entails a value-judgment). Moreover, the philosophical reader need not go on to Part II in order to understand Part I.

But the reader whose interests are mainly theological does need to read Part I in order to understand Part II. Thus he may wonder whether all the technical detail in Part I is really necessary for Part II. It *is* necessary, not only for Part II but also for modern theology in general. Modern theology needs a new logic, and Part I provides the rudiments of such a logic: it enables us to classify with precision the various ways in which language may involve a speaker in something more than a bare assent to facts.[1] Such a classification can only be precise if there is a careful study of many examples, so that each generalization concerning self-involving language can be tested, and the key terms of the classification can be given a clear meaning.

Why does modern theology need a new logic? Part II provides a detailed (though indirect) answer to this question, but here I should indicate the main reason. Older logics deal with propositions (statements, assertions); that is, they deal with relations between propositions and relations between terms of propositions. Modern biblical theology, however, emphasizes *non-propositional* language, both in its account of divine revelation (God's 'word' to man) and in its account of human religious language (man's word to God).[2] In each case the language or 'word' is not (or is not merely) propositional; it is primarily a *self-involving activity*, divine or human. God does not (or does not merely) provide supernatural information concerning Himself, expressed in flat statements of fact; He 'addresses' man in an 'event' or 'deed' which commits Him to man and which expresses His inner Self. Similarly man does not (or does not merely) assert certain facts about God; he addresses God in the activity of worship, committing himself to God and expressing his attitude to God. In so far as God's self-revelation is a self-involving activity ('His Word is claim and promise, gift and demand')[3] and man's religious language is also a self-involving verbal activity ('obedient, thankful confession and prayer'),[4] theology needs an outline of the various ways in which language is self-involving—and, more generally, an outline of the various

---

[1] This is not traditional logic, and some philosophers may object to calling it 'logic' at all. It does seem to me, however, that some of the connections which we shall consider are as timeless and as rigorous as any in traditional logic: indefeasible implications (p. 46 and p. 48, n. 1); performative force and entailment (pp. 59-64). On the other hand, many of the connections obviously differ from those in traditional logic; these belong to what Professor Gilbert Ryle has called, '*informal*' logic (*Dilemmas*, Cambridge, 1954, pp. 111-29).

[2] See, for example, Emil Brunner, *The Divine-Human Encounter*, tr. A. W. Loos, London, 1944, pp. 44-64; cf. Karl Barth concerning God's 'word' to man in *Church Dogmatics*, I, 1, Eng. tr., Edinburgh, 1936, pp. 141-212; cf. also my discussion of Martin Buber, pp. 259-60.

[3] Brunner, op. cit., p. 62.   [4] *Ibid.*

ways in which language is an activity. Theologians are not unaware of this need. A distinguished Barthian once said to me, 'What we require is a theology of the *verb*, rather than the noun or adjective.' We shall see later that the prominence of verbs in explicit performative utterances gives point to this rather enigmatic remark, although grammatical distinctions (verb, noun, adjective) are not fundamental.

2. *Ordinary language and biblical language*

Some theologians may be surprised by the fact that in Part II I appeal to biblical language rather than to everyday language, for analytic philosophers do not usually give much detailed consideration to biblical language. Indeed, this neglect has moved one prominent theologian to indulge in some rather excessive condemnation:

'Linguistic analysis in this context means the scientific study of biblical language with the help of the resources of modern methods in philology, and so on, with a view to discovering what such words as "God" really mean. It is ignorance of and indifference to such scientific and technical language-study which render value-less most of those articles by contemporary linguistic philosophers on the subject of religious statements which from time to time adorn the pages of the philosophical journals. The only linguistic analysts of Christian "religious statements" are Old Testament scholars, or at least those who have listened carefully to what the Old Testament scholars say.'[1]

I am not an Old Testament scholar, but I have tried to listen carefully to what Old Testament (and New Testament) scholars say. My appeal to biblical language, however, is not merely a device for avoiding harsh criticism from theologians. There are sound philosophical reasons for such a procedure. Analytic philosophers insist on an appeal to *ordinary* language; and if a philosopher who studies Christian beliefs wants to use the same method that he employs elsewhere (in his study of history or science or morals or perception), the ordinary language to which he *should* appeal is biblical language.

This will seem paradoxical only if one fails to understand what analytic philosophers mean by 'ordinary' language. Those who appeal to 'ordinary' language are not opposed to all

[1] Alan Richardson, *The Bible in the Age of Science*, London, 1961, p. 149.

language which is unusual or technical, though they are wary about using the technical language of much traditional philosophy. It is not that the man-in-the-street's use of a word is always the final court of appeal. Rather, the philosopher studies how the word is used in its typical settings, whether these uses of the word are everyday or technical, usual or unusual. The meaning of a word or phrase is to be found by first observing it in its natural habitat, before it moves into philosophical captivity. Sometimes the context which is to be taken as typical or fundamental is not obvious. For example, in an analysis of the word 'good', do we begin with 'good sewer-effluent' or 'good man'? Often, however, it is quite clear where we need to begin. If we want to understand the meaning of 'scientific law', it would be folly to begin with the philosopher's favourite, 'All swans are white', as a typical law. We should find out what statements are actually called 'laws' by scientists, and see how these function in scientific language as a whole. Similarly, before we launch into any general discussion of determinism and free will, we should first note in detail how we actually use such words as 'intentional', 'involuntary', or 'motive' in particular contexts. An analysis of legal concepts likewise involves a study of the way in which particular legal words are used in their natural 'habitat', the court-room. Similarly a study of 'historical explanation' will involve an examination of the writings of historians to see how they use such words as 'explain' or 'because'. And an analysis of perception requires an initial survey of the everyday use of such words as 'look', 'appear' or 'real'. In each case, the philosopher may suggest changes in the language, and he may set forth good reasons for such changes. But his recommendations will have little relevance unless they spring from an initial analysis of the 'ordinary' language.

What is the 'natural habitat' in which we should begin a study of what Christians mean by 'God the Creator'? Presumably it is where the words are typically *used*, rather than *talked about*: worship, preaching, private prayer, and Christian religious discussion. The basic context for all of these is a book which is their norm, the Bible. Christians do not agree concerning the nature and scope of the Bible's authority; but both Protestants and Catholics, in different ways, accept it as the norm and background for all Christian discourse. And in both traditions the rise of the 'liturgical movement' and of 'biblical theology' has reinforced this linguistic authority. Hence modern analytic philosophers who investigate Christian conceptions should examine them in relation to biblical language; and they should study the biblical materials with the same devotion to detail which other philosophers require in their analyses of historical, legal or scientific materials. This has not happened. For various reasons, recent analytic philosophy of religion has been preoccupied with one issue, the positivist challenge: If nothing could count against the truth of religious utterance S, and yet S purports to be a statement of fact, S is meaningless. Many interpretations of religious language have been outlined in relation to this challenge, and to the general contrast between scientific and religious language;[1] but the work of *detailed* analysis has scarcely begun. With the exception of Ninian Smart's *Reasons and Faiths*[2] and perhaps O. R. Jones' *The Concept of Holiness*,[3] recent philosophical studies of religious language have not generally been comparable to recent philosophical analyses in other fields—in law[4] or history,[5] for example. (I mean that they have not been comparable in conception and technique; no judgment of merit is implied.) No analytic philosopher, to my knowledge, has investigated the Christian conception of Creation by carrying out a minute examination of biblical language concerning Creation. Smart does not attempt a detailed examination of biblical language in particular, for he is interested (quite legitimately) in a comparative survey of several religions. Jones has considered the Christian conception of holiness in relation to its biblical background, but his study only overlaps slightly with mine.[6]

My main point, in any case, is that the basic 'ordinary' language to which an analytic philosopher should appeal when he considers *Christian* conceptions is biblical language. If analytic philosophers have failed to do this, it is certainly not

---

[1] See F. Ferré, *Language, Logic and God*, New York, 1961, for an excellent survey of recent analytic philosophy of religion; see also section I of my bibliography.
[2] London, 1958.   [3] London, 1961.
[4] E.g., H. L. A. Hart and A. M. Honoré, *Causation in the Law*, Oxford, 1959.
[5] E.g., W. Dray, *Laws and Explanation in History*, Oxford, 1957.
[6] See p. 141, n. 1 and p. 183, n. 5.

B

because their method precludes such an appeal. Let us therefore have a closer look at 'biblical language'.

3. *Biblical language, biblical theology and philosophical analysis*

Since the application of current techniques of logical analysis to biblical language is a new enterprise, it raises new problems of method. There are few philosophical precedents or models to guide the beginner. One thing soon becomes clear, however. Biblical scholars have already carried out an intensive study of words in the Bible, and they are specially qualified for this job by their knowledge of ancient cultures and languages. And, as we shall see, the scholars sometimes go beyond mere historical language-study; in so far as they are theologians, they analyse biblical concepts and conceptions, using methods which occasionally are similar to those of modern philosophical analysis. So the philosopher finds that some of his initial work has been done for him already, by people who are in a better position to do it.

But when a philosopher approaches biblical ideas by making use of the initial work of biblical experts, he should realize that the material which they provide for his analysis differs somewhat from the sort of 'ordinary-language' material which is provided by contemporary scientific books, everyday perception-talk or historical writings. Suppose, for example, that we consult the biblical experts concerning the meaning of the biblical words which are translated as 'holy' and 'spirit'. The biblical scholar or linguist can give us an answer in historical terms: what a word probably meant at a particular period in a particular community; or what a word in a particular biblical passage probably meant to the particular man who wrote it. But the biblical *theologian* assumes that a biblical word as such— abstracted from such particular contexts—has an *essential* meaning. That is, he is interested not only in the meaning which an important theological word had for the community of Israel in 1000 B.C. and 700 B.C. and for the Church in A.D. 75, not only in what meaning the word had for the writer of one verse and for the writer of another verse, but also in an alleged essential meaning which includes its proper meaning for the Christian community today. His procedure depends on a religious assumption or belief: the 'essential' meaning of a key biblical word is the meaning for which a biblical theologian searches because he believes in the *unity* of the biblical revelation and in its contemporary relevance and *normativeness*. He makes an assumption which ensures for him a unity of meaning for the word 'holy' or 'spirit': The New Testament is the norm for the Old Testament (that is, as to which Old Testament connotations of a word are relevant and acceptable);[1] and the whole Bible is the norm for legitimate Christian discourse today. The work of a biblical theologian is not only descriptive, though it depends on historical scholarship; it is also selective, interpretative and *prescriptive*.

Biblical theologians have a second assumption as well. They look for a systematic connection or association between various biblical words (for example, between 'creation', 'covenant' and 'glory'); what they eventually expound is not a relatively simple idea or concept, but a complex biblical conception (for example, the biblical *conception* of Creation). That is, they assume that the unity of the Bible involves not only an essential meaning for particular key-words, but also a close interconnection of meaning among these words. To some extent, such inter-connections can be discovered and described by historical scholars who want to know what associations of meaning a word actually had for a particular biblical writer; for it is clear that these writers were consciously thinking within the broad framework of a religious tradition. But the biblical theologian goes beyond such historical considerations in so far as he selects and prescribes connections of meaning which are to be recognized by Christians today.[2]

All this complicates the task of an analytic philosopher who tries to study biblical language as the context for Christian

[1] Note that the Old Testament was a 'norm' for the New Testament writers in that the relevant and acceptable connotations of an important theological word came mainly from the Old Testament rather than from (for example) classical Greek literature.

[2] Biblical theologians tend not to acknowledge the selective and prescriptive aspects of their work; at the very least, they overemphasize its historical and descriptive nature. If my account of their assumptions concerning 'essential meaning' and 'systematic connection' is correct, an adequate *justification* of their procedure would seem to be required. I have not seen one, and I can not provide one here; complex issues concerning theories of revelation and biblical authority are involved. I think that such a justification could perhaps be given in terms of an appeal to some of the insights of modern literary criticism; see Northrop Frye, *Anatomy of Criticism*, Princeton, 1957. See also A. Farrer, *The Glass of Vision*, London, 1948.

discourse today. For he can only approach the words of the Bible *via* a biblical theology which is prescriptive and selective. In order to study the religious language-in-*use* he must choose a second-order theological language in which men *talk about* this religious language, selecting, interpreting and prescribing. This choice of a biblical theology is not settled by logical analysis; logical analysis presupposes this choice. Before one can proceed with the analysis, one must decide to follow a particular biblical theologian, or to combine ideas from various biblical theologians, or to create a biblical theology for one-self.[1]

In this book I have assumed that, in the total biblical context, there is an essential meaning for the word 'Creator', and a close association of meaning between this word and other words such as 'covenant' and 'glory'; only this two-fold assumption makes it possible to talk about the 'biblical conception' of Creation. Moreover, my philosophical analysis of biblical language in Part II presupposes a particular biblical theology. Like any other biblical theology, mine depends on the descriptive studies of historical scholars; but like any other biblical theology it involves interpretative selections and prescriptions. I have tried to reflect some of the main trends in contemporary biblical theology. But I have not hesitated to introduce some of my own interpretations, especially in chapter 6. The choice or creation of a biblical theology involves many difficult questions of hermeneutics—questions of general theory[2] and questions of detailed exegesis. These questions cannot possibly be discussed in the book itself. But the reader should realize that they exist, and that philosophical analysis by itself does not answer them.

I do not claim that philosophical and theological questions can be kept completely separate. Indeed, although I do not profess to see everything that this book implies for theology, (for it is a new venture in philosophy of religion), I should say

---

[1] My own theology of Creation is a 'creation' in which I am conscious of having been influenced by Barth, Brunner, Bultmann, Bevan, Barr and Buber. (I should perhaps add the names of Pedersen, Foerster and Farrer, lest some Freudian should detect an obsession with 'B'-theologians!)

[2] For an excellent survey of such questions, see James D. Smart, *The Interpretation of Scripture*, London, 1961. For a pungent criticism of current arguments based on the alleged distinctiveness of the Hebrew language, see James Barr, *The Semantics of Biblical Language*, Oxford, 1961.

something more here concerning the relation between philosophy and theology—in the past and in this book. In the past, philosophers have provided for theology a logic, a metaphysic, or an apologetic, or all three of these. What is it that I am trying to do?

(1) *Logic*. The provision of a logic for theology need not involve the dictation of particular answers to particular theological questions. Indeed, a logic may provide a framework within which theologians can *dis*agree intelligibly. For example, Peter Martyr, the Reformation theologian, accepted Thomas Aquinas' Aristotelian logic of 'analogy', but he disagreed radically with Aquinas concerning its application in theology.[1] Similarly my logic of 'onlooks' provides a framework for intelligible disagreement between theologians who are dogmatists or liberals,[2] individualists or communalists,[3] objectivists or subjectivists.[4] On the other hand, a new logic may very well be in tension with earlier theologies in so far as these are bound up with earlier logics. The reader will make his own judgment concerning this when he sees the theories of religious meaning and religious truth which gradually emerge as I apply the logic to the biblical materials. I suspect that theologians in the Aristotelian, Platonic or Cartesian traditions will not be pleased, though I hope that they will be interested.

(2) *Metaphysics*. Philosophy has sometimes provided a metaphysical terminology which allegedly enables exegetes and theologians to 'translate' biblical passages or credal affirmations into philosophical statements. Schleiermacher, for example, reduced propositions concerning God to descriptions of human states of mind which include a 'feeling of absolute dependence';[5] and, more recently, Bultmann has expounded scripture and dogma in terms drawn from Heidegger's existentialism. In this book, however, I am not trying to 'translate' Bible or creed in terms of a metaphysic which arises out of philosophical reflection. Instead, I have taken some of the metaphysical ideas in modern biblical theology and explored these as an analytic

---

[1] See J. C. McLelland, *The Visible Words of God*, Edinburgh, 1957, pp. 82-3: 'For Martyr, the theological analogy of proportionality does not rest on a doctrine of ontological continuity between God and man, but on the *unio hypostica* of God and man in the Person of Jesus Christ.'

[2] See p. 255. [3] See p. 139. [4] See pp. 251-2.

[5] F. Schleiermacher, *The Christian Faith*, 2nd ed., tr. H. R. Mackintosh, Edinburgh, 1928, especially pp. 126, 194.

philosopher. This procedure does not imply any belief that it is possible to *derive* a complete and satisfactory metaphysic from the Bible by itself. Serious difficulties arise if one attempts to derive such a metaphysic from features of the Bible which are merely grammatical or lexical.[1] Moreover, one's theology is bound to be affected by non-biblical metaphysical assumptions from philosophy or from the 'common sense' of one's culture. It does seem to me, however, that it is possible and desirable to let the Bible say the first and decisive word in any Christian metaphysic.

(3) *Apologetics.* Philosophy has sometimes provided not only a metaphysical terminology for interpreting theology, but also an armoury of arguments for defending theology: 'proofs' for the existence of God and 'evidences' for the truth of Christianity. In this book I undertake no such defence. I should make it clear, however, that this omission does not arise from any conviction that Christian apologetics is simply a mistake. I do not have any such conviction. But since my procedure may create the impression that I do, a disclaimer is in order. Though I shall use various techniques of contemporary philosophical analysis, I do not share the assumptions of some of its practitioners. We have seen that the analyst appeals first to 'ordinary' language, language being used in its natural habitat, and he applies various techniques which elucidate the logical structure of this language. For example, he analyses talk about material objects, so as to exhibit what Wittgenstein would call the 'rules' of this 'language-game', the 'moves' which can be made within it. I accept this general approach in philosophy. But sometimes it is accompanied by the following assumption: Any attempt to reject a language-game as a whole (for example, all talk about material objects or all talk about God) is a logical error; since people do in fact talk in a particular way their words do have a use and hence a meaning; there is accordingly no further question as to whether anything real or existing is referred to in the language-game as a whole; a language-game is neither open to any attack from outside itself, nor dependent on any justification from outside itself. This assumption is exemplified in part by Norman Malcolm when he claims that one 'cannot meaningfully say or

---

[1] See James Barr, *op. cit.*, and *Biblical Words for Time*, London, 1962, chs. 6-7.

think' that there is no God, since the word 'God', in the Judaeo-Christian language-game, means 'necessarily-existing being'.[1]

It is interesting to compare Malcolm, the follower of Wittgenstein, with Karl Barth, the neo-orthodox theologian. For Barth makes a similar assumption concerning the biblical 'language-game', which he calls 'the Word of God' or 'Church proclamation':

'In the Word of God it is decided that the knowledge of God cannot let itself be called in question, or call itself in question, from any position outside itself. . . . It is quite impossible to ask whether God is knowable, because this question is already decided by the only legitimate and meaningful questioning which arises in this connexion. The only legitimate and meaningful questions in this context are: how far is God known? and how far is God knowable? These questions are legitimate and meaningful because they are genuine questions of Church proclamation and therefore also genuine questions of dogmatics.'[2]

For Barth, dogmatic theology is similar to what Wittgenstein calls logical 'grammar';[3] it exhibits the conceptual structure of biblical language. One does not attempt to justify or defend biblical language; one merely displays its inner logical connections.

Personally, I reject the philosophical view of language as something to be divided up into language-games which are each self-justifying and autonomous.[4] And I reject the

---

[1] 'Anselm's Ontological Arguments', *The Philosophical Review*, January, 1960, pp. 61-2.

[2] *Church Dogmatics*, II, 1, Eng. tr., Edinburgh, 1957, pp. 4-5. According to John McIntyre, Barth's theological method depends a great deal on his interpretation of Anselm (*St Anselm and His Critics*, London, 1954, p. 25); it is interesting to notice that, as presented by McIntyre (p. 30), Barth's interpretation of Anselm is very similar to Norman Malcolm's interpretation.

[3] L. Wittgenstein, *Philosophical Investigations*, tr. G. E. M. Anscombe, Oxford, 1953, Part I, numbers 371 and 373: *'Essence* is expressed by grammar.' 'Grammar tells us what kind of object anything is. (Theology as grammar.)' Here are some other 'grammatical' utterances:

'One plays patience by oneself' (no. 248).
'Sensations are private' (no. 248).
'Every rod has a length' (no. 251).
'My right hand can't give my left hand money' (no. 268).

Cf. Barth: 'If the knowledge of a "God" is or even can be attacked from without . . . then that "God" is manifestly not God but a false god" (*op. cit.*, p. 7).

[4] I am more interested in disclaiming this view myself than in ascribing it to anyone else. I have occasionally encountered it in philosophical discussion with followers of Wittgenstein, and Malcolm's article does exemplify it to some extent; but it is doubtful whether one should ascribe it to Wittgenstein himself.

theological view that the existence of God and the possibility of knowing God are questions which need not and must not be raised once we have noted that the biblical 'language-game' is in fact played, that 'Church proclamation' does occur. Questions of theological truth are not replaceable by questions concerning the internal logical 'grammar' of biblical language. Nevertheless, it seems to me that the latter questions should be answered *first*. That is, before we ask, 'Does the Creator-God in whom Christians believe actually exist?' we should ask, 'What does "God the Creator" mean in biblical language?' (Similarly, before asking 'Are there ghosts?' we are wise if we ask, 'What is meant by the word "ghost"?')

In this book we shall consider questions of logic and meaning, leaving questions of existence and truth to the last few pages. I have avoided Christian apologetics. Of course, if 'Christian apologetics' means a defence of Christian beliefs not against the charge of falsity but against the charge of *meaninglessness*, then this book *is* a piece of Christian apologetics; for I have tried to elucidate the meaning of Christian beliefs concerning Creation. I have not tried to justify these beliefs, however; I have refrained from traditional apologetics. I have done this, not because I think that an attempt to justify Christian beliefs arises from a conceptual blunder which some modern philosophers or theologians have detected, but because questions of meaning should precede questions of truth (and because no book should be too long!). The clarification of what someone means should help us to understand what sort of 'truth' is alleged, and to decide whether or not to accept his belief as true. But the fact that a word has a meaning does not guarantee that it refers to anything; and the fact that a word has a use does not justify the use.

Now, however, let us leave these general issues. Let us for the time being forget about theology, and let us focus our attention on the self-involving elements in everyday language.

I

SELF-INVOLVING ELEMENTS IN EVERYDAY LANGUAGE

I

THE PERFORMATIVE FORCE OF LANGUAGE

OUR FIRST step in the analysis of self-involving language is an investigation of J. L. Austin's discovery of 'performatives'. In this chapter I shall set forth his main ideas in a somewhat modified form, and I shall subject them to further analysis so as to elucidate self-involving language.[1] ('Performatives' are important in religious language: in Part II we shall see that both God's use of His 'word' in creation, and men's use of their words in talk about God as Creator, are 'performative'.)

1. *Performatives and Infelicities*

Consider the following examples of things that people may say:

'I pledge you my loyalty and support.'
'I accept full responsibility for the accident.'
'I, John, take thee, Ann, to be my lawful wedded wife.'
'I appoint you Governor of Kenya.'
'I name this ship the *Ivernia*.'
'I authorize you to speak for the Party.'
'I order you to stop smoking within ten days.'
'I baptize you in the name of Jesus.'
'I divorce you.'
'I thank you.'

---

[1] Austin's account of performatives is to be found in *How to do Things with Words*, edited from lecture notes by J. O. Urmson, Oxford, 1962. See also *Philosophical Papers* (especially 'Performative Utterances') ed. J. O. Urmson and G. J. Warnock, Oxford, 1961. Sections 1, 3, 5 and 9.2 of this chapter are outlines of Austin's account, with some minor additions and alterations (see p. 28, n. 3; p. 44, n. 2; p. 71, n. 1). Section 2 follows the broad outline of his analysis, but differs in several ways which are extremely important (see p. 35, n. 1, and p. 38, n. 1). The rest of the chapter is entirely my own responsibility. I have not presupposed any previous acquaintance with Austin's work on the part of the reader. Readers who *are* familiar with Austin's account of performatives may be puzzled by my deviations from it; so I have summarized these deviations, for handy reference, on p. 71, n. 1.

'I apologize for my rudeness.'
'We praise thee, O Lord.'
'I judge this dog to be the best in the show.'
'I value your ring at £200.'

In saying, 'I promise . . .', I promise. In saying, 'I appoint . . .',
I appoint. In saying, 'I thank . . .', I thank. In saying, 'I
judge . . .', I judge. That is, each utterance is an example of
doing something in saying[1] something. What I do is made
explicit by the verb: 'promise', 'appoint', 'thank', 'judge', and
so on. I am not stating or reporting that I am doing these things,
as *you* would be if you said of me, 'He is promising . . .', or 'He
is appointing . . .', and so on. Nor am I reporting or stating
something as *I* would be if I myself said, 'I promised . . .', or 'I
appointed . . .', and so on. No, when I say, 'I promise . . .' or 'I
appoint . . .', and so on, my utterance as a whole is neither true
nor false. It is what Professor Austin called a 'performative',
for in saying what I do I *perform* a speech-act of a certain kind.[2]

Each performative, in so far as it is a performative, cannot be
false; but it is liable to other deviations, which Austin whimsi-
cally called 'Infelicities':[3]

Infelicity I.   I may fail to do what I purport to be doing, so
that my utterance is null and void, so that I do not succeed in
thanking or appointing or whatever it is that I am trying to do.
Or, less drastically, my success may be doubtful and challenge-
able. Such a misfortune may occur because there is, in my
society, no established conventional procedure to be invoked—
for example, no divorce merely by saying 'I divorce you'; or
because I am not in a position to invoke an existing procedure
—for example, to 'appoint' a Governor or 'name' a ship; or
because I make what is generally regarded as a mistake[4] in the
procedure—for example, I fail to use the Trinitarian formula in
baptism. Thus there are various conditions to be met if an utterance is to be correctly described as being what it purports to be
—for example, if the utterance, 'I appoint you Governor of

---

[1] I shall restrict my analysis to spoken rather than written language, but this is
merely a matter of convenience.

[2] The term 'performative' is *not* coined from 'formative' and the prefix 'per'.

[3] In *How to do Things with Words* (Lectures II-IV), Austin distinguished six
Infelicities, four of which (his 'Misfires') come under my Infelicity I, and the other
two (his 'Abuses') come under my Infelicities II*a* and II*b*. My exposition here does
not differ from his except in being a simplification.

[4] Austin divided such mistakes into two sorts, according to whether what I say
is incorrect, or incomplete.

Kenya' is to be correctly described as 'appointing'. Where such a condition is a necessary one, a statement concerning it is entailed by a statement which describes the speech-act as being such-and-such a performative—for example, 'I married Ann' entails, 'I was not married to anyone else at the time'. For if I was already married, I did not marry Ann; I merely went through what purported to be a marriage ceremony. On the whole, however, success-conditions for performatives are not usually 'necessary' (in the sense of the word indicated above); and they are not usually so precise. Indeed, some performatives are difficult to muff: If I say, 'I promise to do . . .', there are few[1] circumstances in which I would fail to have made a promise.

Infelicity IIa.   A performative may deviate or go wrong, even though it is successful in avoiding Infelicity I, so that it is neither null nor indefinite. For I may abuse the procedure by not having the intention or attitude which must usually be present if the performative is to be socially useful. For example, I may not intend to do what I promise, or I may praise a man whom I regard with contempt. In saying, 'I promise . . .', or 'I praise . . .', I do promise or praise; this does not depend on my having certain intentions or attitudes. But I imply that I have certain intentions or attitudes; if these are absent my utterance is misleading and it is usually also insincere. It is not just that my utterance provides you with evidence so that you can make an inductive inference to my state of mind, though this may often be the case with many ordinary remarks. It is rather a matter of linguistic convention that certain performatives carry certain implications[2] concerning the speaker's attitude or intention.

Implications of attitude are most prominent in those performatives which Austin called 'Behabitives': 'praise', 'thank', 'apologize', 'commend', 'blame', 'reprimand', 'glorify', 'worship', 'confess', 'welcome', 'protest', 'accuse', etc. Implications of intention are most prominent in those performatives which

---

[1] I might be mimicking someone, or acting in a play, or testing a microphone, or parroting sounds in a language foreign to me. (And what if no one else heard my words, or no one else understood my words—did I make a promise?)

[2] Utterances may have other sorts of implication which are not obviously related to performatives, and which I am ignoring in this book. For example, 'In saying, "There were only two applications this year", he implied that he had reason to expect more, or that there had been more in the past'. I shall consider implications in detail in section 6.

Austin called 'Commissives': 'promise', 'pledge', 'accept', 'undertake', 'engage', 'threaten', 'swear loyalty', 'declare as policy', 'take as wife', etc. We shall examine Behabitives and Commissives in section 2.

Infelicity IIb. A performative may deviate or go wrong, not by being null or by being misleading, but because commitments which are made are not subsequently fulfilled. For example, I may sincerely pledge you my support, and then give you none; or I may accept responsibility for the accident, meaning what I say, yet later refuse to pay damages. Commissives are distinguished by this element of commitment to future conduct—that is, non-verbal conduct, or conduct which is not necessarily limited to the verbal. All performatives involve a measure of verbal commitment or consistency; even when I name a ship, I commit myself to go on referring to it by that name. But Commissives involve commitments which are not merely verbal.

2. *A classification of performatives*

The initial delineation of performatives rested on a contrast with some true-or-false utterances; for example, 'I thank you' was contrasted with 'I thanked you'. This crude contrast requires further refinement and modification. Indeed, we shall eventually see that there is no simple contrast between performative and non-performative language. Our first step, however, is a classification of performatives. We shall soon see that some performatives do have a true-or-false content.

2.1. *Constatives*[1]

Consider the following examples:

'I estimate that the cost to you will be £50,000.'
'I guess that there are 197 beans in the bottle.'
'I warn you that Brown is dangerous.'
'I bet you sixpence that it will rain tomorrow.'
'I argue that inflation brings increasing demand.'
'I state that I was in London on August 1st, 1959.'
'I report that business expanded during 1958.'
'I infer from these premises that Socrates is mortal.'

Note that, as before, in each case I *do* something in saying something: I estimate, guess, warn, bet, argue, state, report or

[1] Readers who are acquainted with Austin's analysis and who are surprised by my inclusion of Constatives as a class of performatives should see p. 38, n. 1.

infer. But if we abstract the content of my estimate, guess, warning, etc., we have an utterance which is open to appraisal in terms of truth or falsity (or similar terms, such as accuracy or inaccuracy, and correctness or incorrectness): for example, 'The cost to you will be £50,000', or 'There are 197 beans in the bottle', or 'Brown is dangerous'. The success of the performative force and the truth (or accuracy, etc.) of the content are independent of each other. For on the one hand it is possible, for example, to say something which is definitely and successfully an 'estimate' or a 'statement', though it is an inaccurate estimate or a false statement. And, on the other hand, the content may be true or accurate, even though the performative deviates in one of the three possible ways: What I report may be true, yet not correctly described as a 'report', because I had no evidence and was only in a position to make a guess (Infelicity I); or, where Brown is in fact dangerous, I may warn you that Brown is dangerous, implying that I believe this, yet not believe this (Infelicity II*a*); or I may bet you sixpence it will rain tomorrow, yet refuse your sixpence when the rail falls (Infelicity II*b*).

In these examples, the distinction between the content and the performative force of an utterance is straightforward; the presence of a content, and the means of 'abstracting' it, are made obvious by the 'that'-clause. Moreover, the 'that'-clause contains an indicative sentence which *by itself* is factual; that is, the sentence is true-or-false, accurate-or-inaccurate, etc. Consider the sentence, 'The cost to you will be £50,000'. Suppose I explicitly make this an estimate, or statement, or report, or inference, or guess, or warning, or bet, or item of argument; that is, I say, 'I estimate that . . .', or 'I state that . . .', etc. These explicit performative labels do not make it inappropriate to go on appraising the content in factual terms. Indeed it may seem pedantic to insist that it is the content, rather than the whole utterance, which is factual. But the performative labels do change things, in two important ways: (i) Each performative verb makes it clearer what sorts of *additional* appraisal are appropriate. For example, the verb 'guess' shows that the utterance, 'There are 197 beans in the bottle' is not only true-or-false, but also lucky-or-unlucky; the verb 'infer' shows that what I say is not only true-or-false, but also valid-or-invalid;

and the verb 'estimate' shows that what I say is not only correct-or-incorrect, but also reliable-or-unreliable. (ii) The *species* of *factual* appraisal which is appropriate sometimes depends, for example, on whether the sentence is a report (typically accurate-or-inaccurate) or a statement (typically true-or-false).

These two complications, however, should not obscure the main point concerning estimates, admissions, reports, guesses, etc.: they have an abstractable *factual* content. Hence philosophers have been justified in grouping all these utterances together and calling them 'statements' or 'assertions'. But these labels may lead us to forget that the utterances which non-philosophers call 'statements' or 'assertions' form only a small segment of the large class. Austin's coined term 'Constative' avoids this difficulty, and yet it reminds us ('Con*stat*ive') that statements are typical specimens.

2.2. *Commissives*

We should not assume, however, that all utterances have an abstractable *factual* content. Consider two of our earlier examples:

'I promise to return this book tomorrow.'
'I pledge you my loyalty and support.'

These are Commissive performatives, for the speaker *commits* himself in more than a verbal way. They have a 'content', for the speaker is undertaking to behave in a specified way in the future; for example, he is undertaking to 'return this book tomorrow'. And it is possible to construct an indicative sentence which is a prediction of what is undertaken, or one which, later, is a report of its occurrence. But the content *within* the Commissive utterance is not factual: it is not appropriately appraised in terms of 'truth' or 'falsity' (or in similar terms such as 'accurate'/'inaccurate', 'correct'/'incorrect'). In using a Commissive-performative form of speech, I *distinguish* an utterance from Constative utterances, which have a factual content. In so far as an utterance is Commissive, it is not true-or-false; it is fulfilled-or-unfulfilled.

Commissives are specially important in this book. We shall see that they provide one main way in which language may be *self-involving*. But let us continue this classification of performatives.

2.3. *Exercitives*

When we consider another class of performatives, the contrast with Constatives is also obvious. Consider three of our earlier examples:

'I appoint you Governor of Kenya.'
'I name this ship the *Ivernia*.'
'I order you to stop smoking within ten days.'

Other examples would be, 'I decree . . .', 'I approve . . .', 'I endorse . . .', 'I authorize . . .', 'I bequeath . . .', 'I give . . .'. Austin called these Exercitives: the speaker, *exercising* authority, brings about a conventional or institutional state of affairs; he does this in *saying* something. For example, you are now Governor of Kenya, or the ship bears the name *Ivernia*, or you are under orders to stop smoking, *because I said so*.

After the Exercitive utterance has taken effect,[1] we may state this fact in a Constative utterance which is true by virtue of the Exercitive's performative force:

'You have been appointed Governor of Kenya.'
'I have named this ship the *Ivernia*.'
'You are under orders to stop smoking within ten days.'

These statements do not correspond to the content of a Constative performative. For example, the content of 'I predict that you will stop smoking within ten days' is not, 'I have predicted that you will stop smoking within ten days'; it is, 'You will stop smoking within ten days'.

One of the Exercitive examples, however, does have an abstractable content which roughly corresponds to the content of Constative utterances.

'I order you to stop smoking within ten days.' (Exercitive.)
'I predict that you will stop smoking within ten days.' (Constative.)

In both cases we may abstract the content, 'You will stop smoking within ten days'. But if you do in fact stop smoking within ten days, this shows that the Constative was *true* and that the Exercitive has been *obeyed*; the Exercitive-performative form distinguishes an utterance from Constative utterances which have a factual content.

[1] That is, after the utterance has occurred without having suffered any Infelicity I; see section 9.3.

C

We may thus say that Exercitives differ from Constatives in two possible ways: (a) Some Exercitives have no abstractable content which corresponds to the abstractable content of Constatives. (b) Some Exercitives do have such an abstractable content, but within the Exercitive it is not appropriately appraised in terms of truth-or-falsity, accuracy-or-inaccuracy, etc.

Note that any Exercitive may suffer an Infelicity I, so that it fails to be what it purports to be, *viz.*, an appointment, a naming, an order. That is, the speaker may fail to bring about the institutional state of affairs which he intended, *viz.*, your appointment as Governor, the ship's christening as *Ivernia*, and your being under orders to stop smoking. But in some cases the speaker may fail to bring about a *non*-institutional state of affairs which he intended, for example, your stopping smoking. This is a failure, not of performative force, but of causal power. The distinction between performative force and causal power will be examined in section 9.

(In Part II we shall see that Exercitives are very important in a study of the biblical conception of Creation. The divine command in Genesis 1 is an Exercitive 'utterance'.)

2.4. *Behabitives*

So far, we have considered performatives whose abstractable content is contained in a 'that'-clause, or a clause which is readily changed into a 'that'-clause. Many performatives, however, do not conform to this pattern. Consider these earlier examples:

'I thank you.'
'We praise thee, O Lord.'
'I apologize for my behaviour.'

Austin called these 'Behabitives', since they related the speaker to another person in the context of human *behaviour* and social relations, without being strongly Commissive. The speaker implies that he has certain attitudes in relation to the person whom he addresses, or towards what he is talking about. In saying, 'I thank you', I imply (but do not report) that I am grateful to you; in saying, 'I apologize for my behaviour', I imply (but do not report), that I have an unfavourable attitude towards my behaviour. Behabitives imply attitudes.[1] (Other typical Behabitive verbs are 'congratulate', 'blame', 'welcome', 'confess', 'bless', 'curse'.)

In the three examples of Behabitives, there is no obvious content to be abstracted. But there are factual presuppositions: that you exist, that the Lord exists, and that I have behaved in some undesignated way. Factual presuppositions are similarly involved in typical Commissive and Exercitive utterances:

'I pledge you my loyalty.'
'I order you to stop smoking within ten days.'

These have abstractable contents ('I shall be loyal', 'You will stop smoking within ten days'), but they also presuppose that you exist. The importance of such presuppositions in religious language is obvious if we consider the following examples:

'I thank *thee*, O God, for my *creation*.'
'I dedicate my life to *thee*, O Lord.'

It is probably true that most human language concerning God is Behabitive or Commissive; but this does not automatically eliminate the relevance of facts—factual presuppositions, and, sometimes, factual content. We may find *special* reasons why the presupposition or content of a religious utterance is not as 'factual' as it might appear to be; but that is another matter.

A Behabitive sometimes has an obvious abstractable element which is more conveniently[2] described as its 'content' rather than its 'presupposition':

'I thank thee that *I am not as other men are*.'
'I commend you in that *you have shown unusual self-restraint*.'

In each case the content is factual. Such Behabitives differ from Constatives, not in that they lack a factual content, but in that the speaker implies an attitude towards the person whom he

---

[1] Austin did not classify Behabitives in terms of attitude-implication. In *In How to do Things with Words*, he characterized the Behabitive as the *expression* of an attitude (p. 159) or the *adoption* of an attitude (p. 162). But his examples of Behabitives (p. 159) are more accurately described as implications of attitudes. See my discussion of 'Indefeasible' implications (section 6.1) and expressions of attitude (chapter 3).

[2] It is a matter of convenience. Border-line cases abound. For example, does, 'I apologize *for being rude*' have a presupposition or a content? Is it closest to, 'I apologize for my behaviour' or to, 'I apologize in that I have been rude'?

addresses, or towards what he is talking about.[1] For example, in saying, 'I thank thee that . . .' rather than, 'I state that . . .', I imply that I am grateful to you; in saying, 'I commend you in that . . .', rather than, 'I report that . . .', I imply that I have a favourable attitude towards your behaviour. This difference between Behabitives and Constatives is what makes the former a type of self-involving language. I shall call an utterance 'self-involving' if it has Behabitive or Commissive force. (Behabitives and Commissives and self-involvement will be explored more fully in sections 6 and 7.)

2.5. *Verdictives*

Another important class of performatives are those which Austin called 'Verdictives', since some of them are verdicts:

> 'I rate Jones above Smith in sheer skill.'
> 'I value your ring at £200.'
> 'I judge this dog to be the best in the show.'
> 'I find you guilty of assault.'
> 'In my opinion, Mary is more beautiful than Jane.'

Verdictives differ from Exercitives. In a Verdictive utterance, I say what *is* so; in an Exercitive utterance, I authoritatively say what is to *be* so because I *say* so. One cannot draw a sharp line between the two, however. On the one hand, many Verdictives are based, to some extent, on the exercise of *authority*; and on the other hand, many Exercitives are based, to some extent, on what *is* so. For example, when Jones grades apples, or Lenin defines 'socialism' or God evaluates the created world, are these utterances to be classified as authoritative Verdictives or as factually-based Exercitives?

The class of Verdictives also has no clear border with the class of Constatives. Nevertheless, a distinction can be made: the abstractable contents of Constatives deal with matters of fact, but the abstractable contents of Verdictives deal with matters of opinion or judgment. Roughly speaking, 'matters of fact' (for example, the number of beans in this bottle) can be settled by some agreed method of common sense or of science. As against this, 'matters of opinion or judgment' (for example, female beauty) either have no agreed method, or have a method

---

[1] The attitude may include feelings. I shall discuss the relations between attitudes and feelings in chapter 2, section 2.2, and chapter 3, section 1.1.

which depends partly on the special conventional authority of some people. This distinction, however, is not clear-cut in everyday life; and even in a court room there may be wrangles concerning a celebrity's alleged 'vulgarity': Is it a matter of fact or a matter of opinion?

Verdictives are closer to Constatives than Commissives and Exercitives are. For Commissives and Exercitives are no ways of referring to what *is* the case, but are used to 'create' something: an undertaking (for example, by a promise) or an institutional relation (for example, by a decree). But consider a typical official Verdictive. The magistrate says, 'I find you guilty of assault'. What makes the man legally guilty of assault? It is partly, of course, the fact that he struck Smith in such-and-such circumstances, etc. But legal guilt also depends on the existence of legal conventions and the exercise of legal authority. That is, the prisoner is guilty of assault partly because the magistrate, acting as an official who applies or interprets the law, *says* so. Of course, the magistrate's utterance is not a sufficient condition; one can say, 'The magistrate said he was guilty of assault, but he was not; the verdict was based on false testimony to the *facts*'. But suppose that we are all agreed as to the facts, and that it is a Chief Justice who gives the verdict, 'I find you guilty of assault'. Then a layman could question the verdict only in very exceptional circumstances—circumstances which undermine the Chief Justice's claim to authority.

(Not every utterance, 'Jones is guilty of assault' is a Verdictive: (i) I might use the words loosely, meaning, 'Jones did in fact hit him', referring to the facts of the case, but not, strictly speaking, to legal guilt. (ii) I might utter these words as a statement of fact, since the facts of the case plus the law (accepted as an institutional fact) eliminate all reasonable doubt, so that (a) Jones would be judged guilty by any reasonable magistrate, or (b) Jones has been judged guilty. (iii) But sometimes I might be agreeing with an authoritative verdict, where my utterance is a matter of performatively *accepting* the authority of law or judge; such an utterance would be an unofficial Verdictive with strong Commissive elements. It would be similar to a religious utterance in which I agree with a divine verdict—for example, with God's judgment that the created world is good.)[1]

[1] Cf. ch. 4, section 2.3.

Though official Verdictives are based on facts, the content is not strictly factual, unless we extend 'factual' to include that which depends partly on the authoritative utterance of the speaker. Unofficial Verdictives (expressions of opinion on matters of opinion) also have a content which is not strictly factual. (Consider, for example, 'Mary is more beautiful than Jane', said by an onlooker at a beauty contest.) Hence Verdictives differ from Constatives in the same sort of way as Exercitives and Commissives do: their content is not strictly factual. (Behabitives, however, differ in that they imply attitudes.)

Thus performatives may be divided into five classes: (In each case Austin's artificial etymology is indicated.)

(1) Con*stat*ives (class includes *state*ments): state, report, guess, warn, bet, estimate, etc.

(2) *Commis*sives (more-than-verbal *commit*ment): promise, pledge, threaten, covenant, undertake, etc.

(3) *Exerci*tives (an *exercise* of authority): order, decree, appoint, name, give, etc.

(4) *Behabi*tives (concerning social *behaviour*): thank, praise, apologize, blame, confess, etc.

(5) *Verdic*tives (class includes *verdicts*): judge, rate, find, grade, value, etc.

Constatives are classified as performatives because we can consider them not only according to their factual content, but also according to their *performative force* (as reports, guesses, warnings, etc.). Moreover, in section 9.2 we shall contrast the performative force of all performative utterances, *including Constatives*, with their causal power.[1]

---

[1] This footnote is for readers who are acquainted with Austin's analysis, for they will be surprised by my inclusion of 'Constatives' as a class of performatives. The surprise is natural, since Austin began *How to do Things with Words* by *distinguishing* performatives from constatives. He suggested two ways in which they differ:

(a) In uttering a performative, I *do* something, whereas in uttering a constative I merely *say* something.

(b) Performatives are open to Infelicities, whereas constatives are true-or-false.

In Lecture XI, however, after a closer scrutiny of (a) and (b), Austin *rejected his earlier performative/constative distinction.* He replaced it by a classification of speech-acts according to their 'illocutionary force', that is, according to what a speaker *does in saying* something. Austin pointed out that this illocutionary force (which I call 'performative force') can be discerned not only in performatives but also in constatives: in saying, 'I state . . .', I state; hence he rejected the initial distinction which he had made in terms of (a), above. In Austin's new classification, typical examples of earlier 'performatives' appear as examples of utterances which have Verdictive, Exercitive, Commissive or Behabitive force; and typical examples of earlier

The division of performatives into five classes is far less neat and clear-cut than one might gather from my brief outline.[1] On the one hand, some performative verbs typically combine various sorts of performative force; the verb 'forgive', for example, is Exercitive (cf. 'pardon'), Commissive (cf. 'accept') and Behabitive (contrast 'blame').[2] On the other hand, some performative verbs have different performative forces in different contexts. For example, consider the verb 'warn':

Constative: 'I warn (cf. report to) you that the enemy are advancing.'
Commissive: 'I warn (cf. make this threat to) you that I will tolerate no interference.'
Exercitive: 'I warn (cf. request) you not to use that path at night.'

'constatives' appear as examples of utterances which have Expositive illocutionary force.

Austin classifies speech-acts-with-their-illocutionary-forces, whereas I refer to my classification as a classification of 'performatives'. Thus when I say that Constatives form a class of performatives, there might seem to be no genuine difference from Austin at all, only two differences of terminology:

(i) I use the label 'performative' rather than 'speech-act-with-its-illocutionary-force'.
(ii) I use the label 'Constative' rather than 'Expositive' for the fifth class (having retained the labels 'Verdictive', 'Exercitive', 'Commissive' and 'Behabitive').

The first difference is merely terminological, but the difference between 'Constative' and 'Expositive' is not. For I distinguish the fifth class from Verdictives, Exercitives and Commissives (though not from Behabitives, see below) by reference to true-or-false content as the criterion, whereas Austin does not. That is, I have not rejected the second half of distinction (b), above; in my analysis, all performatives are open to Infelicities, but some of these (my 'Constatives') differ from others in being appropriately appraised as true-or-false (or accurate or inaccurate, or correct-or-incorrect, etc.). In contrast with this, Austin criticizes the use of any such criterion as a means for classifying utterances; and he does not use any such criterion when he distinguishes his class of Expositives.

I have used the label 'Constative' because I distinguish the class by means of one criterion which Austin used in his original constative/performative distinction and which he later abandoned: the second half of distinction (b), above.

I should make it clear that *some* of Austin's 'Expositives' would not be happily classified as Constatives (my term), for example, 'I interpret . . .' or 'I define . . .'. Moreover, some of his 'Expositives' do not belong to *any* of my classes, for example, 'I begin by . . .' or 'I conclude by . . .'; my classification is not as exhaustive as Austin's.

Note that I distinguish Constatives from Behabitives, not by reference to the absence of factual content in the latter (for some Behabitives do have factual content), but by reference to the absence of any implications of attitude in the former. See pp. 34-6 and 56.

[1] The classification is also not exhaustive: a few of Austin's 'Expositives' (for example, 'I begin by . . .') do not belong to my class of Constatives or to any other of my classes; cf. p. 38, n. 1.
[2] In *How to do Things with Words*, Lecture XII, Austin finds examples of verbs on *every* border-line between the classes which he distinguishes.

Behabitive: 'I warn (cf. confess to) you that I am an unpleasant companion on a tour.'

Such exceptions and complications do not destroy the value of the five-fold classification. Indeed, they would not be recognized as such if the classification were not attempted. But they do suggest that, sometimes, instead of saying, 'Utterance p is a Behabitive (but not a Commissive or Verdictive, etc.)', it will be less misleading to say, 'The performative force of utterance p is primarily Behabitive (but also somewhat Commissive, etc.).'

3. *Autobiographical reporting*

There are some performatives which have not only a content (or factual presuppositions) and a performative force, but also a third aspect, which I shall call 'autobiographical reporting'. Consider the following examples:

'I blame you for his unhappiness.'
'I agree with what you say.'
'I acknowledge Father Browne's authority in spiritual matters.'
'I submit to thee, O Lord.'
'I forgive you.'

In each case, my utterance is a performative. In saying what I say, I blame, agree, acknowledge, submit and forgive. But I also refer to myself, to my mental state or pattern of behaviour; I report that this is such-and-such. I do not merely imply this, or commit myself to some future behaviour; I report it. What I say may be not merely misleading (Infelicity IIa), or eventually unfulfilled (Infelicity IIb); it may be false: a mistake or a lie. (Contrast such cases with 'I thank you' 'I promise', 'I order' or 'I guess' which involve no true-or-false report concerning myself.) The verb 'blame' (or 'forgive', or 'acknowledge', etc.) has a dual aspect; it is both performative and autobiographical. In saying, 'I blame you', I blame you; yet I may have been blaming you without saying anything, so that I report this fact now in the words, 'I blame you'. In saying 'I forgive you', I forgive you; but I also let you know what my attitude is towards you. In saying, 'I acknowledge his authority', I acknowledge it; yet if I have been failing to acknowledge it in practice, what I say is false.

Sometimes these verbs are given both a performative and an autobiographical use in the same particular utterance; but not always. It is possible for a verb to have only a performative use in one context, and only an autobiographical use in another context. For example, a newly-converted rebel might acknowledge the authority of king or God for the first time by saying, 'I acknowledge your authority'; his utterance would not be taken as a lie, a false report, but as an act of submission which is sincere or insincere. On the other hand, I might say to you, 'I acknowledge his authority', in such a context that the performative element is minimal or non-existent and the autobiographical element is primary. The verb 'submit' might similarly be used either to commit oneself to a new mode of behaviour or to report one's habitual conduct. Likewise the verb 'forgive' might be used either performatively or autobiographically; the performative use would be either Commissive, committing oneself to a favourable attitude, or Behabitive, implying that one has a favourable attitude; the autobiographical use would be a report that one has a favourable attitude.

But each of these verbs may have a dual use in a single utterance. A particular utterance is an 'autobiographical performative' when the utterance (or more specifically, its key verb) is given such a dual use. Such utterances differ from the relatively-pure performatives which we were examining in sections 1 and 2, where few of the verbs have an autobiographical use in *any* context. The distinction between pure and autobiographical performatives cuts across the general five-fold classification of performatives, though it is difficult to find an autobiographical Exercitive. (How about 'repudiate'?)

4. 'Acknowledge': an important autobiographical-performative verb

Before we leave the distinction between pure and autobiographical performatives, we ought to give special attention to an important example of the latter, the verb 'acknowledge'. Karl Barth[1] regards this word as the key to Christian religious experience, faith and language, in so far as these are truly biblical. He provides a stimulating analysis of this word, but he does not explicitly note its performative aspect.[2]

---

[1] *Church Dogmatics*, I, 1, pp. 213-60.
[2] For this reason, my analysis is fundamentally different from his, though I am indebted to him for some details.

The verb 'to acknowledge' covers most of what one does in religious utterance, so wide are its strands of meaning:

(i) To admit receipt of a verbal communication (message or letter) or of a gift; this usually involves thanking someone.

(ii) To show by word or other conventional means (for example, a nod or smile) that one has taken note of a person's presence.

(iii) To admit or accept a claim, obligation, authority, or status.

(iv) To admit or tell someone a fact, usually that someone has performed an action which is relevant to one's own behaviour.

(v) To confess a fault or sin to someone.

These varied examples show that 'acknowledge' needs to be classified as both a Behabitive and a Commissive. Note also that what one acknowledges is something personal. As Barth says, 'A fact which is acknowledged is . . . not a fact of nature—we do not acknowledge a landslip or a rainbow or the like—but a fact created and presented by a person or persons. The determination of man's existence by the Word of God is such a creation; it is determination by God's person.'[1]

The word 'acknowledge' has a *performative* aspect. In saying, 'I acknowledge *x*', I acknowledge *x*, and therein I imply that I have certain intentions or attitudes, and I commit myself to certain behaviour. It is true that the implications and commitments are minimal in the case of an extremely formal acknowledgment—for example, of a letter. But here, and in my subsequent use of 'acknowledge', we shall be ignoring such cases.

The word 'acknowledge' usually also has an *autobiographical* aspect, so that states of mind and patterns of behaviour are not only implied and made commitments, but are actually reported. If I actually acknowledge how much you have done for me, I not only say something to you, I also think and act accordingly: I admit the fact in my own private thinking, I am grateful in my attitude towards you, and I try to do something for you in some way.

Note that it is sometimes possible to abstract the *content* of my acknowledgement, as something additional to the autobiographical and performative elements. For example, in saying, 'I acknowledge that Jones saved my life', I do three things:

---

[1] *Church Dogmatics*, I, 1, p. 234 (translation slightly rearranged). Barth is referring to the rainbow in a secular context; in a biblical context it *is* something to acknowledge, for it is a sign of a covenant.

I perform the verbal act of acknowledging.
  (performative element)

I report (perhaps falsely) my own state of mind in relation to Jones.
  (autobiographical element)

I refer to the fact that Jones has saved my life.
  (factual element)

Similarly, in saying, 'I acknowledge the Holy Spirit as the source of life', I perform the verbal act of acknowledging, I report (perhaps falsely) my own attitudes, and I refer to something which presumably is a putative fact. As we noted earlier, the discovery that much religious language is Behabitive or Commissive does not, by itself, show that such language lacks putative factual content. The same point applies to the discovery of autobiographical elements in religious language; these need not be the *only* factual aspect to religious language.

What is it to behave and think 'accordingly' when I acknowledge something? The answer to this question is usually quite clear where an action which I acknowledge is described in 'institutional' terms—for example, where I acknowledge that you have 'given' or 'loaned' me five shillings, or that I have 'rebelled'. But where an action is described in non-'institutional' terms (for example, 'You pulled me out of the water when I was drowning') the language does not itself include a reference to appropriate thought and behaviour. Where I acknowledge an action, this often involves interpreting it in 'institutional' terms, at least implicitly; for example, I might look on your rescue as a sort of 'gift' of life to me, though notions of property and ownership are not strictly applicable. Similarly, as we shall see in chapter 4, a biblical acknowledgment of God as my Creator includes an interpretation of His action as a gift and as a decree.

What I mean by 'institutional' terms will become more clear in sections 8 and 9. But here our next step is to make another important distinction among performatives. So far we have classified them as Constatives, Commissives, Exercitives, etc., and we have distinguished pure performatives from autobiographical performatives. Now we shall distinguish explicit performatives from non-explicit performatives.

5. *Non-explicit performatives*

Nearly all our examples of performatives have had one feature in common: they have been self-labelling and explicit. The verb, in the first person present indicative tense,[1] has labelled the utterance as to its performative force, for example, 'I *thank* you', or 'I *blame* you'. In other possible examples, the label occurs, but it is not a verb in that tense:

> 'You are hereby *appointed* Governor of Kenya.'
> 'Please accept my *apologies* for my rudeness.'
> 'My *estimate* of the cost is £50,000.'
> 'I take pleasure in *reporting* that business has increased during 1960.'

But a performative need not be self-labelling and thus perfectly explicit. It is possible to appoint, apologize, estimate, report, etc., without using the words 'appoint', 'apology', 'estimate', 'report' or any similar self-labelling words. Such utterances, however, may be ambiguous as to their performative force, and this ambiguity is overcome by means of explicit performatives. Suppose I say, 'I shall be brusque with him'. I can make my meaning explicit by saying, 'I predict that I shall be brusque with him', or 'I intend to be brusque with him', or 'I promise to be brusque with him'. A similar possible ambiguity, concerning 'You ought to take the job', can be cleared up if I include in my utterance the word 'advise', or 'urge' or 'warn'. And we may also recall how 'The cost to you will be £50,000' could be an estimate, a guess, a warning, a report, or an undertaking. Such utterances are non-explicit performatives.

In addition to the five-fold classification of performatives, we now have two main ways in which to distinguish among performatives:[2] they may be autobiographical or pure, and

---

[1] In *How to do Things with Words* (pp. 56, 64) Austin pointed out that pure-performative verbs are sometimes given an *habitual* present-tense meaning. Consider, for example, 'I *bet* sixpence every day', or 'I always *thank* shopkeepers for courtesies'. These are not performatives, except in that they may be declarations of policy; in saying 'I bet', I do not, in this case, actually bet; in saying, 'I thank', I do not, in this case, actually thank. What I say is an autobiographical report, concerning bets or thanks which I perform in *other* cases by saying 'I bet' or 'I thank'.

[2] Both distinctions are Austin's, but I have labelled one side of each dichotomy differently: (i) He called non-explicit performatives 'primary' or 'primitive' (*op. cit.*, p. 72). This nomenclature raises difficult questions concerning the *history* of language, whereas the label 'non-explicit' does not. (ii) Austin contrasted pure performatives with those which are partly 'descriptive' (*ibid.*, pp. 79, 83), having linked 'descriptive' closely with 'constative' (p. 77). This is misleading, for a pure performative may very well be descriptive or constative: 'I report that . . .'. The correct opposite to 'pure' here is '*self*-descriptive'; hence my label, 'autobiographical'.

they may be explicit or non-explicit. Note that all pure performatives are explicit, but not all explicit performatives are pure, for some are autobiographical (for example, 'blame'). Also note that some autobiographical performatives, unlike 'blame', are non-explicit as to their performative force:

'I appreciate your kindness.' (a thank-you?)
'I feel sorry about what happened.' (an apology?)

Once we grant that utterances may have a performative force even though they do not contain an explicit performative word, it is reasonable to say that *every* utterance is a performative. Indeed, I think that an Austinian analysis of language does lead logically to the claim that any particular utterance, in its particular context, has a particular performative force (or purports to have this force—cf. Infelicity I).

At this point a critic might object: 'You began in section I by contrasting performative with non-performative utterances; yet now you undermine your contrast by saying that *all* utterances are performatives.' This objection involves a misinterpretation of the argument. We now can see that when the notion of 'performatives' was originally introduced, I referred to some performatives (Exercitives, Commissives, Behabitives and Verdictives) which have an explicit performative force, and to some Constatives which have a non-explicit performative force. Thus the original contrast had two aspects: (a) non-Constative versus Constative performative force and (b) explicit versus non-explicit performative force. Both distinctions are distinctions between different kinds of performative force; hence neither distinction is undermined by the claim that every utterance has a particular performative force (or purports to have this force). This is all that I mean when I say that every utterance is a performative. (In some cases our description of an utterance's performative force may have to be vague: for example, 'It's an imperative' or 'It's an undertaking'; and in some cases we may be uncertain concerning the performative force. But performative force does not differ from other aspects of meaning in being open to vagueness and uncertainty.)

It is important to insist that performative force need not be explicit. But we must be careful to distinguish the performative force which depends primarily on the special context of a particular utterance from the performative force which depends primarily on the words of the utterance; in the latter case, the same words would have this force if uttered in many different sorts of context. This distinction will be examined more carefully in part of the next section.

6. *The implications and commitments of performatives*

I shall now try to classify performatives in terms of their implications and commitments. Since implications of attitude are characteristic of Behabitives, and commitments to behaviour are characteristic of Commissives, I will restrict the analysis to these two classes (or aspects) of performative language. Behabitives and Commissives require special consideration because of their importance as self-involving elements in everyday language and in biblical language concerning Creation; but the study of implications and commitments will lead to some general conclusions which are relevant to all performative language. We shall begin with implications, with what Austin calls 'that rather woolly word "imply" '.[1] A classification of implications should help us to distinguish different strands in the 'wool'.

6.1. *Classification of implications*

Consider the following examples:

(1) 'I commend Smith for being submissive and restrained.'
(2) 'Smith is loyal and honest.'
(3) 'Smith is submissive and restrained.'

If I say (1) in any standard[2] context, I imply that I have a favourable attitude towards Smith. It is no use for me to protest, 'I didn't mean to imply . . .', for I did imply it, whether I meant to or not. And if I say, 'I commend Smith for being submissive and restrained, but I do not have a favourable attitude towards him in this regard', my utterance is self-stultifying. It is self-stultifying in the same sort of way as the utterance, 'I state that Jones was in the house at the time of the murder, but I don't believe that he was'. Where the performative force of an utterance is explicit, its implications are corres-

---

[1] *Philosophical Papers*, p. 224.
[2] That is, I am not acting in a play, testing a microphone, mimicking, etc.; and I am not speaking in an ironical tone of voice, giving the word 'commend' a meaning which contrasts with its ordinary, non-ironical meaning. In all subsequent analysis we shall ignore both sorts of exception.

pondingly strong and definite. Let us call this sort of implication 'Indefeasible'; it makes no sense to disclaim what is implied.

Let us now consider the words of (2), 'Smith is loyal and honest'. In nearly[1] every standard context, when I say (2), I imply that I have a favourable attitude towards Smith, and I cannot claim that I do not imply this. But it does make sense to disclaim what is implied: Suppose that I say, 'Smith is loyal and honest, but I do not have a favourable attitude towards him in this regard'. This is not necessarily a self-stultifying utterance; my peculiar morality may lead me to say just this. Yet there is an implication which needs to be disclaimed: I use the word 'but'. On the other hand, the implication is not Indefeasible, for I can disclaim what is implied. Let us call this 'Prima-facie' implication.

Now let us consider the words of (3), 'Smith is submissive and restrained'. In most contexts the words do not even have a Prima-facie implication; for I may utter them and then go on to disclaim a favourable attitude without even using the word 'but'. There is no implication to disclaim. Indeed, I can utter the words of (3) and then say, 'I did not imply that . . .', for the words as such do not carry such an implication. Occasionally, my utterance may provide very good evidence that I have a favourable attitude towards Smith; but if you infer this, your inference depends more on an empirical generalization than a linguistic convention, for example, a generalization such as, 'Most people who, in such-and-such circumstances, say that someone is submissive and restrained, have a favourable attitude towards him'. Compare this with, 'most people who in certain circumstances grit their teeth are in pain.' Note that just as I might have deliberately deceived you by gritting my teeth, so I might have deliberately deceived you by saying, 'Smith is submissive and restrained'; but I did not definitely *imply* that I was in pain or that I felt favourably towards Smith. My utterance did not have the performative force of a commendation. Though example (2) ('Smith is loyal and honest')

---

[1] Exceptions: (i) Both speaker and *hearer* belong to a social group which differs so radically from most of society that the usual favourable implications of 'honest' and 'loyal' do not exist at all. (ii) A more likely exception: The context makes it clear that the speaker is referring to a specific *sort* of honesty (concerning property) and of loyalty (to the Crown) which is undesirable for the purposes (stealing the Crown Jewels) which the speaker has in mind.

is usually a non-explicit Behabitive, example (3) ('Smith is submissive and restrained') is not usually a Behabitive at all.

In a special context, however, the words of example (3) might have the performative force of a commendation. Suppose that the utterance, 'Smith is submissive and restrained' forms part of a eulogy; then it is part of a larger speech-act which, as a whole, has the performative force of a eulogy and implies a favourable attitude towards Smith. My audience would legitimately expect me to disclaim any particular favourable implications if I do not mean them. Here, as in the case of Prima-facie implications, there is something to disclaim which one can disclaim. But the implication depends, not on the words of the particular utterance, but on its special Behabitive context. Hence I shall call this 'Contextual'[1] implication. Note that some sentences in the eulogy may have Prima-facie implications independently of their special Behabitive context, for example, 'Smith is loyal and honest'.

The distinction between Prima-facie and Contextual implication is not always clear-cut. Sometimes the latter occurs where the context is a definite performative act such as a service of worship, an oath of allegiance before a magistrate, or a eulogy at a testimonial dinner. But where the context is less definite, the Contextual implications may need to combine with weak Prima-facie implications of an utterance; hence the resulting implication cannot be neatly classified. Nevertheless it is extremely important to make the distinction between Prima-facie and Contextual implications, especially in any detailed analysis of religious language. For it is a truism that any utterance which forms part of an act of worship is itself an act of worship. Even the parish announcements occur in this special

---

[1] My 'Contextual implication' should not be confused with P. Nowell-Smith's 'contextual implication': 'A statement *p* contextually implies a statement *q* if anyone who knew the normal conventions of the language would be entitled to infer *q* from *p* in the context in which they occur' (*Ethics*, 1954, p. 80). My account of implication differs from this in three ways: (i) Many implications (Indefeasible or Prima-facie) are as independent of context as logical relations within everyday language *can* be; only one species of implication deserves the label 'Contextual'. (ii) It is not the statement *p* that implies *q*; it is the *speaker*. In saying *p*, the speaker implies *q*. (Nowell-Smith's examples were usually presented in the latter form, however.) (iii) Implications occur not only when people make statements, but also when they promise, apologize, vote, etc.

Nowell-Smith has recently modified his account in these three respects—a fact which reassures me concerning my own account. See 'Contextual Implication and Ethical Theory', *Aristotelian Society Sup. Vol.*, 1962.

performative context, and thus become acts of worship. But sometimes an utterance within a service of worship may have its own independent performative force and implications—for example, 'We thank thee, O Lord'. Now suppose that, as part of a service of worship, I utter the words, 'All things were made by the word of the Creator'. My utterance carries an implication that I have a reverent attitude towards the Creator. Does this implication depend entirely on the context of worship, or does the word 'Creator' have independent implications? If it does, are these implications like those of the word 'honest', or do they depend in some way on the biblical *tradition*? We shall return to this problem later.

In the preceding paragraph I referred to 'weak' Prima-facie implications. Some Prima-facie implications may be weak in a special way, which we shall now consider. Take the formula, 'In saying x, I (do not) imply that y'. Usually the verb 'imply' is used, in sentences which follow this formula, to report something *public*. That is, my use of the word 'imply' is equivalent to *your* use when you say, 'In saying x, Evans implies (does not imply) that y.' Implications usually depend entirely on linguistic conventions plus context, and not on the speaker's private intentions. Implications usually have to do with what *is meant* by an utterance, not with what the speaker means;[1] if the speaker means something else and does not intend to imply such-and-such this makes no difference: he *does* imply such-and-such. There are exceptions to this, however. A word may have two fairly distinct uses, only one of which involves implications concerning the speaker's attitude. For example, I might say, 'That is a very valuable picture; I'm not implying that I like it; I just mean that people would pay plenty for it'. Here the words, 'I'm not implying . . .' are used to express my intention (what I mean), not to report something public (what is meant, whether or not I meant it). The implication of the utterance here depends, in part, on the intention of the speaker. Compare the word 'valuable' with 'cunning', 'caricature', 'carnal' or 'suggestive'. Such words differ from some other words which have Prima-facie implications in that one can not only *disclaim what is implied*, but also *deny that one implies it*. I shall

[1] This distinction will be explored more fully in sections 7.2.2 and 9, and in chapter 2, section 3.5.4.

D

call such implications 'Speaker-dependent Prima-facie implications'. They differ from Indefeasible implications, of course, for these do not allow me even to disclaim what is implied. And they differ from Contextual implications, which require a special context before it is necessary or even appropriate to deny that one implies such-and-such.

I have suggested four technical names for the main ways in which a speaker may imply intentions or attitudes:

(1) Indefeasible implications: 'I commend Smith for being submissive and restrained.'
(2a) Speaker-independent Prima-facie implications: 'Smith is loyal and honest.'
(2b) Speaker-dependent Prima-facie implications: 'That is a very valuable picture.'
(3) Contextual implications: 'Smith is submissive and restrained.' (uttered as part of a eulogy)

The relation between context and implications now requires further investigation. First of all, it is important to consider *descriptive* contexts.

The speaker-independent Prima-facie implications of an utterance can sometimes be set aside. Suppose, for example, that I say, 'Smith is honest and loyal' in a special 'descriptive' context in which I have said, 'Please ignore the implications which these words usually have concerning the speaker's attitudes; I'm not commending Smith's character or deploring it; I'm just trying to describe him.' Here the Behabitive utterance occurs in a total linguistic context which is descriptive; the speaker does not try to deny that the utterance has implications; he simply sets these implications aside. Note that a context may be descriptive without my explicitly saying, 'Take what I say descriptively, setting aside any implications concerning my attitudes . . .'. For example, when my friend wants to be able to identify Mr Smith at the station, I say, 'He is very tall, handsome, and grey-haired, and he has a little moustache'. Here I am using the word 'handsome' descriptively, setting aside any implications concerning what sort of features I like. Such non-explicitly descriptive contexts are far from rare. A great deal of our talk about people takes place within them. I usually try to find, not so much the word which fits my personal attitude to Smith, as the word which fits him.

Thus contexts may affect implications in two opposite ways. On the one hand, a word or utterance may gain Behabitive or Commissive force because it occurs in a special Behabitive or Commissive context. And, on the other hand, another word or utterance may have its Behabitive or Commissive force set aside because it occurs in a descriptive context. (Note that where the force is Indefeasible, it cannot be set aside, for example, 'I commend you . . .'.)

The examples of 'contexts' have so far been restricted to *occasions* for utterances. On the one hand, the context might be a eulogy (Behabitive), an oath of allegiance (Commissive), or a service of worship (Behabitive-Commissive); on the other hand, it might be a social-worker's case-book report (descriptive). Each context is itself a particular linguistic act on a particular conventional occasion, and we say that the utterance occurs 'within' the context, using the word 'within' in a spatio-temporal sense. But sometimes an utterance has special implications, not so much because of the occasion when it occurs, but because of the literary, sociological, philosophical or religious *tradition* 'within' which a man speaks. For example, the word 'political' occurs in a Marxist context if it has the meaning which is built up in the writings of Karl Marx and his followers or interpreters. The word 'natural' occurs in a Thomist context if it has the meaning which is built up in the writings of St Thomas and his followers or interpreters. Similarly, it seems to me, the word 'Creator' occurs in a biblical context if it has the meaning built up in the Bible as a whole, as the Bible is interpreted according to some tradition of interpretation.

In Part II I shall explain more fully what is involved in this notion of a 'biblical context'. But at this stage it does seem to me to be important and legitimate to distinguish between two sorts of Contextual implication: 'Occasional' and 'Traditional'. Thus implications need to be classified in the following way:

(1) Indefeasible.
(2) Prima-facie: (*a*) Speaker-independent.
(*b*) Speaker-dependent.
(3) Contextual: (*a*) Occasional.
(*b*) Traditional.

Both 3*a* and 3*b* may vary in their degree of speaker-dependence. As an Occasional context, a testimonial dinner provides such strong implications of approval that the private intentions of the speaker are more or less irrelevant to the Behabitive force of his words; similarly a clinical report provides an unambiguously descriptive context. But other Occasional contexts may allow the speaker himself to determine, in part, the Behabitive implications of his words. Traditional contexts vary in a similar way. On the one hand a Traditional context may be involved by a public Occasional context; for example, an utterance within the Occasional context of a Christian act of worship involves the speaker in a Traditional biblical context. On the other hand, a speaker is often free to decide whether or not he wishes his utterance to have (for himself and for others) the meaning provided by some Traditional context.

Many implications fall on border-lines between the classes which I have suggested. But at least it is more useful to be able to locate them on border-lines than not to be able to locate them at all. And if it is true that in saying, 'God is my Creator' I imply that I have certain intentions and attitudes, it is important to be able to designate which class or classes of implications are involved and which are not involved.

We now turn from the implications of Performatives to consider their commitments. These are similarly in need of classification, but I shall deal with them more briefly.

6.2. *Classification of commitments*

It is possible to distinguish commitments in a three-fold way which bears some resemblance to the classification of implications. Consider the following examples:

(1) 'I acknowledge you as my king.'
(2) 'You are my king.'
(3a) 'Yes, this boy is in fact my son.' (uttered in a law-court testimony, an Occasional context, where my utterance commits me to accepting responsibility for the boy)
(3b) 'It is unnatural to use spermicide in birth-control.' (uttered in the Traditional context of Thomism)

Case (1) is an Indefeasible commitment. If I add, 'but I've not committed myself to behave accordingly', my disclaimer is false. (We are assuming here that the word 'acknowledge' is not being used merely formally.)[1]

[1] Cf. p. 42.

Case (2) is a Prima-facie commitment. I can sensibly add a disclaimer: 'But I've not committed myself to behave accordingly'. The disclaimer, however, is needed; without it, I will naturally be taken to be committing myself to act accordingly.

Case (3a) is an Occasional-Contextual commitment. The example shows that an utterance which has a non-explicit Constative performative force of some kind or other may also gain Commissive force, without ceasing to be factual. This is possible because the utterance occurs in a special Commissive context. A descriptive context, on the other hand, may involve the setting aside of Prima-facie commitments. For example, you ask me for some information about Mr Jones, and I reply, 'He's a middle-aged solicitor in London and he's my legal guardian'. Here I am not Commissively acknowledging my status in relation to Jones; I am just describing him.

Case (3b) is a Traditional-Contextual commitment. In the context of the Thomist tradition, the utterance commits the speaker to refrain from particular actions; an 'unnatural' action is one which ought not to be carried out. (In Part II I shall argue that if the utterance 'God is my Creator' occurs in the biblical context, it commits the speaker to various modes of action; the commitment is Traditional-Contextual.)

The classification of commitments as 'Indefeasible' and 'Prima-facie' does not correspond exactly to the classification of implications. In the rest of this paragraph, I shall explain the difference, since it is of general interest to philosophers who are exploring the logic of self-involvement in everyday language. Readers whose interests are mainly theological may find it convenient to omit this, however, for it is not necessary as a prolegomenon to Part II. *Indefeasible commitments* are commitments where I cannot deny that I have committed myself to conduct C. These Commitments seem to resemble implications where I cannot deny that I have implied that I have attitude A; but such implications are not indefeasible, they are speaker-independent Prima-facie implications. *Prima-facie commitments* are commitments where I can deny that I have committed myself to conduct C. These commitments seem to resemble implications where I can deny that I have implied that I have attitude A; but such implications are speaker-dependent Prima-facie implications. Note, however, that we distinguish

Indefeasible implications from speaker-independent Prima-facie implications in terms of the question, 'Can I disclaim what I have implied?'; the two sorts of implications are similar in that I cannot deny that I have implied that I have attitude A, but they differ in that where the implication is Indefeasible I cannot disclaim my attitude A. Now what would be a parallel distinction between commitments? What would it be to disclaim my conduct C before I do anything? The conduct, unlike the attitude, lies entirely in the future. I cannot disclaim it in the way that I can disclaim an attitude in the present. There *cannot* be any commitments where I can disclaim my future conduct in the way that I may disclaim having an attitude at present. Indefeasible commitments are as 'indefeasible' as they *can* be.

The classification of implications and commitments may therefore be summarized as follows (omitting Contextual cases):

Implications

   (1) Indefeasible: I *cannot* disclaim having attitude A.
                  I *cannot* deny that I imply that I have attitude A.

   (2a) Speaker-independent Prima-facie: I *can* disclaim having attitude A. I *cannot* deny that I imply that I have attitude A.

   (2b) Speaker-dependent Prima-facie: I *can* disclaim having attitude A; and I *need* to. I *can* deny that I imply that I have attitude A; and I *need* to.

Commitments

   (1) Indefeasible: I *cannot* deny that I commit myself to conduct C.

   (2) Prima-facie: I *can* deny that I commit myself to conduct C; and I *need* to.

6.3. *Performative force: words, context and speaker*

We have seen that context may be important in relation to the implications of Behabitives and Commissives and to the commitments of Commissives. Context is also important in relation to other performatives. Where the words of an utterance would usually give it a performative force which is Exercitive, Verdictive or Constative, the utterance may lose such force or gain additional force because it occurs in a special Occasional context. For example, an utterance which would usually be a prediction (Constative force) has the force of an order (Exercitive) when it is part of an order-of-the-day. Likewise the utterance, 'That is your watch', which is usually a Constative, may become a Verdictive when the speaker is a judge. We noted cases where, 'You are guilty of assault' is not a Verdictive but a Constative. And the implication of personal veracity and certainty is stronger in the context of a witness-box testimony than in a casual conversation.

The analysis of Behabitives and Commissives indicates some general features of performatives, which I shall sketch here:

(I) The *words*. The utterance may, by itself (apart from exceptional contexts),[1] carry a performative force. This force is either Indefeasible or Prima-facie (that is, disclaimable).

(II) The public *context* or conventional occasion. This is always relevant, if only to the extent of its not being exceptional. And sometimes a special context may give a particular utterance a force which it would not usually have, or set aside a force which it would usually have.

(III) The *speaker's intention*. Sometimes an utterance has alternative performative forces, and the speaker can specify which force he intends his utterance to have. And sometimes the (Traditional) context depends in part on the speaker's intention.

I shall not attempt to illustrate these three factors at work in all performatives. We have examined Behabitives and Commissives, and I am confident that the same three factors are present, in subtly-varying ways, in other performatives—and indeed in language generally.

7. *Performative language, self-involving language and 'evaluative' language*

We are now in a position to apply the analysis of performatives to a perennial problem: the nature of 'evaluative' language. We have seen that the specific *nature* of the attitudes (or intentions) which I imply, and of the behaviour to which I commit myself, depends on the nature of specific Behabitive

---

[1] Cf. p. 46, n. 2.

and Commissive force of the utterance: thanking or commending, promising or submitting. And we have seen that implications and commitments may be classified *logically* as Indefeasible, Prima-facie or Contextual. Where the utterance contains an explicit-performative word, its implications and commitments are Indefeasible. Sometimes words which are not explicit-performatives carry Prima-facie implications or commitments (for example, 'honest' or 'king').

Now let us reconsider another point. Except when a typical Constative utterance occurs in a special Behabitive or Commissive context, it carries only the implication that the speaker believes what he says and only the commitment to a minimal verbal consistency. For example, in many contexts if I say, 'Jones is next door', my utterance implies no intentions or attitudes, and it is non-committal. I am not implying anything concerning myself except that I believe that he is next door; and I am not committing myself to anything except verbal consistency, for example, not saying, 'Jones is here'. Let us give such utterances a label. If we were concerned only with the absence of any implications of attitude, I could call such utterances, simply, 'Constatives'. For Constatives and Behabitives form mutually-exclusive classes of utterance; I have made it a matter of definition that an utterance which has a factual content but which also carries implications concerning the speaker's attitudes is not a Constative but a Behabitive. But a Constative which has *Commissive* force does not cease to be a Constative; the two classes are not mutually exclusive.[1] So let us talk about *sorts* of performative *force*, and not merely about classes of utterance. Then we may define a technical term, 'flat Constative', as follows: A flat Constative is a Constative (for example, a statement, assertion, or prediction) which does not have Behabitive or Commissive force.

7.1. *The 'autonomy of value'*

With this definition we can provide a new interpretation for the philosophical slogan which, in various guises, has dominated both modern ethics and modern theology: No statement entails

---

[1] Cf. p. 52, example (3a): 'Yes, this boy is in fact my son' (uttered in a special Commissive context). Note that the content of this utterance *qua* Constative is factual; but the 'content' *qua* Commissive (that is, *what* is undertaken) is not factual.

a value-judgment. The theological relevance of this slogan should perhaps be noted here. On the one hand, critics[1] of Christianity argue that even if Christian doctrines were true, they would be merely statements of fact which do not affect the logical independence of human value-judgments; whether or not God is Creator of all things, I can make the same value-judgments; indeed, God as Creator is morally relevant to me only in so far as I judge Him to be so. On the other hand, modern Protestant theologians[2] have claimed that a genuinely religious utterance cannot be merely a statement of fact (extremists leave out the word 'merely', or allow only autobiographical statements); if I can give mere assent to an utterance about a Creator, my utterance is not genuinely religious; human commitments, attitudes or feelings are somehow involved in the meaning of religious language; no genuinely religious utterance is entailed by a mere statement of fact.

Philosophers have suggested various criteria for distinguishing between 'statements' and 'value-judgments'; but it seems to me that the preceding analysis of performatives provides a new formulation which is fundamental: Behabitives are utterances in which the speaker implies various mental states (intentions, attitudes) other than, or in addition to, belief; Commissives are utterances in which the speaker commits himself to future patterns of more-than-merely-verbal behaviour; flat Constatives are utterances which have a factual content,[3] and which are neither Behabitive nor Commissive. Thus *no flat Constative entails a Behabitive or Commissive*; that is, *no flat Constative entails a self-involving utterance*. (In chapter 2 we shall consider expressions of feeling as another sort of self-involving utterance, but in

---

[1] E.g., R. W. Hepburn, *Christianity and Paradox*, London, 1958, ch. 8; also (with A. Flew), 'Problems of Perspective', article in *The Plain View*, Winter, 1955.

[2] I am referring to such a varied group as F. Schleiermacher, *On Religion*, tr. J. Oman, New York, 1958; R. Otto, *The Idea of the Holy*, tr. J. Harvey, 2nd. ed., Oxford, 1923; E. Bevan, *Symbolism and Belief*, London, 1938; P. Tillich, *Systematic Theology*, I, London, 1953; J. Baillie, *Our Knowledge of God*, Oxford, 1939; K. Barth, *Church Dogmatics*, Eng. tr., Edinburgh, 1936ff.; E. Brunner, *Dogmatics* I and II, London, 1949 and 1952; D. Bonhoeffer, *Creation and Fall*, London, 1959; G. S. Hendry, *God the Creator*, London, 1937. There are of course enormous differences among these theologians; but there is a general agreement in the claim that human commitments or attitudes or feelings are involved in the meaning of religious language.

[3] The class of 'flat Constative' will not be restricted to cases where the factual content has been *established*. A scientific hypothesis may be a 'flat Constative', though in ordinary language we contrast a 'hypothesis' with a '*statement* of fact'.

this chapter I am only using 'self-involving' to cover Behabitive and Commissive force.)

The range of self-involving (Behabitive and Commissive) utterances is broader than the range of utterances which the man in the street would call 'evaluative'. Indeed, it is even broader than the vast range of language which some philosophers cover with their technical use of the word 'evaluative' or 'value-judgment'. For many purposes of philosophical analysis one probably should not call language 'evaluative' unless some additional conditions are fulfilled; self-involving performative force should probably not be regarded as a sufficient condition for language to be 'evaluative'; but it is a necessary condition. Self-involving performative force is what makes 'evaluative' language differ from other language in such a way that there is an 'autonomy of value'.

Often a self-involving utterance is not self-labelling as to its performative force, but the occurrence of certain 'value-words' is a fairly reliable indication that the utterance has one or other of the self-involving performative forces. For example, the word 'good' indicates commendation ('good student') or recommendation ('good show') or worship ('God is good') or endorsement ('good cause'). Much value-judgment analysis has concentrated unduly on such value-words rather than on the various explicit performatives which clarify them; hence there has been a tendency to assimilate value-judgments to particular performative verbs: 'commend', 'subscribe' or 'command'. In a list of value-words we must include not only the very general ones like 'good', 'ought', 'beautiful' or 'important', but also the more specific ones like 'cruel'; the latter form a surprising proportion of the words in the dictionary.[1]

In so far as a 'value-judgment' or 'evaluative utterance' is a Behabitive or Commissive utterance, it is clear what is the basis for the 'autonomy of value'. The philosophical slogan 'No statement entails a value-judgment' is a particular way of pointing out that no utterance which does not have certain implications or commitments entails an utterance which does. The slogan draws our attention to cases where the first utter-

---

[1] For example, under 'ca' in the *Shorter Oxford English Dictionary*: 'cabal', 'cad', 'cadge', 'caggy', 'cajole', 'calamities', 'candid', 'cant', 'caricature', 'carl', 'carnal', 'carp', 'cattish', 'cavil'. Most of these, however, carry Prima-facie implications which are weak.

ance is a flat Constative. But the same logical point applies elsewhere: No 'flat' Exercitive or Verdictive entails a Behabitive or Commissive.

7.2. *Performatives and entailment*

Indeed, the 'autonomy of value' is only a particular version of a very general and fundamental feature of language, which performative-analysis reveals. Let p and q be any two utterances. Then p entails q when two conditions both hold:

(1) The performative forces of p and q are the same (or are related in the special way which we shall consider in section 7.2.3.).
(2) The abstractable contents cp and cq are such that cp and not-cq are incompatible when cp and not-cq are given the same performative force.

The first requirement is not prominent where 'entailment' is discussed in formal logic, for the logician assumes that p and q are both statements (which have truth-conditions), and he focuses his attention on the second requirement. But in the analysis of everyday language, it is unhelpful to restrict 'entailment' to relations between the 'statements' which the formal logician considers. For one promise may entail another promise, or one command entail another command. Moreover, the 'autonomy of value' slogan would be unilluminating if entailment-relations were restricted arbitrarily to relations between statements. For we would not understand *why*, for example, a (flat) statement cannot entail a promise. Nor would the restriction rule out putative entailment-relations which the 'autonomy of value' rightly prohibits: for example, between two utterances which have the same truth-conditions but which differ in that the second has Behabitive force whereas the first does not.

The particular non-entailment which is emphasized by the 'autonomy of value' is an instance of a more general feature of language: If an utterance does not have performative force F^1, it does not entail an utterance which does have performative force F^1.[1] Since a flat Constative, by definition, does not have Behabitive or Commissive force, it cannot entail an utterance which does. That is, in other terminology, 'No statement entails

[1] Unless the utterances are related in the special way which we shall consider in section 7.2.3.

a value-judgment'. *The non-entailment which is stressed by the
'autonomy of value' depends on a difference in performative force between
two utterances.* Austin's discovery of performatives thus enables
us to shed new light on a problem which has generated philosophical controversy for centuries.[1]

We shall now consider three sorts of performative-entailment:
(i) where the explicit performative force is the same in each
utterance; (ii) where the performative force of the premise is
non-explicit, but the performative force of the conclusion is
explicit; (iii) where the explicit performative force in the utterances is not the same. (Non-philosophers can omit this rather
technical discussion of performative-entailment, and move on to
section 7.3.)

7.2.1. *Entailment between explicit performatives*

Here are some syllogisms which involve explicit performative
verbs:

(a) 'I predict that I shall make all x's f.'
(b) 'a is an x.'
(c) 'I predict that I shall make a, f.'

(a) 'I promise that I will make all x's f.'
(b) 'a is an x.'
(c) 'I promise that I will make a, f.'

(a) 'I command you to make all x's f.'
(b) 'a is an x.'
(c) 'I command you to make a, f.'

In each syllogism, (a) and (b) entail (c); for (a) and (b) are
incompatible with not-(c). Note that not-(c) may take any one
of three distinct forms:

(i) 'I predict that I shall not make a, f.'
    'I promise that I will not make a, f.'
    'I command you not to make a, f.'
(ii) 'I do not predict that I shall make a, f.'
    'I do not promise that I will make a, f.'
    'I do not command you to make a, f.'

(That is, I refuse to predict, promise or command; or I disclaim
predicting, promising, or commanding.)

---

[1] Austin himself did not, to my knowledge, apply his analysis of performatives to
the problem of the 'autonomy of value'. Indeed, his analysis seemed to him to
suggest the following 'moral': 'The familiar contrast of "normative or evaluative"
as opposed to the factual is in need, like so many dichotomies, of elimination'
(*How to do Things with Words*, p. 148).

(iii) 'I did not predict that I would make a,f.' ⎱
       'I did not promise that I would make a,f.' ⎰ said later
       'I did not command you to make a,f.' ⎰
(Compare with another later utterance said by you concerning
me: 'He did not predict (promise, command) . . .'.)

The third form of not-(c) introduces difficulties which we shall
not consider here. If we confine our attention to the first two
forms of not-(c), it is obvious that (a) and (b) entail (c) by
virtue of the abstractable contents of (a) and (c) in relation to
(b), and by virtue of the explicit performative force which is
common to (a) and (c).

If the performative force of (a) and (c) is not explicit, an
entailment-relation is possible; but this is because we *assume* a
common performative force. Consider this syllogism:

(a) 'I made all x's f.'
(b) 'a is an x.'
(c) 'I made a,f.'

Here (a) and (b) entail (c), for (a) and (b) are incompatible
with not-(c): 'I did not make a,f.' We assume, having no reason
to think otherwise, that (a) and (c) have the same Constative
force; we assume, for example, that they are both statements.
But consider this syllogism:

(a) 'I will make all x's f.'
(b) 'a is an x.'
(c) 'I will make a,f.'

If both (a) and (c) are Commissive[1] expressions of intention,
then (a) and (b) entail (c). But if (a) is a prediction[2] and (c) is
an expression of intention, the entailment does not hold. For
example, the invalid syllogism might be:

(a) 'I will fail all the examinations.'
       (performative force of a prediction)
(b) 'One examination is on Kant.'
(c) 'I will fail the examination on Kant.'
       (performative force of an expression of intention)

Here (a) and (b) are not incompatible with not-(c), 'I will not
fail the examination on Kant', the performative force of which

---

[1] In chapter 2, section 1, we shall see that expressions of intention fall into the
class of Commissives.
[2] In everyday language, 'I will . . .' and 'I shall . . .' are often used interchange-
ably. If 'I will . . .' could only be used for expressions of intention and 'I shall . . .'
could only be used for predictions, no questions would arise concerning performative force in 'I will'-syllogisms and 'I shall'-syllogisms.

is made explicit by 'I intend not to fail the examination on Kant' (or perhaps, 'I do not intend to fail the examination on Kant').

Obviously the relation between non-explicit and explicit performatives requires further attention.

7.2.2. *Entailment and non-explicit performatives*

Consider the following suggestion concerning possible entailment-relations:

(1) If the utterance, 'I will go' has promissory force, then it entails, 'I promise to go'.
(2) If the utterance, 'Smith is loyal and honest' has commending force, then it entails, 'I commend Smith for being loyal and honest'.
(3) If the utterance, 'Smith is restrained and submissive' has commending force, then it entails, 'I commend Smith for being restrained and submissive'.
(4) If the utterance, 'You are my king' has acknowledging force, then it entails, 'I acknowledge that you are my king'.

In each case we have a particular utterance which by itself has non-explicit performative force, and an utterance which makes explicit the former's force on a particular occasion. Let us call this 'P?-P entailment'; the question-mark indicates non-explicit performative force. Another example would be:

(5) If the utterance, 'I will make all x's f' has promissory force, then, 'I will make all x's f, and a is an x' entails 'I promise to make a, f'.

There are two formidable objections to the use of the word 'entail' in such cases. First, surely the utterance by itself (for example, 'I will go') should entail such-and-such, without having to include the hypothetical clause, 'If the utterance . . .'. Second, except in (2) the performative force is speaker-dependent; the speaker can deny that his utterance has such-and-such force; he can deny that it carries such-and-such implications or commitments.

Thus the two-fold objection to 'P?-P entailment' is that it makes entailment hypothetical and speaker-dependent. But someone might reply with the following argument, asking us to consider this case of ordinary entailment:

(a) 'All Japanese are pacifists nowadays.'
(b) 'Yoshida is a Japanese.'
(c) 'Yoshida is a pacifist nowadays.'

Suppose that, in conversation, I utter (a) and (b); later on I say, 'Yoshida is not a pacifist nowadays'; you protest, 'You're contradicting what you said earlier'. I could legitimately reply, 'No, I didn't mean "all" in its strict sense'. Thus even a traditional syllogism perhaps needs to be expressed in a hypothetical form:[1]

If 'all x's are f', has non-exceptional and omnitemporal force, then 'all x's are f, and a is an x' entails 'a is f'.

And whether or not 'All x's are f' does have such force seems to depend, in some cases, on how the speaker regards[2] his utterance—what *he means* by 'all', rather than what *is meant*.[3]

This speaker-dependence of 'all', however, does have limits. For example, suppose that I am being sued for slander, and I admit that I said, 'All the women at 2 Main Street are prostitutes', I cannot claim that my words had the meaning, 'Most of the women . . .'; and what *I* personally meant is largely irrelevant. In most cases and in most contexts 'all' has a strict public meaning, independent of a particular speaker's intended meaning, and (largely) independent of context. So in spite of some similarity between P?-P entailments and ordinary entailments, it is perhaps best not to use the word 'entail' for the former except where P? is contradicted by not-P regardless of the speaker's intentions. (Indeed, in section 9.1. I shall suggest an alternative way of referring to the P?-P relation.)

The main point, however, is clear. The performative force of a particular utterance may depend mainly on the words, or the context, or the speaker's intention; but in *every* case the following remains true: If an utterance does not have performative force F[1], it does not entail an utterance which does have performative force F[1]. Since a flat Constative by definition does not have Behabitive or Commissive force, it cannot

---

[1] This form is not the one (which leads to an infinite regress) in which an argument's rule of inference is made a premise in the argument. The point here is that if a term in everyday English were so precise in its everyday meaning that the corresponding term in formal logic is its exact equivalent, no such hypothetical form would be needed. But in everyday language, the meaning of 'all' sometimes does depend on the intention of the speaker, or on the special context.

[2] Cf. R. M. Hare, *The Language of Morals*, p. 25.   [3] Cf. p. 49.

entail an utterance which does. That is, in other terminology,
'No statement entails a value-judgment'. The non-entailment
which is stressed by the 'autonomy of value' depends on a
difference in performative force between two utterances.

7.2.3. *Entailment and different performative forces*

We have considered examples of entailments where the
performative forces, whether explicit or non-explicit, are
identical in premise and conclusion. There are some cases,
however, where the forces may be different, yet an entailment-
relation is still present. Some performative words such as
'command', 'promise', 'grade', 'praise' and 'state', when used
descriptively, refer to a genus which includes a species:
(respectively) 'decree', 'pledge', 'rank', 'commend' and 'report'.
Hence 'I decree that x' entails 'I command that x'; 'I pledge
that x' entails 'I promise that x', etc. (Note that the genus-words
are paradigms of the five classes of performative: 'command' is
an Exercitive, 'promise' a Commissive, 'grade' a Verdictive,
'praise' a Behabitive, and 'state' a Constative.)

The logical point here may be expressed as follows: Where p
entails q, though p has performative force F^1 and q has performative force F^2, it must be true that 'p had force F^1' entails
'p had force F^2'. For example, '*I decree* that all spies be executed'
entails 'I *command* that some spies be executed'; for 'p was a
decree' entails 'p was a command'.

Apart from the genus-words to which I have referred, however, most performative words differ subtly from one another
in such a way as to make entailment-relations between them a
rarity. Where F^1 has 'more' force than F^2, F^1 may nevertheless
lack some meaning which F^2 has. For example, 'recommend'
has stronger Behabitive force than 'propose', but the latter
involves *bringing up* something or someone for consideration;
hence 'I recommend that x' does not strictly entail 'I propose
that x'.

We need not consider such subtleties in any further detail
here. But they do indicate the general lines for a comprehensive
study of entailment in everday language.

7.3. *The 'autonomy of value' and freedom*

Since the 'autonomy of value' depends on a difference in
performative force between two utterances it is a *logical*

doctrine. The 'freedom' or 'compulsion', the 'can' or 'cannot' with which it deals, is logical or linguistic; it is not psychological or moral. This point should be clearly understood. I have interpreted the slogan, 'No statement entails a value-judgment' as 'No flat Constative entails a self-involving utterance (that is, a Behabitive or Commissive)'. Some Kantian philosophers might mean a great deal more than this by the 'autonomy of value'. Consider this argument:

'No flat Constative entails a value-judgment.'
Therefore: (1) 'No external state of affairs affects a man's freedom in making a (truly) moral decision.'
Or:(2) 'A man ought not to allow any external state of affairs to affect his freedom in making a moral decision.'

We may or may not agree with (1) or (2); but the argument as such is spurious. The absence of an entailment-relation between a flat Constative and a self-involving utterance involves a 'freedom' from logical compulsion; but this has nothing to do with psychological freedom or moral freedom. If I utter sentence X, in which I do not imply anything concerning my attitudes or intentions, and do not commit myself to any future conduct, I am under no logical compulsion to utter or to accept sentence Y, which does have such implications or commitments. This 'freedom', however, is separate from my freedom in having a particular attitude, or in forming a particular intention, or in performing a particular deed. Suppose, for example, that I meet an unusual man who moves me to profound reverence. I am logically 'free' to accept certain flat Constatives (X) concerning this man, and yet to reject an utterance (Y) which implies that I have an attitude of reverence towards him. But this has nothing to do with two questions:

(1) The psychological (or philosophical) question: In what way am I 'free' when I respond reverently to the man's personality, and when this response issues in moral decisions?
(2) The moral question: To what extent ought I to let an external reality influence me profoundly in my moral decisions?

No answers to these questions are dictated by the lack of entailment-relation between a flat Constative and a self-involving ('evaluative') utterance. Indeed, with reference to (1), it might be the case that, although my logical freedom to

E

say, 'X.not-Y' remains, the personal qualities reported in X produce my reverent response in such a way that I do not 'choose' or 'decide' to revere the man at all.[1] And with reference to (2), it may be argued that true moral freedom consists in an 'openness' to certain external realities; such a view may be obscure and debatable, but it is not ruled out because of my logical 'freedom' to say, 'X.not-Y'.

In Part II we shall see that the *logical* character of the 'autonomy of value' is important in considering Creation. We shall discover evidence against the view that the utterance, 'God is my Creator' is a flat Constative. But let us suppose for the moment that such a view is correct; that is, let us suppose that in saying, 'God is my Creator', I am logically free to reject any self-involving utterances which might seem to be entailed. It is still an open question whether or not the experience which gives rise to my utterance leaves me psychologically free not to involve myself on a deeply personal level; there may be little room for choice or decision in the matter. And it is still an open question whether or not I ought to allow the alleged external Reality to influence me in my moral commitments.

But let us leave the 'autonomy of value' so that we may consider a group of words which is important in any study of self-involving language. (We shall see later that these words are sometimes specially prominent in expressions of attitude and in biblical language concerning Creation.)

8. *Institutional-relation words*

Consider the following examples:

'He is my king (lord, master, legal guardian, husband).'
'I am your subject (servant, ward, wife, estate manager, official spokesman, slave).'
'Mr MacTavish is my main creditor.'
'Mr Iqbash is the founder of our secret society, which exists by his authority alone.'

---

[1] It seems to me that R. M. Hare (*The Language of Morals*) links the *logical* autonomy of value-judgments too closely with *choice* in so far as the latter is a *psychological* matter. A. Flew has even argued for the occurrence of *unconscious* decisions which are 'logically inescapable', apparently arguing from a logical point (the autonomy of value) to a psychological conclusion. ('Problems of Perspective', *The Plain View*, Winter, 1955, p. 154.)

The key words here are words for *status* or *role* within the institutional structure of human society. The utterances involve the speaker in Prima-facie commitments. Unless he disclaims these commitments, his utterances are legitimately taken as acknowledgments of status or role. Such institutional-relation words include as part of their meaning some indication of conduct which is thought to be appropriate. As D. Emmet has said, 'A role has some norm of behaviour built into it'.[1]

This comes about because 'social life depends on certain expectations as to how people are going to behave, and the fact that these are sufficiently often fulfilled for individuals to plan their own conduct accordingly. . . . Some of these mutual expectations become standardized in terms of socially recognized rights and obligations. When a person is acting in a sphere where these hold, he is carrying out what sociologists call a *role*. A role is a part someone plays in a pattern of social activities. . . . The position a person occupies, in virtue of which he has certain capacities afforded to carry out his role, is called his *status*. A "status" is thought of as a position someone holds which carries with it certain rights and obligations, whereas a "role" is thought of as a form of action in which these are put into operation.'[2]

Hence, according to Professor Emmet, 'Social relationship can seldom be described in terms which are valuationally aseptic. . . . The ways in which a social relationship is described will suggest that certain obligations are appropriate to it, even if these vary from one society to another. It may, of course, be possible to talk about ways in which other people see their roles in purely descriptive terms; but the description is likely to contain some expressions connected with our own conceptions of what is appropriate behaviour in such roles.'[3]

It is important to notice that the institutional-relation words involve commitments which are Prima-facie, not Indefeasible. Suppose that a girl has decided to elope, rejecting the authority of her legal guardian. She says to an older friend:

> 'Yes, he is my legal guardian and I'm his ward, but I'm not going to seek his permission.'

Friend: 'But you just admitted that you are his ward.'

[1] *Function, Purpose and Powers*, London, 1958, p. 10.
[2] *Ibid.*, pp. 26-7; my italics for 'status'.   [3] *Ibid.*, p. 10.

Reply: 'I was just stating a legal fact. I didn't commit myself to acting as his dutiful child.'

Note also that the Commissive force of institutional-relation words may be set aside in a descriptive context. Indeed, the descriptive context is perhaps typical; the Commissive force is strongest in *face-to-face* contexts, where I say, 'You are my legal guardian' or 'You are my Lord'.

Yet we should pay attention to the radical difference between institutional-relation words and some other words. It is important to distinguish two sorts of words which may be applied to human actions: 'institutional' and 'causal'. When I say, 'Jones has *appointed* me to be his estate-manager', I refer to an act in institutional terms, and thereby acknowledge my own status and role (unless I disclaim the Prima-facie commitment). But if I say, 'Jones *built* my house', or 'Jones *made* my wooden leg', I refer to an act in 'causal' terms; here the language itself involves no such commitments. In chapter 4 we shall see the immense importance of the contrast between institutional and causal language in biblical talk about God the Creator. In so far as biblical men referred to the act of Creation in institutional terms, and especially as they addressed God personally in these terms, they committed themselves to certain behaviour. But they also use causal terms (for example, 'make') which do not carry a self-involving force when they occur in everyday language. (Chapter 4 will deal mainly with institutional terms and chapter 6 with causal terms.)

We have seen that when words are used performatively, institutional relations are sometimes established and sometimes invoked. Our next task is to consider another sort of *use* for words, a causal use. In particular, we shall distinguish the use of words as Exercitive utterances in establishing or invoking institutional relations from the use of words as causal instruments in bringing about results which are not necessarily institutional. This distinction, which we shall later apply to 'Creation by the word', is a particular species of a more general distinction: between the 'performative force' and 'causal power' of words.

9. *Performative force and causal power*

The first step is a clarification of philosophical talk about the 'meaning' and 'use' of words.

9.1. *Performative force and meaning*

It should be realized that the performative force of an utterance on a particular occasion is part of its meaning.[1] If someone hears what I say but does not recognize the performative force of my utterance, he has failed to grasp the full meaning of my utterance. For example, if on a particular occasion I say, 'You may go' (S), the performative force of my utterance is perhaps made explicit by, 'I order you to go' (P). Consider some other examples of non-explicit utterances (S) whose performative force on a particular occasion is made explicit by an explicit performative (P):

(S) 'I'll be there.'
(P) 'I promise to be there.'
(S) 'Smith is honest and loyal.'
(P) 'I commend Smith for being honest and loyal.'
(S) 'You ought to take the job.'
(P) 'I advise you that you ought to take the job.'
(S) 'People ought to be kind to animals.'
(P) 'I subscribe to the principle that people ought to be kind to animals.'

In each case, what is the relation between S, the initial utterance, and P, which makes explicit its performative force on a particular occasion? Here we must distinguish two meanings of 'mean': (i) What *I* mean in saying S may be made explicit by P; that is, I *intend* S to have the meaning made explicit by P. (ii) What the words of S mean may be made explicit by P; that is, the words of S are such that a reasonable person, who knows the relevant linguistic conventions, would in the specific context *take* S to have the meaning (that is, the performative force) which is made explicit in P; otherwise S does not *have* this meaning, even though I mean (that is, intend) S to have this meaning. Often, of course, an utterance has the meaning which I intend it to have; I successfully use S in such a way that it has the intended performative force. And sometimes, as we have seen,[2] the public performative force depends partly on the speaker's intention. In any case, the analysis of the

---

[1] Austin restricted the 'meaning' of an utterance to its 'sense and reference' (roughly my 'content') and so he *contrasted* 'meaning' and force (*How to do Things with Words*, pp. 33, 100, but see p. 148). Such a restriction of the meaning of 'meaning' does not seem to me to be warranted.
[2] P. 49.

meaning of S must include not only its content but also its performative force.

9.2. *Use: performative and causal*

There is, however, another sort of *use* which utterances may be given, which is not part of their meaning:[1] not a performative but a *causal* use. For example, I may say, 'Jones is treacherous' in order to warn you (performative use) and in order to alarm you (causal use). Or I may say, 'I commend you for your diligence' so as to please you; the commending is performative and the pleasing is causal. I may say, 'I believe in God the Father Almighty, Maker of heaven and earth' as a profession of faith, and also as a means of inspiring someone else. I may order you to run as a means of getting you to run. I may reprimand you in order to deter you from future misconduct. I may use certain words in order to thank God and also in order to stir up grateful feelings in myself.

Sometimes the causal result of an utterance is not intended: I may name the ship the *Ivernia* and, incidentally, annoy people who wanted a royal name. Indeed, *any* utterance may have a causal result, intended or unintended; where the result is intended, we can quite properly speak of the utterance's being *used* as a means to the particular end. But this use is not in itself part of the meaning of the sentence, though it usually depends on the meaning, and not just on the words as sounds. Whether or not what I say is (that is, is correctly described as) a warning, a commendation, a profession of faith, an order, a reprimand, and so on, depends on conventions of language and society. But whether or not what I say alarms, pleases, inspires, and so on, is simply a matter of fact. The performative force is usually independent of the causal power: I may warn you, yet not alarm you, order you to run, yet not get you to run, give thanks, yet evoke no feeling of gratitude. A warning is not merely an attempted alarming, or an order merely an attempted getting-to-do. And causal power is usually independent of particular performatives. I can usually bring about the desired effect in some way, by using a different performative or by some non-verbal action.

---

[1] The modern philosopher's slogan, following Wittgenstein, has been, 'When you look for the meaning, ask for the use', or variants of this. The slogan can be a source of error if we include the *causal* use as part of the meaning.

Of course, there are many performatives which require a minimal degree of apprehension by some hearer, for example, 'admit', 'warn', 'apologize', 'thank', 'promise'; but this is a pre-condition of *both* the performative force and the causal power; it is not something which blurs the distinction between the two. On the whole, the distinction[1] is clear and sharp. Moreover, it is extremely useful in the study of various topics with which we are not concerned in this book, for example, the sacraments ('valid' and 'efficacious' celebrations), or justification by grace ('imputed' and 'infused' righteousness), or the uses of moral language ('imperative' and 'emotive' theories).

9.3. *Exercitives and causal power*

There is considerable chance of confusion, however, where the performatives are Exercitives, where the speaker brings about a conventional state of affairs in saying what he does:

---

[1] The argument in section 9.2 has been taken from Austin, *How to do Things with Words*, Lectures VIII–X. He spoke of 'illocutionary force' rather than 'performative force', and he contrasted '*il*locutionary acts' (what one does *in* saying something) with '*per*locutionary acts' (what one does *by* saying something). For an early sketch of a distinction similar to Austin's illocutionary/perlocutionary distinction, see R. M. Hare, 'Freedom of the Will', *Arist. Soc. Sup. Vol.* 25, 1951, pp. 207ff.

Readers who are familiar with Austin's work may find it useful at this point to have a list of my deviations from Austin, which occur in sections 1, 2, 3, 5 and 9. Note that the differences of terminology in A, B and C occur for the sake of simplicity and in D for the sake of accuracy; deviations E, F and G occur because I disagree with Austin.

	How to do Things with Words	*Self-Involvement and Creation*	(*page*)
A	Infelicities	Infelicities	
	'Misfires'/'Abuses'	I/II (a and b)	28, n. 3
	(4 kinds) (2 kinds)		
B	'explicit'/'primary'	'explicit'/'non-explicit'	44, n. 2
C	'illocutionary'/'perlocutionary'	'performative'/'causal'	71, n. 1
D	'pure'/'descriptive'	'pure'/'autobiographical'	44, n. 2
E	A Behabitive is the expression of an attitude or the adopting of an attitude.	A Behabitive implies an attitude.	35, n. 1
F	The distinction of 'constatives' as a class of factural or true-or-false utterances is abandoned.	A class of 'Constatives' is distinguished from Exercitives, Verdictives and Commissives in that Constatives have an abstractable factual content.	38, n. 1
	AND	AND	
	The philosophical contrast between 'factual' and 'evaluative' utterances should be eliminated.	The philosophical contrast between 'factual' and 'evaluative' utterances is reinterpreted and reaffirmed. Performative force (that is, Austin's 'illocutionary force') is *part* of meaning.	60, n. 1
G	Illocutionary force is *distinguished* from meaning.		69, n. 1

for example, 'appoint', 'order', 'name', 'authorize', 'decree'. Suppose that we read the following: 'The royal decree took effect on August 1st, 1641'. The phrase 'took effect' may suggest causal efficacy, but this is not the efficacy which is actually meant. For whether or not a decree 'takes effect' is a matter of its success in being a decree, its not being null and void; its taking effect on August 1st means that from that day certain actions were legal, in order, obedient, etc., and other actions were not, *if* these actions took place; the 'taking effect' does not mean that certain legal or obedient actions did in fact take place.

Yet the success in being a decree does depend on its conformity with a recognized procedure, and its being performed by someone who is entitled to issue decrees, which in this case is closely related to whether or not some men recognize Charles' authority as King. It is possible to recognize authority and yet to disobey; indeed, if I do not recognize an authority, I am not willing to call my action 'disobedient' or 'illegal'. But recognition of authority usually involves some degree of obedience in actual conduct. And certainly the purpose of a decree is not merely that men may henceforth *regard* one action as 'obedience' and another action as 'disobedience', but that men may do the one and not the other. Exercitive performatives are usually uttered with the intention of bringing about certain results.

The relevance of 'intended results', however, need not blur the distinction between the performative force and the causal power of a particular Exercitive utterance. The utterance 'On the double', for example, may succeed in being an order (as was intended) and it may succeed in getting me to run (as was intended); but the two intentions are distinct. We can also distinguish two sorts of description of the result of the utterance. On the one hand, the action which results may be described in non-institutional language—for example, as 'running', which might be produced by non-institutional means (for example, by a swarm of bees). On the other hand, the action which results may be described in institutional language—for example, as 'obeying the Sergeant-Major's order'. As such, the action or state must have been brought about by a successfully Exercitive utterance; if what he said

was not an order, what I did was not an act of obedience to
an order.

The fact that the causal use or power of an utterance is not
part of the meaning of the utterance may be obscured by the
fact that the word 'mean' sometimes means 'intend'. For
example, consider the following:

'When I said, "The door is open", I meant you to close the door.'

Presumably I intended to get you to close the door, and I used
what I said as an attempted means to this end. But what I
intended, the causal result which I hoped to bring about,
is not part of the meaning of what I said. The example is
perplexing, however, for 'I meant you to close the door'
might also mean 'I meant you to take my utterance as a request
to close the door'. In this case what I 'meant' obviously is
related to the (intended) meaning of the utterance. Perhaps
the distinction can be seen more easily in another example:

'By saying, "We met at the Stork Club", I meant to embarrass
you.'

Here what I 'meant' is what I intended to bring about causally
by means of my utterance; it is clearly not part of the meaning
of the utterance itself. (The achievement of the result does
depend on your understanding the meaning of the utterance,
or on a third person's understanding; but this does not make it
part of the meaning.)

In typical cases where words have causal power there is a
hearer who understands the meaning of the utterance to some
extent, and who freely cooperates to some extent by allowing
himself to be influenced by the words-with-their-meaning. It
is true that an utterance may produce results irrespective of
its meaning, merely by being a sound: it may annoy a sleepless
man or bring about mechanical changes in a recording machine.
But this sort of causal power is irrelevant in an analysis of
language.

Such causal power is also virtually irrelevant in an analysis
of the biblical conception of Creation. (The notion of Spirit-
wind as Creative power is an exception.[1]) What is relevant is a
fanciful sort of magic in which there is no intelligent hearer

---

[1] See chapter 4, section 3.2.

who understands the words and cooperates freely, yet in which
the *meanings* of words are important. Suppose that whenever
you said, 'Table, rise three inches', it did. Or, better still,
suppose that whenever you said, 'One orange', an orange
would suddenly materialize in your hand. This action would
be somewhat similar to divine Creation of inanimate things
as portrayed in the Bible. The orange example also seems to be
an analogy for Creation of human beings as well, where this is
conceived as a bare causing-to-exist, without any human understanding or cooperation being required. A much better
analogy, however, would be provided by the Queen, if her
saying, 'One Governor of Kenya' both brought a man into
existence and appointed him to his task; by her word she would
'create' him in both ways at once; her word would have both
causal power and Exercitive force.

10. *A summary*

At this point it may be useful to schematize some of the
analysis by drawing an outline of the language-'map' which
has emerged so far. Four main areas have been explored:
performative language, implications and commitments, conditions for entailments, uses of language.

Performative Language
which may be

explicit or non-explicit   pure or autobiographical

can be classified as:
Constative
Verdictive
Exercitive
Commissive . . .⎫
Behabitive   . . .⎭ . . . self-involving

Implications	*and*	*Commitments*
Indefeasible		Indefeasible
Prima-facie:		Prima-facie
(a) Speaker-independent		
(b) Speaker-dependent		
Contextual:		Contextual:
(a) Occasional		(a) Occasional
(b) Traditional		(b) Traditional

Conditions for Entailment

Entailments depend on $\begin{cases} \text{Performative force} \\ \text{Abstractable content} \end{cases}$

Uses of Language
Performative
Causal

11. *Non-verbal performatives and correlative performatives*

The main outline of a performative language-'map' can now be seen. But two special areas remain to be sketched in. The first is non-verbal performatives.

11.1. *Non-verbal performatives*

So far, we have only considered performatives which consist of words. Some performatives, however, are non-verbal. Sometimes an institutional act can be performed not only verbally but also non-verbally. I acknowledge status by bowing or saluting; I welcome by shaking hands; I bless by laying on of hands; I marry by mingling blood; I command by pointing; or I mourn by rending garments. Each action, like a performative utterance, has a performative force.

In my initial presentation of performative utterances, I distinguished them from other utterances by noting that they are deeds: in saying, 'I promise . . .', I promise; in saying, 'I welcome . . .', I welcome, etc. But we soon saw[1] that *all* utterances are deeds, all utterances have performative force; the original examples had been self-labelling and explicit, but *performatives may be non-explicit.* Here, when I call some *non*-verbal behaviour 'performative', this is all that is meant: the behaviour has performative force, it is an institutional act. Verbal and non-verbal performatives may thus be schematized as follows:

(a) Verbal:

Explicit: In saying, 'q', I do q.
       (In saying, 'Welcome', I welcome.)

Non-explicit: In saying such-and-such, which has the force of saying 'q', I do q.
       (In saying, 'How nice to see you',
                  I welcome.)

---

[1] See p. 45.

(b) Non-verbal: In doing p, which has the force of saying 'q',
I do q.
(In shaking hands, I welcome.)

Note that I have *not* contrasted (a) with (b) in the following way, which is epigrammatic but misleading:

(a) In saying, I do.
(b) In doing, I say.

For what I 'do' in (a) and what I 'say' in (b) is the *same*: I perform an institutional act; my behaviour in each case has the particular performative force which would be made explicit by an explicit performative utterance.[1] A performative action is *made explicit* verbally, but the action itself need not be verbal; it may be non-verbal.

11.2. *Correlative performatives*

Performatives, whether verbal or non-verbal, are sometimes 'correlative'. Consider the following examples:

Jones' utterance:	*Smith's reply:*
(1) 'I order you to go.' (Exercitive)	(1) 'Yes, sir.'
(2) 'I appoint you governor.' (Exercitive)	(2) 'I accept the office.'
(3) (i) 'I judge Brown to be a scoundrel.' (Verdictive)	(3) (i) 'I agree.'
(ii) 'I give you this watch.' (Exercitive)	(ii) 'I thank you.'
(4) 'I promise never to let you down.' (Commissive)	(4) 'I trust you.'

Let us consider Smith's replies. Each one is a self-involving acknowledgment of Jones' performative utterance. Smith's replies are Behabitive or Commissive, or both; he implies an attitude, or he commits himself to an attitude or to future conduct, or he does both. Each self-involving reply is a performative utterance which is 'correlative' to one of Jones' performative utterances. If Jones' performative actions were non-verbal, Smith's replies could still be 'correlative'. Consider the following examples:

Jones' non-verbal action:	*Smith's reply:*
(1) Jones points at Smith and then at the door.	(1) 'Yes, sir.'

---

[1] There are exceptions. For example, my gesture or utterance may have the performative force of an insult, although there is no explicit performative form in English: 'I insult you'. (The example is Austin's.)

(2) Jones places his ceremonial sword in Smith's hand.

(2) 'I accept the office.'

(3) (i) Jones glances at Brown and then scowls deliberately.

(3) (i) 'I agree.'

(ii) Jones puts his watch on Smith's wrist.

(ii) 'I thank you.'

(4) Jones shakes Smith's hand as he looks steadfastly into his eyes.

(4) 'I trust you.'

What makes two performatives 'correlative'? Smith's reply is 'correlative' to Jones' verbal or non-verbal performative because in each case *Smith implies that he takes Jones' action to have a performative force which makes the reply an appropriate one*; that is, Smith implies either that he supposes (perhaps mistakenly) that Jones' action actually *has* this performative force, or that he *ascribes* this force to Jones' action. Note that if Smith had replied negatively in each case, his replies could still have been correlative:

(1) 'No, sir.'
(2) 'I decline the office.'
(3) (i) 'I disagree.'
    (ii) 'I refuse to accept it.'
(4) 'I refuse to trust you.'

Here, too, Smith implies in each case that he takes Jones' action to have a performative force which makes the reply an appropriate one. If, for example, Smith does *not* take Jones' pointing gestures as an order, it would be inappropriate—indeed, it would be misleading—to say *either* 'Yes, sir' *or* 'No, sir'.

In Chapter 4 we shall see that correlative performatives are extremely important in the biblical conception of Creation. Indeed, we shall see that the divine 'word' of Creation is logically similar to Jones' utterances, and the human word concerning Creation is logically similar to Smith's replies. For divine Creation is Creation by the divine 'word' or 'utterance', which has not only the causal power to bring things into existence but also the performative force of an institutional act; and the human utterance concerning this divine performative is a self-involving acknowledgment which has correlative performative force.

God's 'utterance':

(1) 'I order you to exist as my servant.' (Exercitive)

Man's reply:

(1) 'Yes, Lord, I acknowledge my status.'

(2) 'I appoint you as my steward over nature.' (Exercitive)

(2) 'I accept this role.'

(3) (i) 'I judge creaturely existence to be good.' (Verdictive)

(3) (i) 'I accept this authoritative verdict.'

(ii) 'I give you existence as a blessing.' (Exercitive)

(ii) 'I thank thee.'

(4) 'I pledge you my steadfast love.' (Commissive)

(4) 'I put my trust in thee.'

In Chapter 4 we shall consider these correlative divine and human performatives in detail, referring to the biblical evidence. Here I wish merely to point out that the human self-involving acknowledgments of God's Creative action imply an interpretation of this action in *performative* terms—as an order, an appointment, a verdict, a gift, a pledge. The performative interpretation need not be literal; in this book it will definitely *not* be literal. But since *some* sort of performative interpretation is implied, the analysis of self-involving elements in the biblical conception of Creation must deal not only with *human* self-involving language *concerning* Creation, but also with the *divine* performative 'word' *of* Creation.

These brief studies of non-verbal performatives and correlative performatives bring the analysis of performatives, if not to completion, at least to a suitable close. We have seen that Behabitive and Commissive performatives are self-involving. Now we shall consider another way in which language may be self-involving: when it is used to express feelings.

2

EXPRESSIONS OF FEELING

WE HAVE considered two uses of language: performative and causal. Now I shall try to show that there is another distinct use: for expressing feelings. This use is important in any consideration of self-involving language. It is also important in any consideration of the Christian idea of Creation. Eminent and influential thinkers such as Schleiermacher[1] and Otto[2] have interpreted the idea of Creation in terms of feelings. And we shall see that biblical language concerning Creation is often used to express feeling, especially in so far as Creation is viewed as a revelation of divine glory; one understands this glory in so far as one responds, and the response is, in part, a feeling. Moreover (and this is more important), an examination of expressive behaviour and other ways in which *feelings* are *revealed* will shed light on the biblical view of how the Creator's inner *Self* is *revealed*.

Since current philosophical literature does not seem to provide even a framework within which to begin an analysis of expressions of feeling, my account in this chapter will involve a rather detailed and complex analysis. Even so, it is only an initial and tentative exploration of the area. We shall see that verbal expressions of feeling, like Behabitive and Commissive utterances, are self-involving, and that they involve a distinct use of language, alongside the performative and causal uses. A great deal of the analysis, however, will be concerned with *non-*verbal expressions of feeling. There are two reasons for this. First, verbal expressions of feeling are properly understood only

---

[1] F. Schleiermacher, *The Christian Faith*, 2nd ed., tr. H. R. Mackintosh, Edinburgh, 1928, pp. 149-56.
[2] R. Otto, *The Idea of the Holy*, pp. 9-11, 20-21, 77-80. N. Smart, like Otto, interprets the idea of Creation in relation to numinous feelings; but he emphasizes the *expression* of feelings. (*Reasons and Faiths*, London, 1958, ch. 1.)

in relation to non-verbal ones. Second, the examination of non-verbal expressions of feeling and other feeling-revealing-behaviour is extremely relevant to theology; as I said above, the analysis will shed light on the biblical view of how the Creator's inner Self is revealed.

The first task is to distinguish the use of language to express feelings from its performative use. I shall examine the distinction where at first sight it may seem that the two uses merge: in 'expressive' language. I shall compare 'expression of feeling' with 'expression of opinion' and 'expression of intention'. Though the word 'express' rightly suggests important similarities between these, there is a basic difference: whereas expressions of opinion and intention are performative utterances, the phrase 'expression of feeling' classifies an utterance in a different sort of way.

1. *Expressions of feeling, opinion and intention*

Expressions of feeling, opinion and intention do have many similar logical features, which should be noted before we explore the differences:

(1) I cannot express your opinion, intention, or feeling, though I can report these; 'expressions of . . .' are first-personal.[1]

(2) The range of first-personal matters which can be expressed is limited to what is 'private'. I can report on my own activities or behaviour, but I do not 'express' these. What I express is 'private' in that, to a large extent, I am the primary authority concerning it; on the whole, it is for me to say what my opinions, intentions or feelings are.[2]

(3) A common element in the concept of 'expressing' is 'making public', as opposed to 'concealing'. I may know what I think of Smith, or what I intend to do next, or how I am feeling, and yet not express my opinion, intention or feeling—that is, not publicize it. In such a case, I have formed an opinion or intention explicitly but privately, or I have knowingly restrained my inclination to certain specific feeling-expressing behaviour.

---

[1] In exceptional cases I can express your opinion, intention or feeling; when you *accept* what I say as being an expression of your opinion, intention or feeling. Such 'proxy-expressions', like proxy-promises, proxy-thanks, proxy-commands, etc., are indirectly yet essentially first-personal.

[2] My behaviour *may* reveal an opinion (belief, assumption) or intention or feeling of which I am unaware, but which I would acknowledge if it were pointed out; such cases are being ignored in the analysis here.

(4) When I 'express' an opinion, intention or feeling, I often 'articulate' that which is otherwise vague. Sometimes I have thought about Smith, or considered what to do, or have a feeling, but in each case the opinion, intention or feeling was vague until I expressed it. Of course, I may have a definite, articulated opinion, intention or feeling which I have not expressed (that is, not publicized).

(5) The phrases 'expression of opinion', 'expression of intention' and 'expression of feeling' each refer to a class of speech-act (although the third is not restricted to speech-acts). In saying, 'I think that Smith is unreliable', I express an opinion. In saying, 'I intend to visit Burford to-morrow', I express an intention. In saying, 'What a magnificent view!' I express a feeling. Each utterance may suffer from what looks like performative-Infelicity IIa: I may be *insincere*, lacking the opinion, intention or feeling which I express. Nevertheless the utterance in such cases remains an expression of opinion, intention or feeling, just as 'I promise to do . . .' is a promise even when it is insincere. Thus the phrase 'expression of . . .' seems to be used to classify utterances as to their performative force.

Such an interpretation is feasible for expressions of intention and opinion. To say, 'Jones expressed his intention to do x' is to classify Jones' utterance as a Commissive, a minimal undertaking. And the utterance, 'Jones expressed the opinion that p' has two uses: (a) Sometimes it is used to classify Jones' utterance as an unofficial Verdictive; that is, it is used to indicate that Jones' utterance was concerned with a matter of opinion: a matter concerning which Jones (and others) are only entitled to give an opinion. (b) Sometimes it is used to classify Jones' utterance according to the degree of backing which he gave to it, even where it has to do with a matter of fact; for example, what Jones said was, 'I think that the Germans are planning another offensive'; in such cases the utterance is to be compared with Constative performatives: testimony, guess, assumption, etc.

In our classification of performatives, however, there is no obvious place for expressions of feeling. And further differences appear when we examine the notion of 'sincerity' in expressions of opinion, intention and feeling. The sincerity of my expression of opinion does not depend on its correspondence with an inner mental activity, state or event, in addition to my saying something and meaning it. Consider the following pairs of examples:

1.(1) 'This morning I was thinking about Smith.'
  (2) 'This morning I was thinking that Smith is unreliable.'
2.(1) 'I think that this morning I was thinking about Smith.'
  (2) 'I think that Smith is unreliable.'

Examples 1.(1) and 1.(2) are autobiographical reports which are true or false, depending on whether or not my words correspond with some mental event or thinking activity which took place this morning. But the sincerity of the words 'I think' in examples 2.(1) and 2.(2) does not depend on a similar correspondence; there need not be such an event or activity concomitant with, and in addition to, the utterance of the words. The sincerity depends, rather, on something mysterious: on whether I now *mean* what I say. (This meaning of 'mean' should be distinguished from another,[1] where I 'mean what I say' in the sense that I intend the words to have their conventional meaning—perhaps in order to deceive someone!)

Such a rough sketch of 'sincerity' in expressions of opinion (or in expressions of intention, which are similar in this respect), obviously raises many problems.[2] But perhaps it provides an adequate basis for showing how such sincerity differs from the 'sincerity' which is involved in expressions of feeling. Suppose that I insincerely express profound sadness concerning your departure. Here what is lacking is the feeling which, in some sense, 'corresponds' to my expression of feeling; it is not just a matter of privately refraining from meaning what I say. For an expression of opinion or intention to be sincere, what is required is that I privately mean what I say; the concomitant occurrence of certain internal thinking activity may be relevant, but it is neither a necessary nor a sufficient condition for sincerity. But for an expression of feeling to be sincere I must not only 'mean' what I say or do but also *have* the feeling; and if I have the feeling, my expression of feeling is sincere. The sincerity of my expression of opinion or intention does not depend decisively on what true-or-false reports can be made concerning

[1] See chapter 1, section 9.1.
[2] For example, if the question is whether or not I now mean what I say when I express an opinion or intention, I am in a better position than you are (and a different position from yours) to know whether or not I now mean what I say. What is it to 'mean what one says'? That is, what is it to be sincere, to involve oneself personally as well as linguistically? In section 2 of ch. 7, *Some Further Problems*, I shall argue that a study of linguistic self-involvement in religious language fails to answer important questions concerning the nature of personal or 'existential' self-involvement in religion; but such a study is an indispensable prerequisite.

me—for example, concerning what I was thinking just now, or what I have been planning to do. The sincerity of my expression of feeling, however, does depend decisively on what true-or-false reports can be made concerning what I feel. The function of an expression of opinion or an expression of intention is Verdictive or Commissive; it is not to give an autobiographical report but to give an unofficial verdict (or qualified backing), or a minimal undertaking. The function of an expression of feeling, however, cannot be separated so definitely from reports of feeling.

Note that a speaker does not 'create' his opinion or intention merely by uttering certain words in a certain context, as a speaker may 'create' his promise; what he thus creates is his expression-of-opinion and expression-of-intention. But he can 'create' his opinion and intention by uttering certain words in a certain context and *meaning* them, whereas he cannot create a feeling in this way. He may evoke a feeling, in himself or in others, by uttering certain words; and he may also evoke an opinion or intention in a similar way; but such causal 'evoking' is different from 'creating' one's own opinion or intention by saying certain words and meaning them.

Thus with reference to feelings (but not to opinions or intentions) there is an 'expressive' use of language which is different from both the performative and the causal uses of language. This expressive use is often closely associated with performative uses. For example, we shall later see that if I 'express an attitude' I 'express' an intention or opinion (performative use) and I sometimes also 'express' a feeling (expressive use).

The contrast between expressions of feeling and expressions of opinion or intention should not mislead us into thinking that feelings as such are sharply distinct and separable from opinions and intentions. There are intimate connections between feelings and opinions, and between feelings and intentions.

First let us consider feelings and opinions. I feel hopeful, wistful, or anxious about what I think may happen, but I feel regretful, nostalgic or disappointed about what I think has happened; this difference arises because of the meaning of the words 'hopeful', 'regretful', etc. Similarly I feel jubilant about such things as victories, but I feel gleeful about such things as practical jokes. I feel sympathy for someone who I think is in trouble; I feel admiration for someone whom I think to be superior to me, and I feel jealousy towards someone who I think is enjoying favours which I desire. That is, what one thinks to be the occasion or the object of a feeling partly determines (logically) what sort of a feeling it is. A feeling is linked with its own context of opinion, or more generally, with its own context of thought; for the person may conceive the total situation to be such-and-such, and regard his conception as an opinion,—but perhaps as knowledge, or as mere guess-work.

The link between feeling and context-of-thought is not absolute. On the one hand, it makes sense to say, 'I think he's dangerous, but I don't feel afraid', or 'I think he's superior to me in brains and character, but I don't admire him'. And on the other hand, it makes sense to say, 'I feel afraid, though I think, indeed I know, there's no danger', or 'I feel jealous, but I don't think he has given me any reason to feel that way'. That is, a feeling may be irrational in that one does not even have the appropriate opinion;[1] this is a different matter from its being unjustified in that one's opinion is mistaken, though one's feeling is appropriate to the opinion. Indeed, there are very few feelings, except specific feeling-sensations of warmth, pressure, movement and pain, which do not necessarily indicate some opinion. Usually I 'feel . . . about . . .'. (We shall consider some exceptions later.)[2]

Now let us consider feelings in relation to intentions. Public behaviour, or a tendency or inclination to public behaviour, usually enters into the meaning of feeling-words. For example whereas two colour-sensations, or a colour-sensation and a sound-sensation differ intrinsically, fear and anger do not; they differ in terms of felt tendencies or inclinations to action, or in terms of actual actions (flight *versus* attack). Since this behaviour is usually, to some degree, intentional, feelings are linked with intentions. Moreover, there is an even closer link between feelings and intentions. We shall see later that a full-fledged expression of

---

[1] Note that there is an ambiguity in the notion of 'opinion' or 'thought' here. It would be very odd to say, 'I feel afraid, but I have no thoughts (i.e. mental occurrences) concerning possible danger'. When I deny that I *think* there is danger, I am not denying the occurrence of certain 'thoughts' as mental events; I am refusing to express the opinion that there is danger; the 'I think' is not autobiographical, but Verdictive.

[2] See sections 2.1 and 3.5.3.

feeling is an action performed with the intention of showing someone how one feels. Such an expression of feeling is an intentional act, unlike a mere symptom of feeling.

2. *The range of feelings*

Before we compare expressions of feeling with symptoms of feeling (or with manifestations of feeling and reports of feeling), we should be more definite concerning feelings as such.

2.1. *A classification of feelings*

The word 'feeling' is so comprehensive and so vague that a great many different classifications of feelings are feasible, and perhaps none can be both exhaustive and precise. Nevertheless, I am proposing a four-fold classification of feelings: as Moods (joyful, hopeful), Responses (amazed, disgusted), Sensations (pain, warmth) and Bodily States (tired, excited). This classification has the merit of being useful in an analysis of 'expressions of feeling'. (We shall also find it useful when we consider the feelings which are expressed in response to the Creator's glory.) Obviously other classifications, for other purposes, are possible.

A list of *Moods* might include joy, hope, serenity, satisfaction, uneasiness, gloom, anxiety and wistfulness. Such feelings might also have been called 'feeling-tones' or 'states of mind'; but 'Mood' seems to be the most suitable label.

Responses include being amazed, disgusted, astonished, horrified, surprised, and dismayed. Such feelings are usually brief and episodic in contrast with Moods; usually one can say precisely *when* one felt amazed or disgusted or astonished. And such feelings are a response *to* something or other. I feel amazed *at* such-and-such, whereas I may feel joyful without there being some definite event or object which is the occasion of the feeling.

Sensations are feelings which can be located. Examples are pain, pressure, movement, warmth, tingles, itches, thrills, shocks, throbs. If I ask, '*Where* do you feel the pain?' my question makes good sense, and you may answer, 'In my leg'. But it makes no sense to ask, 'Where do you feel joyful?' (Mood) or 'Where do you feel amazed?' (Response).

Bodily States are feelings which are indicated by such words as 'tired', 'tense', 'uncomfortable' or 'excited'. It does make sense to ask, 'Where do you feel tired, (or tense, or uncomfortable, or —less plausibly—excited)?' The answer, however, may be, 'All over, not in any particular place'. And these feelings characteristically have a *behavioural* aspect, so that I may be tired, tense, etc., without *feeling* so. That is, Bodily States have two aspects: bodily sensation and bodily condition or behaviour.

Feelings are subtly different in various ways, and this four-fold classification would need to be refined and modified in any thorough analysis of feelings;[1] but it may suffice for our purposes here.

2.2. *Feelings and attitudes*

Before we consider the various ways in which feelings are revealed, we need to examine the range of feelings in another way, by considering feelings in relation to attitudes. In the rest of the chapter, some attitudes will be included within the range of feelings, whereas others will not. How is it that some attitudes *can* be included? How are they related to feelings? In this section I shall try to answer these questions. I shall also lay the basis for further analysis of attitudes in chapter 3 (section 1.1).

Let us set aside feelings which are Bodily States and Sensations, and consider Moods or Responses. What criteria can be suggested to show that some words are intrinsically words for feelings, whereas other words refer to something which may or may not involve feelings? Two tests may be used (where 'W' is a word):

Test I: If I feel W, I am W.
Test II: If I am W, I feel W.

Test I is fairly straightforward. If I feel joyful, I am joyful; if I feel hopeful, I am hopeful. Thus various words for Moods

---

[1] Various complications arise. (i) The classification does not provide a neat place for every feeling. For example, where shall we place fear and anger? They seem to be Responses, but they differ from Responses and resemble Bodily States in one important way: It would be odd to say that I *am* amazed (Response), yet do not *feel* amazed; but if I am tired, afraid, or angry, I may nevertheless not *feel* tired, afraid, or angry. And what about dizziness—is it a Bodily State like feeling excited, or is it a Sensation like feeling warm? (ii) A word which designates a feeling may usually refer to a Mood, yet sometimes refer to a Response: 'satisfied'. Or a feeling-word may sometimes refer to a Bodily State, sometimes to a Mood, and sometimes to a Response: 'excited'. Also, there are dispositions to feelings, some of which are themselves feelings: dispositions to certain Moods ('sanguine') to certain Responses ('irritable') to certain Bodily States ('excitable'), or to certain Sensations ('ticklish').

pass the Test. Similarly, if I feel amazed, I am amazed; if I feel disgusted, I am disgusted; if I feel astonished, I am astonished. Thus various words for Responses pass the Test. But if we consider words for some attitudes, we find that they fail Test I. When I feel conciliatory, I may nevertheless not be conciliatory; when I feel friendly, I may nevertheless not be friendly; when I feel submissive, I may nevertheless not be submissive.

Now let us note one important difference between Moods and Responses. Where W is a Mood-word, 'feel' involves more than 'am': if I say that I 'feel' joyful, I indicate not only that I am joyful but also that I experience strong inner commotions of some sort, going on now. But where W is a Response-word, 'feel' and 'am' are virtually equivalent: there is little difference between saying that I 'feel' amazed and saying that I 'am' amazed. Thus Response-words obviously pass Test II: If I am amazed, I feel amazed; if I am disgusted, I feel disgusted, and so on. Mood-words also pass Test II, however, though less obviously. For if I am joyful, to *some* extent I feel joyful; if I am serene, to some extent I feel serene; if I am hopeful, to some extent I feel hopeful, and so on.

The two Tests help us to distinguish Mood-words and Response-words from such attitude-words as 'hostile', 'submissive', 'condescending', 'conciliatory', or 'uncompromising'; for these words fail both Tests. But some attitude-words do have an intrinsic logical connection with feelings. If I feel jealous (resentful, grateful, indignant) I am jealous (resentful, grateful, indignant); these attitude-words thus pass Test I. And perhaps the words 'indignant' and 'thankful' pass Test II: If I am indignant or thankful I feel indignant or thankful. Also, the words 'grateful', 'jealous' and 'resentful' approximate to Test II in varying degrees; here we have Moods which are logically connected with attitudes, or attitudes which are logically connected with Moods. We may consider gratitude, jealousy, resentment and indignation either as species of feeling or as species of attitude. In this chapter we shall think of them as feelings which can be 'expressed', like other feelings which do not involve attitudes. In chapter 3 we shall consider them as attitudes.

Note that even where an attitude-word does not have an intrinsic logical connection with a Mood, a particular attitude may in fact involve a Mood. For example, the utterance, 'I feel sympathetic (reverent, forgiving, respectful, apologetic, submissive)' does not entail 'I am sympathetic (reverent, etc.)'; nor does 'I am sympathetic (reverent, etc.)' entail 'I feel sympathetic (reverent, etc.)'. But Jones' particular sympathy for Mrs Brown may, in fact, include a Mood. In so far as it does, we can consider that the element of feeling in the attitude is 'expressed' in whatever way a non-attitudinal feeling is 'expressed'.

Now that we have some idea of the range of feelings, we can consider various ways in which feelings are revealed.

3. *Feeling-revealing behaviour (FRB) : symptoms, manifestations, expressions and reports*

Suppose that you say, 'Jones is feeling sad' (or happy, annoyed, afraid, ashamed, indignant, amazed, tired, excited). Someone may ask you, 'How do you know?' or 'On what basis do you believe so?' Your answer will involve some reference to Jones' observable *behaviour*. You may refer to someone else's report, but this depends ultimately on some reference to Jones' behaviour. In using the word 'behaviour', I do not wish to restrict the reference to deliberate actions; I include a wide range of observables, extending, for example, from the pallor of Jones' cheeks to his uttering the words 'I feel sad'. The one element common to all the behaviour is that Jones' feelings are *revealed* to someone. I wish to give the word 'reveal' a comprehensive reference too, so that Jones might (for example) reveal his annoyance either involuntarily by his flushed face, or voluntarily by saying 'I feel annoyed'.

In an analysis of feeling-revealing behaviour (FRB) one is tempted to assume that there are two clearly-distinct classes of FRB: (i) Some FRB is natural and spontaneous; it is neither deliberate nor dependent on learning; it provides inductive evidence for the presence of certain feelings: for example, my facial pallor, of which I am not even aware. (ii) Some FRB is conventional and artificial, it is deliberate and dependent on learning; it means a certain feeling because it is a code-signal: for example, I say to you, 'I feel annoyed'. But FRB does not all fall neatly into one or other of these classes. A much more complex analysis is required. I shall divide FRB into four classes, with further sub-divisions. The reader will see that even these distinctions are not sharp or self-evident, but require considerable reflection.

Our first task is to distinguish expressions of feeling from reports of feeling.

3.1. *Expressive FRB contrasted with reportive FRB*

If I say, 'I feel annoyed' in a matter-of-fact tone of voice, or write these words on a piece of paper which I hand to someone, I do not express my feeling; I merely report it. But if I say, 'I feel annoyed' in an annoyed tone of voice, I both report my feeling and express it. Similarly, if I say, 'He is sad' (or 'He is dead') in a regretful tone of voice, I both report his feeling (or his death) and express my feeling.

What is the difference between an expression of feeling-F and a report of feeling-F? I propose to distinguish them in the following way: *An expression of feeling-F is often part of the meaning of 'feeling-F', but a report of feeling-F is not.* For example, laughing is part of the meaning of 'amused', but saying 'I am amused' is not.

Such a distinction obviously requires clarification, especially the phrase, 'part of the meaning'. When I speak of 'part of the meaning', what I have in mind is not a behaviourism which *equates* feelings with external behaviour, but something else. Consider the process by which we learn the meaning of various feeling-words. One learns that they are applied when several of a whole complex of behaviour-patterns are observable in others or in oneself; or, in the case of oneself, one may have a felt tendency to some of this behaviour, a tendency which is controlled or resisted. No one pattern of behaviour (or felt tendency to such behaviour) is a necessary and sufficient condition, but in the absence of *all* of these, the particular feeling-word is inapplicable. The meaning of a feeling-word (for example, 'grief') is intrinsically related to typical revelations of that feeling. For example, what distinguishes 'grief' from 'nostalgia' is not an inner sensation abstracted from all behaviour, but the differing expressions of feeling which typically reveal grief and nostalgia.[1] (This point is specially obvious if we consider artistic expressions

---

[1] The context of thought is also important; for example, it would be odd to apply 'nostalgia' to a feeling concerning something which happened recently.

of feeling, where what the precise feeling is can not be divorced from its expression.)

Note that in the case of feelings it is often impossible to make a clear distinction between 'evidence' for the feeling and 'criteria' for the feeling. Elsewhere this is sometimes possible: for example, I can distinguish evidence for the fact that Jones has meningitis (severe headaches) from criteria for this (the result of a test of the spinal fluid); similarly a loud noise may be evidence that a car accident has occurred, but the noise is separable from what we mean by 'car accident'; and your panting for breath may be evidence that you have been running, but it is not part of what we mean by 'running', it is not a criterion of running. But is Jones' melancholy tone of voice evidence for melancholy or a criterion of melancholy?

If we call it 'evidence' for melancholy, we must realize that a peculiar tone of voice is part of what we mean by 'melancholy'. Consider a somewhat similar case: when Smith opens the door for me, he provides evidence of his courtesy; yet his action is also part of what we mean by 'courtesy'; the two are not mutually exclusive. Jones' tone of voice differs, however, from Smith's door-opening, which is evidence concerning how Smith will probably *behave on other occasions*; Jones' tone of voice is evidence concerning something which includes an *inner, contemporary* experience. The experience is not 'inner' in the way that a bulging cheek reveals a candy *inside* little Johnny's mouth. Jones' tone of voice is evidence for something which I can not observe, unlike such observables as Smith's later behaviour or Johnny's candy. Furthermore, we can not abstract *what* the something is from the concrete 'evidence'. It is true that a man often does not *have* to express his feelings; but the nature of the feeling is logically connected with the ways in which he would express it if he did express it. We cannot describe a feeling-experience 'in itself', without reference to any observable behaviour in which it is expressed, or would be expressed. (Similarly, as we shall see in chapter 5, the inner nature of God is unobservable, and we can not describe Him 'in Himself'; that is, we cannot describe God without reference to observables in which He expresses Himself, or would express Himself.)[1]

[1] Chapter 5, section 1.3.

If we call Jones' tone of voice a 'criterion' of melancholy, we must realize that it is neither a sufficient nor a necessary[1] condition for the application of the word 'melancholy'. He may use this tone of voice, and yet not be melancholy; or he may be melancholy, and yet not use this tone of voice. Yet if he *is* melancholy, the meaning of the word which is applied to him is understood by reference to various expressions of melancholy which include this tone of voice.

Now let us consider *reports* of feeling, for example, where I say, 'I feel cross (anxious, melancholy, afraid, etc.)'. I have argued that, in a sense, a cross tone of voice is part of the meaning of 'cross'; but my *saying* 'I feel cross' is not, in this sense, part of the meaning of 'cross'. Similarly it is not part of the meaning of 'feeling nostalgic' that one says, 'I feel nostalgic'; but it is part of the meaning, on a particular occasion, that one feels that which is expressed by such songs as 'The Hills of Home', or by certain poems. (One may consider another case which is somewhat analogous, but which does not involve feelings: It is not part of the meaning of 'fast talker' that one says, 'I'm a fast talker'; but one's rapid utterance of these words, or any other words, *is* part of the meaning.)

An expression of feeling differs from a report of feeling, but it can be *used* as a report of feeling; that is, it can be used as an alternative to a verbal report, as a code-sign. What an expressive smile means as a *report* can be stated in a sentence, for example, 'I feel happy'. That is, I may use the smile as an alternative to saying, 'I have the sort of feeling which is expressed in a host of varied ways (including smiling) which are covered by the word happy'. The word 'happy' is vague, however, compared with various precise expressions of feeling. What the particular smile means as an *expression* of feeling cannot be translated into a verbal *report*;[2] the smile is behaviour on the basis of which an observer may judge that I am feeling that which is expressed by my particular smile.

This distinction between reportive use and expressive use

---

[1] I am not assuming that the contrast between 'evidence' and 'criterion' is usually sharp. For example, is the philosopher's perennial example, 'All men are mortal' an empirical generalization or is it partly a definition of 'men'?

[2] Note that I may *express* in words a feeling which is very similar to the particular feeling which the smile expresses. Likewise, Proust may use words to *express* a feeling which is very similar to that which is expressed in a musical theme.

may seem overly-refined and pedantic in the case of smiles. But consider a subtle shrug of the shoulders, or a jazz trumpeter's extemporaneous outburst of melody. One may interpret these as code-reports, in vague and general terms: 'I feel indifferent', 'I feel exultant'. (Similarly a hand-movement may be a code-sign for 'I am going to turn right'.) But *qua* expressions of feeling, the specific behaviour or sound expresses a specific feeling: the feeling which such behaviour or sound expresses. (Note the circularity.) Of course, I may find expressions of feeling which are similar enough to the particular shrug and particular melody for the same verbal label to be applicable: 'indifferent', 'exultant'. Indeed, I may refine my reportive language so that I can greatly narrow the range of feelings-with-expressions which is covered by one word; instead of saying that I feel 'sad', I may say that I feel 'nostalgic', 'forlorn', 'mournful' or 'penitent'. But the distinction between expressing feelings and reporting feelings is not thereby eliminated. Nor is it eliminated by the fact that I may do both by the same behaviour, for example, by directing a frown at you which expresses my displeasure and signals my displeasure. An expression of feeling is not replaceable by behaviour which is merely a report of feeling. (In chapter 5 we shall see that God reveals Himself in particular observables which *express* His inner nature; hence these observables—the starry heavens or the Cross—are not replaceable by mere reports.)

We have noticed that expressions of feeling are often used to report feelings. Reports of feeling, however, are not typically expressive. Indeed, the vocabulary of feeling-words (words used to report feelings) is not expressive, on the whole; consider 'displeasure', 'anxiety', or 'surprise'. This vocabulary may be regarded as a basic language, to which expressions of feeling are the code-signals; in a similar way the words 'right', left', 'stop', etc., form a basic language for the code-signals of car-driving.

Since typical expressions of feeling are part of what is meant by the feeling-word, and since they may be given a reportive use, an expression of feeling is sometimes—in a curious way—*self-referring*. If I report, 'I feel displeased', I refer in part to frowns or tendencies to frown. If I frown at you, I 'say' in code, 'I feel displeased', thus referring in part to my frown! If I improvise on a trumpet, to reveal to you how I feel at the moment, this is much more than reporting 'I feel exultant', for I express (or try to express) the precise sort of exultation which I feel. But it *is* a way of reporting how I feel; so my expression of feeling refers, in part, to itself,—as if I said, '*This* is what I feel'. (In chapter 5 we shall see that God's self-revelation in expressive observables comes as if He said, '*This* is what I am'.)

Of course, much expressive behaviour is not reportive; it is *acted* in contexts where the observers know that it is being acted, for example, on the stage. Moreover, my complex artistic expression of feeling sometimes may be intended mainly as a means of *clarifying* for myself what I feel, rather than as a means of communicating what I feel to someone else. Also, some behaviour which people might call 'expressive' is used to *evoke* feelings in others more than to reveal or communicate the agent's own feelings. These links between expressions-of-feeling and acting, private clarifying, and evoking are important; indeed, they generate some of the perennial problems of aesthetics. But I shall not consider them here, since I am primarily interested in expressions of feeling as a means of communication.

Our contrast between expressions of feeling and reports of feeling raises one final difficulty which should be faced: sometimes the words 'express' and 'report' are virtually equivalent. Thus I may say, 'Jones expressed surprise . . .', where Jones merely *said*, 'I am surprised . . .' without being *expressive* at all. But this use of the word 'express' to refer to someone's non-expressive utterance need not obscure our analysis, once we have noted it and set it aside. The main contrast remains: An expression of feeling-F is often part of what we mean by 'feeling-F'; but it is not part of the meaning of 'feeling-F' that one reports (or is inclined to report) 'I feel F'.

3.2. *A four-fold classification of FRB*

Feeling-revealing behaviour (FRB) is not limited to expressions of feeling and reports of feeling. We need to be able to compare these with symptoms of feeling and manifestations of feeling. Such a comparison involves a complex classification of FRB. This four-fold classification is not intuitively obvious, and it will require considerable analysis before the distinctions become clear; but an initial outline is perhaps helpful:

Class I: Symptoms of feeling. Two sorts of symptoms may be distinguished:

(1) Jones' face goes white, though he is not aware of this; if Jones did become aware of how white his face is, he could not control this. In the context, I judge that he is afraid.

(2) Jones' hands are trembling; he is aware of this, but he cannot stop the trembling, or even modify it. In the context I judge that he is afraid.

Class II: Manifestations of feeling. Here are some examples of manifestive FRB: I drag my feet or slouch when I am tired; I grit my teeth when I am in pain; I shake my arms or legs when I am irritated; I jump about when I am excited.

It is important to distinguish four sorts of manifestive FRB, for example, four varieties of feet-dragging: (Similar examples could be given for slouching, muscle-tensing, etc.)

(a) Jones drags his feet, not noticing that he is doing so, and thus he reveals his tiredness (of which he may or may not be aware in some other way at the time).

(b) Jones drags his feet, and he is aware of this; and he goes on doing it, though he could stop or change his feet-dragging. He has not any intention of showing someone else that he is tired. (Indeed, he may think that he is unobserved.)

(c) Jones drags his feet deliberately so as to show the sergeant-major that he is tired; he does not intend the sergeant-major to recognize his intention, but to take the behaviour as a case of (b), or—even better—as a case of (a).

(d) Jones drags his feet deliberately so as to show the sergeant-major that he is tired, intending that the sergeant-major take his behaviour as having this intention.

Note that all this behaviour is a 'manifestation' of feeling; but in (a) the behaviour manifests the feeling, whereas in (c) and (d) the man manifests the feeling; (b) is on the borderline.

Class III: Expressions of feeling. Here are some examples of expressive FRB: frowns, smiles, wails, laughs, tones of voice, verbal exclamations such as 'Ouch!' or 'Damn!', impromptu compositions on the piano or the trumpet, poetic laments.

It is important to distinguish expressive FRB into four kinds, which correspond to the four kinds of manifestive FRB. Consider, for example, four varieties of frowning:

(a) Jones frowns, not noticing that he frowns, and thus he betrays his displeasure (of which he may or may not be aware in some other way at the time).

(b) Jones frowns, and is aware of his frown, and is able to stop or modify his frowning; but he has no intention of showing anyone that he is displeased. (Indeed, he may think that he is unobserved.)

(c) Jones frowns deliberately so as to show me that he is displeased, but not intending that I should take his frown as having this intention; that is, he intends me to take the frown as a case of (a) or (b).

(d) Jones frowns deliberately so as to show me that he is displeased, intending me to take his frown as having this intention.

Note that sort (c) is rare and overly-subtle in the case of Class III, though not in Class II.

Class IV: Reports of feeling. These need no further elaboration here.

I do not claim that the divisions suggested here are very clear-cut. The subdivisions of Class III, for example, flow into one another: a particular laugh might lie on the border-line between IIIa and IIIb (Could Jones help laughing?) or between IIIb and IIId (Was Jones' laugh directed at Smith?) Moreover, we shall see that it is extremely difficult to specify the difference between Classes II and III. But this classification of FRB does provide a useful framework within which we may analyse expressions of feeling. In chapter 5 we shall see that many of the logical features of feeling-revealing behaviour shed light on Creation as divine 'soul-revealing behaviour'.

3.3. *Manifestive and expressive FRB contrasted with symptomatic FRB*

There is an important contrast between Classes II and III on the one hand, and Class I on the other. It is true that not all manifestive and expressive FRB is deliberate or even voluntary, for some may be unnoticed and involuntary: IIa and IIIa. But this does not mean that cases of IIa and IIIa should be assimilated with Class I. There is an enormous difference between behaviour which can, and behaviour which cannot, become a deliberate manifestation or expression of feeling— that is, an *activity*. For example. I notice that my hands are trembling and my heart is pounding, and I realize that I am afraid; but I do not similarly notice that I am dragging my feet or laughing (when in cases (b) or (d) I actively drag my feet or actively laugh) and thus realize that I am tired or amused. For once I become aware of my dragging feet or my laughing and continue it, instead of stopping it or modifying it, I do not use *inspection* to discover how I feel; I know how I feel because I am intentionally doing that which manifests or expresses such-and-such a feeling. Thus it is a necessary condition for FRB which is a 'manifestation' or 'expression' of feeling that one *can* be the agent of the FRB.

This does not help us to distinguish manifestations (II) from expressions (III), though it does serve to distinguish both from what I call 'symptoms' (I). Moreover, much FRB in Classes II and III can be not only controlled and directed, but also *simulated*. Thus, unless I am sure that Jones' feet-dragging or tone of voice is unconscious (IIa or IIIa), I need to know whether or not Jones is simulating the FRB, whether or not he is pretending to be tired or annoyed. Although intentions are irrelevant to Class-I FRB, I need to know Jones' intention in these other cases; that is, I need to know whether or not the FRB is genuine or sham.[1] Similarly, where FRB is reportive, I need to know whether or not an attempt is being made to deceive me.

FRB in Classes IId, IIId and IV has this in common: in each case the agent initiates *activity* so as to *induce* me to believe that he has certain feelings. This important similarity makes it difficult to distinguish these classes of FRB. We shall begin with Classes IId and IV. (In Part II we shall see that divine self-revelation in Creation is an *activity* initiated by God so as to *induce* men to belief concerning Himself. A detailed analysis of FRB in Classes IId, IIId and IV thus provides a logical framework which is useful in theological analysis.)

3.4. *Manifestive FRB contrasted with reportive FRB*

The main difference between Class IId and Class IV would seem to be this:[2] If Jones drags his feet to show me that he feels tired, or grits his teeth to show me that he feels pain, my judgment depends on an *inductive generalization*—like the

---

[1] H. P. Grice discusses this need to know that I am not shamming, but he tries to use it to make a distinction which is very similar to my distinction *between* Classes II and III, or II and IV. 'Meaning', *The Philosophical Review*, July, 1957.

[2] We have already relied on this sort of distinction, in discussing the implications of performatives. See pp. 29, 47.

inference from panting-for-breath to running, or from bulging cheeks to candy. But if Jones says, 'I feel tired' or 'I feel a pain', my judgment depends on *conventions of meaning*, like the judgment based on his saying, 'I've been running' or 'I've a candy in my mouth'.

If we are to say that manifestive FRB (feet-dragging, teeth-gritting) involves an inductive generalization, we need to recognize differences from other cases:

(1) Manifestive FRB differs from much inductive evidence in that it is often an *activity* which may be *simulated* and so an observer needs to know whether or not it is sham or genuine.[1] But manifestive FRB is not alone in this; the same thing is true when an observer sees me panting for breath.

(2) Manifestive FRB differs from much inductive evidence in that it is *part of the meaning* of what is inferred; but the case of 'courtesy' is similar in this respect.[2]

(3) Manifestive FRB differs from much inductive evidence in that it need not rest on causal connections;[3] but it is not unique in this.

(4) Manifestive FRB differs from much inductive evidence in that what is inferred is (a) not observable by me and (b) not specifiable except with reference to specific FRB which *is* observable. This is a crucial difference, which we should constantly remember if we continue to speak of manifestive FRB as 'inductive evidence'—as I propose to do.

The contrast between manifestive FRB and reportive FRB in terms of inductive generalizations versus conventions of meaning may be challenged in another way: We may begin to wonder whether, in general, judgments based on conventions of meaning are clearly distinguishable from judgments based on inductive generalizations. This raises one of the most important, and most difficult, problems in philosophy; I shall only sketch an answer which may be adequate for the purposes of this book.

In our discussion of performative force,[4] we found that three distinct questions may be asked concerning an utterance; this applies to reports of feeling as well:

---

[1] Cf. section 3.3.   [2] Cf. section 3.1.
[3] It might be maintained that where a manifestation is not an activity (IIa), a cause-effect account is applicable, especially where the feeling is a sensation; on such an account, my feeling of pain causes me to grit my teeth. But this raises problems of mental-physical causation which need not be considered here.
[4] Pp. 69, 73.

G

(i)   What *is* meant, in this society, by this behaviour? That is, what would a reasonable person, who knows the relevant linguistic conventions in this society, take as *the meaning* of this action?

(ii) What does the *agent mean* by his action? That is, what does *he* take to be *the meaning* of his action?

(iii) What does *he intend* by his action? That is, what *results* is he trying to bring about?

A mistake in language or code occurs when (ii) differs from (i). For example, if a Canadian in England says, 'I feel sick', not taking this as an indication of nausea, he has made a mistake. And if he moves his arm straight out from the car window beside the driver's seat, this *means* (in England), 'I am going to turn right', whether or not *he meant* this.

Many actions do not come under questions (i) or (ii), but only under question (iii). For example, if Jones puts his hand in his pocket, intending to get his handkerchief out, there is usually no 'public meaning', and thus no possible conflict between the public meaning of this act and what he takes to be its public meaning. Complications arise, however, where Jones' intention is to get me to believe or infer something from his action. Consider some earlier examples:

> Jones pants for breath so that I will think he has been running.
> Jones drags his feet so that I will think he is feeling tired.
> Jones grits his teeth so that I will think he is feeling pain.

Here there may be a difference between what Jones intends me to think and what I actually do think (cf. question (iii)), and this difference is not utterly independent of questions concerning public meaning. If Jones makes a mistake, is it a mistake concerning the external behaviour which *usually* occurs along with tiredness or pain? Or is it a mistake concerning the external behaviour which a reasonable person would *take as evidence* for tiredness or pain? Or is it a mistake concerning the external behaviour which a reasonable person would *take as having the meaning*, 'I feel tired' or 'I feel pain'?

In border-line cases the answer is not obvious. Suppose that Brown makes his coat pocket bulge outwards, intending to get me to think that he is pointing a revolver at me. (He may, or may not, be pointing a revolver.) Suppose that he fails:

I do not think that he is pointing a revolver at me. His mistake may be described as a failure to make a bulge which revolvers usually make; or as a failure to make a bulge which a reasonable person would take as evidence for a revolver; or as a failure to make a bulge which a reasonable person would take as a gesture which means, 'Stick-em-up'. There seems to be no sharp line to be drawn—neither here, nor in the case of many other actions *directed* at another person with the intention of inducing belief. Often it is the *context* which changes an action which provides evidence based on an inductive generalization into an action which has a public meaning.[1] Thus the public meaning of one action may be extremely context-dependent; the public meaning of another action may be virtually Indefeasible; the public meaning of a third action may be somewhere in between. No sharp line can be drawn. Thus when some FRB is called 'manifestive' rather than 'reportive', this may be because it never has a public meaning; but it may be because its occasional public meaning is fairly context-dependent.

The broad contrast nevertheless remains: whether or not behaviour B is *evidence* for X does depend on the frequency of conjunction between B and X, and often also on a causal connection between X and B. Neither of these factors is required if behaviour B *means* X: causal connection is irrelevant; and even if an utterance is often made mistakenly or deceitfully, it still can retain its public meaning.

In chapter 5 we shall consider the biblical view of world-Creation as an action in which God reveals His inner glory. We shall find that human beliefs concerning Creation depend on what men take to be the *public meaning*, the performative force, of some aspects of world-Creation. For example, the regular movements of the stars are not inductive evidence for the existence of a hidden Designer; rather, they are taken to mean the faithful pledge of God to men.

3.5. *Expressive FRB contrasted with manifestive FRB*

We have seen that the difference between reportive FRB and manifestive FRB is surprisingly difficult to elucidate. The difference between expressive FRB and manifestive FRB is even more elusive. Here too it is Class IId which causes most of

[1] Cf. pp. 47-9, concerning Contextual implication.

the trouble. We shall consider various ways in which a contrast may be attempted.[1]

3.5.1. *Spontaneous versus artificial FRB*

At first sight, it would seem that expressions of feeling differ from manifestations of feeling in that I deliberately initiate the expressive behaviour so as to reveal my feelings to someone else. But such a contrast is challenged by Classes IIIb and IId. Class IIIb reminds us that a great deal of 'expressive' behaviour is not primarily a means of expressing one's feelings *to* other people (even if we exclude from consideration the acting, self-clarifying and evoking which were mentioned on p. 93). Much expressive FRB is 'spontaneous' rather than 'artificial': that is, it is not a matter of my deciding to initiate certain behaviour (for example, a laugh) but rather of my being able to control and direct the behaviour to some extent as it happens. Class IId reminds us that manifestive FRB, on occasion, may be 'artificial'.

Indeed, a distinction between spontaneous and artificial FRB is not very precise or easy to apply; it depends on the extent to which the FRB is 'natural', in the sense of being instinctive or habitual. And what is habitual for one person is not for another. Thus even Class-IV 'reportive' FRB may sometimes be 'spontaneous'.

Nevertheless the spontaneous/artificial distinction does enable us to make a rough contrast between Classes II and III: In Class II any artificial FRB is almost bound to be misleading (false, deceitful)—for example, if I initiate (rather than continue or fail-to-modify) my feet-dragging. But in Class III, FRB frequently can be artificial without being misleading—for example, I deliberately smile at you to show that I am pleased, though I rarely smile spontaneously. No sharp distinction is possible here, however. It is not difficult to imagine similar cases for Class-II FRB: for example, I am actually tired and I deliberately drag my feet to show you that I am tired, though I rarely manifest tiredness in this way.

3.5.2. *Reportive use of unlearned FRB*

Let us try another method of distinguishing Classes II and

[1] Sections 3.5.1, 3.5.2 and 3.5.3 are not used in Part II, though they are of considerable philosophical interest. Readers whose interests are mainly theological may find it convenient to read only the summary on page 103.

III. First we note a similarity: Though much Class-III FRB is learned by imitation, some (for example, smiles, laughs and wails) resembles Class-II FRB in being relatively *unlearned*. That is, a baby's smile, laugh and wail reveal his feelings without his having imitated anyone. Similarly a child does not need to learn to drag his feet when tired or to tense his muscles when in pain. In contrast with this, the particular tones of voice or exclamations which express particular feelings vary from culture to culture and even from family to family. They are learned by imitation, though this is not mainly conscious.

Now let us try to specify the difference between II and III: Class-III FRB is often behaviour which is learned by imitation, whereas Class-II FRB is not. And where Class-III FRB is *unlearned*, it differs from (unlearned) Class-II FRB in that *later* it becomes a *conventional* means of revealing feeling. That is, after one has word-labels which one may apply to feelings in *reporting* them, unlearned Class-III FRB may be used like a code, as an alternative to a verbal report of one's feelings. For example, I may smile at you instead of saying, 'I'm happy'.

But there is no reason why any item of Class-II FRB might not come to have the function of a sign in a code; for example, the doctor says, 'Whenever my finger hurts, let me know by gritting your teeth'. Class-IId FRB, like Class-IIId FRB, is deliberate; and where both are relatively unlearned, the former differs only in that it is much less *frequently* used as a code-signal. All we can say is that Class-III FRB often has a reportive use, whereas Class-II FRB does so less frequently. (We must also remember the difficulty in drawing a sharp line between Classes II and IV.)[1]

Note, moreover, that even if some Class-II behaviour did come to have a reportive, code-signal use, this use would not by itself make the behaviour an *expression* of feeling. That is, if some unlearned FRB is to become an expression of feeling, it is not a sufficient condition that it be used as a code-signal.

3.5.3. *FRB and the classification of feelings*

One possible way of contrasting Classes II and III has been ignored so far. Perhaps the class of feelings which are expressed differs from the class of feelings which can only be manifested.

[1] Cf. section 3.4.

For typical Class-II feelings are Bodily States (tiredness, excitement) and Sensations (pains, itches). Typical Class-III feelings are Moods (joy, anxiety, excitement-*concerning-y*) and Responses (amazement, horror, being-thrilled-*at-z*). Certain feelings (Bodily States and Sensations) are typically manifested because they are not feelings with a thought-content, not feelings *about* such-and-such. Other feelings (Moods and Responses) have a thought-content usually, and can be expressed. (They can also be manifested, in so far as they include behaviour associated with Bodily States or Sensations; for example, anxiety may be manifested by muscular contortions, just as tenseness or pain can.) Moreover, feelings which are typically manifested have a *cause*—for example, a needle being jabbed into one's arm; whereas feelings which are also expressed usually have an *occasion*—a situation as conceived by the person. Feelings which are manifested are typically connected with specific sensations; feelings which are expressed are typically connected with thought and intention.

Consider a grimace. A grimace may or may not be expressive. Surely in order to be expressive it must reveal to us, to some extent, what the man feels *about* something—his rebellion, or horror, or disgust, or resignation. Where the 'something' is a specific pain-Sensation, its acuteness and location are *manifested* in the grimace. Yet often what the grimace *expresses* does not include a specific pain-Sensation, but does include a total situation-as-conceived by the person; the feeling which it expresses is a Response or a Mood.

I am not suggesting that there are two sorts of feeling, such that any particular feeling is clearly of one sort or the other, or such that a list of feeling-words could be neatly divided into two. Even 'I feel tired' may involve more than 'My legs and arms are tired' and include something like, 'I think I need a rest'; and tiredness can be revealed in a very expressive way. Moreover, many feelings which can be expressed can also be manifested—for example, anxiety, joy, awe or erotic love. Nevertheless we do seem to have discovered a useful way to distinguish manifestive FRB from some expressive FRB: in so far as a feeling is a Sensation or a Bodily State, and in so far as it has a cause but not an occasion or thought-content, it is not expressed but only manifested.

Yet it would be wrong to suppose that all feelings which are expressed must have a thought-content. My serenity (cf. other Moods) need not be a feeling *concerning* anything; and the feelings expressed in a sonata need not have a programmatic content. We have not yet discovered a clear-cut way of distinguishing expressive FRB from manifestive FRB.

On the other hand, our conclusions so far are sufficiently relevant and significant to be worth summarizing:

(1) Manifestive FRB is more typically spontaneous than expressive FRB is; and where manifestive FRB is artificial, it is more likely to be misleading.

(2) Expressive FRB is often learned by imitation, whereas manifestive FRB is characteristically unlearned; where expressive FRB is unlearned, it differs from manifestive FRB in that it frequently is given a reportive use.

(3) Manifestive FRB is usually associated with Sensations and Bodily States, in so far as these lack thought-content.

3.5.4. *The meaning of expressive FRB*

In section 3.4 we noted that reportive FRB differs from manifestive FRB in having a public meaning which depends on conventions. Does *expressive* FRB differ from manifestive FRB in a similar way? We have seen that both expressive and manifestive FRB may be given a reportive use (the former more frequently) and thus acquire a public meaning. But does expressive FRB, *qua* expressive, have a public, conventional meaning which is distinct from the meaning of reportive FRB, yet analogous to it?

Consider the following examples:

'In our society, Jones' tone of voice means that he feels annoyed, but he himself meant that he felt apologetic.'
'That musical phrase in the song means "I feel anguish", but the words suggest that the composer may have meant, "I feel resignation".'[1]

In each case there is a contrast between what *is meant* and what *he meant*. But in so far as we *state* the contrast in words, the contrast is made in terms of *reportive* use. On the other hand, what the particular tone of voice or musical phrase *means*,

[1] For an able defence of the unfashionable view that music has a 'vocabulary' with definite 'meanings', see D. Cooke, *The Language of Music*, Oxford, 1959, chapters 2, 3.

whether to society or to the agent, is not reducible to its reportive meaning. We have seen[1] that what is expressed is peculiarly linked with its concrete, particular expression. Sometimes, of course, a gesture may be almost equivalent to a verbal report; but we would say that such a gesture is hardly expressive at all. And an expression of feeling in a new or alien artistic medium may not have any stateable reportive use so far as I am concerned; in such cases, however, I would say that I cannot 'understand' it, I cannot discern any 'meaning'.

Is it possible to 'understand' or 'misunderstand' a sonata, a statue or a dance? It is true that some works of art may not be open to being understood or misunderstood, especially those produced by creative artists who are wedded to anti-expressive aesthetic theories. But it seems to me that many works of art have meaning, and that one may have varying degrees of success in understanding this meaning.

Two factors are involved here: (1) Once I am told that a gesture in an alien culture is a way of reporting sadness, I can begin to appreciate its relative expressiveness, whereas previously I simply could not understand it. Similarly, in understanding harmonic progressions of an alien musical culture, it is sometimes helpful to learn what *words* are associated with these progressions, in songs. An understanding of the rudimentary reportive meaning is usually necessary for an understanding of expressive meaning; but it obviously is not enough. (2) I may misunderstand some expressive FRB because my general experience of life, my cultural environment, and my basic attitudes do not enable me to have a feeling sufficiently analogous to that which is expressed. Hence there may be a big difference between the expressive meaning which the FRB has for the agent and its expressive meaning for me. It may not be possible to *state* this difference at all; it is not a difference which depends on *conventions* itself; and the difference may occur when the agent and I agree concerning the rudimentary reportive meaning (for example, 'I feel sad').

The insight which is required in order to appreciate the expressive FRB of other people is similar to that which is required by the creative artist in his work. If he is choosing between alternative modes of expression—for example, two

[1] Section 3.1.

gestures, or two harmonic progressions—his choice partly[1] depends on some sort of 'comparison' between each of these and the inner feeling which he is trying to express. One gesture or harmonic progression seems more appropriate or more adequate than the other. This 'comparison' is a curious phenomenon. It is not as if there were a one-to-one correspondence between the inner feeling and its external expression, as a mirror reflects a face, or a peg fills a hole. For the nature of the inner feeling depends, subtly, on its external expression (or its imagined external expression). Consider another case: I am trying to express my mood in words, or by improvising on the piano, and then you speak, or play some chords; I say, 'That's better; *that's* what I feel'. Now that the feeling is more adequately expressed it is not the same feeling, though we might *report* it in the same way. Yet the choice between alternative expressions was not arbitrary; the inner feeling provided some sort of basis for preference. Similarly my inner feelings provide some basis for *understanding* the expressive FRB of another person—a basis which may be relatively adequate or inadequate.

We are now in a position to suggest three differences between expressive FRB and manifestive FRB: (1) Expressive FRB is open to understanding and misunderstanding in so far as it typically has a (rudimentary) reportive meaning which I may or may not understand. (2) Expressive FRB is open to understanding and misunderstanding in so far as I can appreciate its expressive meaning only to the extent that I fulfil two requirements: (i) My personal life-experience and attitudes must give me some affinity and rapport with the agent who is expressing the feeling. (ii) I must have sufficient insight to appraise the adequacy of the 'correspondence' between the expressive FRB and the inner feeling. (3) Since the same FRB may have very different expressive meanings for different people, we can only speak of *the* expressive meaning if we make one man's understanding authoritative. Often we do choose the agent. (Such a choice was assumed in point (2).) We should realize, however, that a choice is involved; in some aesthetic criticism,

---

[1] In so far as his work of art is expressive; I am not maintaining that art is *always* expressive, and certainly not that it is *only* expressive. Nor am I implying that an artist whose work *is* expressive must always have the feeling at the moment of composition.

the agent's final authority concerning meaning is *not* assumed.

(In chapter 5 we shall see that in so far as God's self-revelation in Creation is expressive, it resembles expressive FRB in these three respects: (1) the link with reportive meaning, (2) the need for rapport with God, and the variations in the adequacy of 'correspondence' between God's inner nature and various expressions of this nature, and (3) the acceptance of God's authority concerning the meaning of world-Creation.)

4. *Expressive language*

In the previous section we examined expressive behaviour in general, without paying any special attention to expressive language. Almost any words can be expressive by virtue of the tone of voice used; a great actor can express the whole gamut of emotions by reading the dictionary. Hence we may wonder whether any words are distinctively expressive, as some words (for example, 'promise' or 'order') are distinctively performative.

4.1. *Feeling-words, Aptness-words, Behabitive words, and exclamatory words*

Before we answer this question directly, it will be useful to note three classes of words which are closely connected with feelings, but which are not themselves distinctively expressive of feeling:

(1) *Feeling-words.* Some words, as we have seen, are used to describe feelings or expressions of feeling; for example, 'sad', 'nostalgic', 'joyful', 'cross', 'wistful' or 'surprise'.

(ii) *Aptness-words.*[1] Some words are used to describe events, actions or things which are *apt* to be an occasion of certain feelings; for example, 'amusing', 'alarming', 'thrilling', 'depressing', 'exciting', 'grim', 'mysterious', or 'fascinating'. Note that since expressive FRB may *evoke* a feeling, an Aptness-word can be applied not only to non-expressive events or things, but also to expressive FRB: both a storm and a *sonata* may be 'thrilling'; both an execution and a *facial expression* may be 'grim'; both a limb and a *dance* may be 'seductive'. The converse, however, is not true: feeling-words are not generally applied, except metaphorically ('wistful' clouds) to inanimate occasions of feeling.

---

[1] Cf. P. Nowell-Smith's 'Aptness-words' (*Ethics*, p. 72); but he distinguishes these sharply from 'Descriptive-words'.

(iii) *Behabitive words.* When I say, 'I thank you', I imply that I have an attitude of gratitude towards you, and this attitude characteristically[1] involves a feeling. Similarly other Behabitives, such as 'apologize', 'commend', 'welcome', 'deplore', 'honour', or 'worship', imply feeling-attitudes.

If I say 'That sigh is *sad*' (feeling-word) or 'That song is *amusing*' (Aptness-word) or '*Thank* you for the song' (Behabitive word), my utterance is not particularly expressive. But if I say, 'That song is splendid!', I have used a word which seems to be expressive in itself, reinforcing the expressiveness of my tone of voice. Other similar words are 'beastly', 'magnificent', 'vile', 'glorious', 'wonderful', 'horrid' and 'holy'. How do such words differ from 'sad', 'amusing', or 'thank you'?

The difference from typical Aptness-words, such as 'amusing' or 'alarming', is not so great as one might expect. If I refer to a procession as 'magnificent' or to Jones as 'splendid', I need not be having a feeling of wonder (awe, excitement, etc.) at the time of the utterance. Usually the word is used in the same way as an ordinary Aptness-word. I describe X as being an occasion of certain feelings (usually Responses, sometimes Moods); and I imply (Prima-facie) that I have had, or would have, such feelings in relation to X, without implying that I have these feelings at the time of utterance. The word 'splendid', however, differs from 'thrilling' in that it carries a stronger Prima-facie implication of my concurrent *attitude*; in saying, 'Smith is a splendid fellow', I imply that I have a favourable attitude towards Smith, one which characteristically involves certain feelings; and the implication is more difficult to set aside in a descriptive context than the implication of such words as 'honest' or 'loyal'. (On the other hand, the implication *can* be set aside, so it is not quite Indefeasible.)

The main point about 'splendid' and 'magnificent', however, is that these words can be used as *exclamations*, where one actually responds to something: 'Splendid!' 'Magnificent!' In this they resemble such words or phrases as 'damn', 'hoorah', 'alas', 'good heavens', 'bravo', and 'O dear', and such behaviour as booing, hissing, applauding, or rending garments. There is a convention that these are to be used as both signals of feeling and expressions of feeling in the presence of that which evokes

[1] And perhaps logically—see section 2.2.

a feeling-Response. In such circumstances it is deceitful to use an exclamatory word if one does not have the feeling which is signalled; and it is linguistically odd to utter the word in a non-expressive tone of voice. Though the degree and subtlety of the utterances' expressiveness depend mainly on the tone of voice, the exclamatory word does reinforce the expressiveness in some way.

Exclamatory words usually have a performative function as well: compare '*magnificent*' with 'excellent', '*vile*' with 'bad', and '*bravo*' with 'commend'; in each case the expressive word has a performative function, but it differs in that it also has the function of expressing (and also signalling) a feeling-Response. We have seen that some exclamatory words ('splendid', but not 'hoorah') have an ordinary descriptive function as Aptness-words. In chapter 5 we shall consider the divine 'holiness' and 'glory' revealed in Creation, and we shall find that these words, like 'splendid', require analysis as Behabitive words, Aptness-words and exclamatory words.[1]

4.2. *Expressive language and impersonal language*

Exclamatory words are expressive by convention. But usually where language expresses feeling (especially feeling-Moods), it is not that particular words, in themselves, are expressive by convention—as particular words, in themselves, are *performative* by convention. Rather, the way in which the words are combined conveys the speaker's or writer's concurrent Mood.[2] (Here tones of voice and exclamation marks are far less important.) Most language is to some extent expressive. At one extreme, some poetry is intended to be primarily expressive of feeling; at the other extreme, some scientific and philosophical disciplines have as an ideal the elimination of the expressive element, so that language is used impersonally.[3]

The contrast between expressive utterances and impersonal (inexpressive) utterances is not the same as the contrast between Behabitive and Commissive utterances and flat Constatives.

---

[1] Chapter 5, section 1.2.

[2] If someone asks, '*How* is a mood conveyed by the way in which words are combined?', I would refer him to the literary critic, who takes over from the philosopher at this point.

[3] This chapter, for example, is extremely impersonal, though it is *about* expressions of feeling!

In the first place, the distinctions do not coincide. I might report an accident in such a way that my report has no Behabitive or Commissive force, but nevertheless conveys my melancholy mood. Conversely, I might commend you in a very inexpressive way, implying that I have a favourable attitude, but not expressing any feelings. In the second place, the distinctions (if we ignore exclamatory words) are of a different logical type. It is a convention of language that in saying, 'I commend you. . .', I imply that I have a favourable attitude to you. It is not in the same way a convention of language that in saying,

> 'She, she is gone, when thou knowest this,
> What fragmentary rubbish this world is.'

I|express a particular feeling-Mood. (It is, however, a convention of language that in saying 'Splendid!', with reference to something present now, I both signal and *express* a feeling-Response.)

Expressive language, like Behabitive and Commissive language, is self-involving, and it is related to the 'autonomy of value'. We have seen that the 'autonomy of value' in relation to performatives means, 'No flat Constative entails a Behabitive or Commissive'. But the 'autonomy of value' in relation to expressive language means, 'No impersonal utterance entails an expressive utterance'; that is, if my utterance does not express any particular feeling, I do not contradict myself if I reject an utterance which does. More generally, if I choose to restrict myself to impersonal language, I am under no logical compulsion to use expressive language. Perhaps I cannot communicate something adequately to you without using expressive language: the splendour of a sunset, the majesty of a symphony, or the glory of God. Perhaps I feel a psychological compulsion to communicate such things; perhaps I judge that I ought to try to communicate such things; but in so far as I make my language impersonal, I am under no logical compulsion.[1]

We have been comparing expressive language with performative language. But language can be used not only to express feelings and to perform institutional acts but also to produce various effects in people. There are three distinct ways in which language may be used:

[1] Cf. chapter 1, section 7.3.

   (a) Performative.
   (b) Expressive.
   (c) Causal.

The connection with feelings is different in each case:

   (a) If my utterance has Behabitive force, I may *imply* that I have a feeling.
   (b) I *express* a feeling.
   (c) I *evoke* or produce a feeling, in myself or in others.

So-called 'emotive' theories of moral language or religious language cannot even begin to achieve clarity unless these basic distinctions are recognized.

Since there are three distinct ways in which language may be used, and since these uses are not mutually exclusive, three distinct questions can be asked concerning any utterance:[1]

   (a) What was its performative force?
   (b) What feeling did it express?
   (c) What effects in people did it produce?

Unlike the answer to (c) the answer to (a) is given with reference to linguistic conventions (though we have seen that sometimes a special context, or the speaker's intention may also be relevant to performative force). Where the utterance is a stock exclamation ('Splendid!', 'Hoorah!'), the answer to (b) depends partly on a linguistic convention, and partly on the tone of voice used. Where the total utterance expresses a Mood, and does so because of the way the words are combined, the utterance is expressive in ways which it shares with other expressive FRB:[2] in order to understand the expressive meaning I need to know roughly what sort of feeling is being reported (for example, that it is a sad feeling); and I need to have a background of experience and an affinity of attitude such that my own feelings have been sufficiently analogous to the particular feeling which is being expressed.

5. *A note concerning 'rapportive' language*

At this point I wish to propose a new technical term: Where an utterance referring to an agent's action is *understood* only

---

[1] The answer to (b) may be 'None', and the answer to (c) may be 'None worth noting'.
[2] Cf. section 3.5.4.

to the extent that one has an affinity and a rapport with the agent, the utterance is 'rapportive'. Actions typically call for 'rapportive' utterances when they are *expressive* or when their *rationale* is *profound*. In Part II we shall see how both these elements are involved in the action of world-Creation. I have already indicated something of the relation between rapportive language and expressive actions. Here I shall outline the relation between rapportive language and the rationale of actions.

In ordinary life, I usually can understand the intention, rationale or point of someone else's action without much reflection, for I have done something fairly similar myself, and my ways of thinking are fairly similar. Indeed, I learned as a child to describe my own action in intentional terms by applying these terms to myself and to *others*.[1] But if the agent is a very sensitive man, or a man from a very different culture, or a man whose maturity and 'depth' of personality greatly exceeds my own, I have considerable difficulty in understanding some of his actions.[2] The rationale of his action is not obviously intelligible, for I do not share his views concerning what is relevant and important as a reason for action, and I do not share his interpretation of what it is that he is doing or trying to do. My understanding of his action is limited by my own individual conception of what actions are intelligible. If I am to understand his action, I must deliberately stretch my imagination so that I may understand his reasons and his way of viewing his action. Understanding depends on rapport; and since it does, my success or failure in understanding an action may provide evidence concerning the sort of person *I* am. For example, when critics review a biography, they sometimes comment on what the book reveals concerning the personality of the *author*:

'The life of a poet should not be written by a man with a pedestrian mind.'
'Only a man of Mr Brown's spiritual depth could probe so deeply into the mind of Pascal.'

In so far as my explanation of someone else's action is rapportive, and in so far as it reveals my individual personality,

[1] Cf. P. F. Strawson, *Individuals*, London, 1959, pp. 110-12.
[2] S. Hampshire considers a similar difficulty in *Thought and Action*, London, 1959, pp. 195-8.

it differs from typical scientific explanations of actions or of anything else.[1] Since self-involving utterances (Commissive, Behabitive or expressive) also differ from typical scientific explanations, one might infer that rationale-explanations are necessarily self-involving. But such an inference would be incorrect. For when I explain the rationale of an action, I need not thereby agree with the agent's reasons or his interpretation of his action; I need not even imply that I agree. And my explanation may be quite impersonal, without any expression of feeling whatsoever. Since my explanation is rapportive, it probably is self-*revealing*; but it need not be linguistically self-*involving*. It is true that, in order to understand Jones' action, I have had to involve myself personally in a venture of imaginative sympathy and identification with him. But this self-involvement which is necessary in order to establish sufficient rapport with Jones is a different matter from any linguistic self-involvement in the words of the explanation. The classification of an utterance as rapportive does not indicate a *use* of language alongside the performative, causal and expressive uses. It is a classification in terms of *conditions of understanding*. My verbal explanation of Jones' action may be both rapportive and self-involving; it may be either rapportive or self-involving; or it may be neither rapportive nor self-involving.

At this point we should distinguish three different ways in which my utterance concerning Jones' action may differ from a typical scientific statement:

(i)   It may be self-involving: Behabitive, Commissive or expressive.
(ii) It may be self-revealing in that it manifests or betrays my personal character.
(iii) It may be rapportive; it may be intelligible to me only to the degree that I have some rapport and affinity with Jones.

Note that rapportive utterances are usually self-revealing; but I do not propose any serious classification of utterances as 'self-revealing'; this feature is merely an incidental characteristic of rapportive language, and of other everyday language.

I have indicated that rapportive language has to do with

[1] For an interesting discussion of differences between rationale-explanations and causal-law-explanations, see W. Dray, *Laws and Explanation in History*, Oxford, 1957, ch. 5.

rapport and also with *affinity*. Various qualifications and objections arise if it is claimed that, in general, one must be *like* another person if one is to understand the rationale of his action. It is true that an affinity of temperament and life-experience seems virtually essential in some cases ('Only an alcoholic can understand an alcoholic'); but a great biographer, novelist or counsellor may have an amazing ability to understand people who are extremely different from himself. We shall not investigate such complications and exceptions here. The main point which I wish to make is this: It is difficult to understand the rationale or intention of an action where the agent is more mature, profound or 'spiritual', or when the agent's action is something which one has not performed oneself (for example, climbing a mountain, painting a picture or cuddling a baby). In Part II we shall consider the extreme case of an action which is difficult to understand: world-Creation; for I am not divine, and I have not created a world! Not only is the rationale of the action perplexing; world-Creation is an expressive action as well. Thus there are two reasons why an understanding of the action requires some degree of rapport and affinity with the Agent. We shall see that an utterance in which one refers to the rationale or to the expressiveness of world-Creation is characteristically rapportive.

Before we begin chapter 3, it may be helpful to schematize the three main classifications which emerge from the analysis so far. In this chapter I have classified feeling-revealing behaviour; I have distinguished four different ways in which a word may be connected with a feeling; and I have completed a general classification of language.

Feeling-Revealing Behaviour

Syptomatic
Manifestive   conventional exclamatory words
           language
Expressive   poetic expressions of mood
        non-linguistic behaviour
Reportive

Words and Feelings

An exclamatory word ('splendid') expresses a feeling.
A feeling-word ('sad') reports a feeling.

A Behabitive word ('apologize') may imply a feeling.
An Aptness-word ('thrilling') describes something which is
apt to evoke a feeling.

A Classification of Language

PERFORMATIVE LANGUAGE:	Constative ('state')
which may be	Verdictive ('grade')
explicit or non-explicit	Exercitive ('order')
pure or autobiographical	Behabitive ('praise') .... ⎫ Self
	Commissive ('promise')... ⎬ involving
	⎭ Language

EXPRESSIVE LANGUAGE............................⎭

RAPPORTIVE LANGUAGE

Some notes concerning the Classification of Language:

1. All language is performative.
   Some language is expressive, but some is not.
   Some language is rapportive, but some is not.
2. An expressive utterance may be Behabitive or Commissive;
   but it may not.
   An expressive utterance is often rapportive, but it need not be.
3. A rapportive utterance may be self-involving; but it may not.
   Language is classified as 'rapportive' or 'non-rapportive'
   according to conditions of understanding, not according to
   use. (The three uses of language are performative, expressive
   and causal.)
4. Any utterance may have a *causal power*, whatever its performative force, and whether or not it is expressive or rapportive.
5. Any utterance may be *self-revealing*, whatever its performative
   force, and whether or not it is expressive or rapportive.

3

EXPRESSIONS OF ATTITUDE

In the analysis of performative language (chapter 1) and expressive language (chapter 2), I have often referred to *attitudes* without examining them in any detail. Chapter 3 will fill in this gap in the analysis. I shall also make use of the earlier chapters so as to explain what it is to '*express an attitude*', for this involves a combination of the performative and expressive elements in language.

Attitudes are far more varied and complex than one might suppose at first glance. Consider the question, 'What is your attitude to Smith?' Four somewhat different sorts of answer may be given, which may or may not be correctly described as 'expressions of attitude', but which are ways of indicating to someone what my attitude is:

1. A report on my feelings: 'I feel very grateful to him.'
2. A report on my pattern of behaviour: 'My attitude, I've come to realize, has been rather condescending.'
3. An expression of opinion: 'I think he's very clever, but unreliable on detail.'
4. An expression of intention or declaration of policy: 'I'm supporting him in this, whatever people say.'

Examples of the four different sorts of answer might be given in reply to the religious question, 'What is your attitude to God?':

1. 'I have a feeling of reverence towards God.' (a report of my feelings)
2. 'I've come to realize that my attitude towards God has been respectful but not submissive.' (a report on a pattern of behaviour)
3. 'I think He's remote from daily life.' (an expression of opinion)
4. 'I submit to God's will in all things.' (a declaration of policy, including an expression of intention)

The four sorts of answer illustrate four elements in attitudes: feelings, behaviour, opinion, and intention. These elements are closely related, but it is possible to distinguish them, by giving examples which involve one element primarily, without excluding the others. The examples may be considered as illustrations of different *sorts* of attitude: a feeling-attitude is one in which feeling is specially prominent, a behaviour-attitude is one in which behaviour is specially prominent, and so on. When I speak of 'sorts' of attitude, this is not to be interpreted as if the mere presence of a feeling, or of some behaviour, or of an opinion, or of a policy, is in each case a sufficient condition, or a necessary condition, for the presence of an attitude.

1. *Four sorts of attitude*

We shall consider the four sorts of attitude in turn, comparing each with the others.

1.1. *Feeling-attitudes*

Sometimes, if you ask me about my attitude to Smith, I let you know what *feeling* Smith, or the thought of Smith, arouses in me: gratitude, indignation or sympathy. These, like reverence towards God, are attitudes which involve feelings. But attitudes may involve feelings in at least six different ways, which should be distinguished (where 'W' is an attitude-word):

(i) (Test II).[1] 'I am W' entails, 'I feel W'. W—perhaps 'indignant', 'grateful' and 'thankful' (not 'reverent', 'friendly' or 'sympathetic').

(ii) Usually, if I am W, I feel W. W—'jealous', 'resentful', 'reverent', 'friendly', 'sympathetic', 'loving' (not 'submissive' or 'condescending').

(iii) (Test I).[1] 'I feel W' entails, 'I am W'. W—'jealous', 'grateful', 'resentful' (not 'reverent', 'friendly' or 'sympathetic').

(iv) If on a particular occasion I feel W, this feeling is an expressible Mood. W—all the above, plus 'submissive', 'apologetic' and 'forgiving'.

(v) I can be said to feel W 'fervently', 'vehemently', or 'ardently'. W—most of the above, plus many others.

(vi) I can be said to 'feel' W.
W—virtually any attitude-word, even such words as 'conciliatory', 'condescending', 'uncompromising', or 'respectful', which refer primarily to patterns of observable behaviour.

[1] Chapter 2, section 2.2.

I propose to call those attitudes which come under (i), (ii) or (iii) 'feeling-attitudes'. Such attitudes are usefully contrasted with the second sort of attitude, which is predominantly behavioural—for example, 'condescending, 'submissive', 'servile', or 'respectful'. In feeling-attitudes, the stress is on inner states of mind to which I have a measure of privileged access, whereas in behaviour-attitudes the stress is on my public conduct, which I observe in much the same way as outsiders do. Even if I have not felt superior to Smith, my bearing and my remarks may have been condescending, without my even realizing it; in contrast with this, I am in a strong position to deny that I have been indignant, grateful, jealous, reverent or sympathetic if I did not *feel* indignant, grateful, etc. (apart from psychoanalytic considerations). Nevertheless, the distinction between feeling-attitudes and behaviour-attitudes is not a sharp one, for public behaviour is usually involved, to some extent, in the meaning of words for feelings (for example, 'fear' and 'anger') and of words for feeling-attitudes (for example, 'indignant', 'grateful', 'jealous' or 'sympathetic'). And even attitude-words which are relatively pure in their behavioural sense, for example, 'condescending', can be modified in the direction of feeling: 'I feel condescending'; it usually makes sense to say that one 'feels' a tendency to behave in such-and-such a way. (Compare (vi), above.)

We saw earlier[1] that there is a close (but not absolute) connection between feelings and opinions. Feeling-attitudes similarly involve a context of opinion or thought. Likewise feeling-attitudes may be linked with intentions and policies. For a declaration of policy involves a commitment, and the commitment-making force of a word may enter into the very meaning of the related feeling-word. For example, if someone says, 'I felt devout', and uses the word 'devout' strictly rather than as a vague equivalent for 'pious' or 'religious', he is reporting that he had the feelings and intentions appropriate to the making of a sincere vow. Perhaps he actually did dedicate himself by a vow, perhaps he felt as if he had dedicated himself by a vow, or perhaps he felt that he wanted to dedicate himself by a vow. In any case the meaning of 'I felt devout'

[1] Chapter 2, section 1.

is connected with Commissive acts of self-dedication.

1.2. *Behaviour-attitudes*

In some attitudes, it is not feeling but behaviour which is specially prominent. When asked about my attitude, I tell someone how I have been behaving in relation to Smith, or to God: I have been condescending, respectful, conciliatory, submissive, self-abasing, servile, prudish or hyper-critical. Since behaviour-attitudes have already been compared with feeling-attitudes, let us now compare them with the other two sorts of attitude.

Consider an expression of opinion: 'I think he's very clever, but unreliable on detail'. This may provide evidence concerning my behaviour-attitude; indeed, it may be regarded as an instance of my behaviour-attitude. But the behaviour-attitude does not consist entirely of such verbal behaviour; it also includes my non-verbal behaviour. Indeed, I may have a behaviour-attitude without expressing any opinions. Some attitude-words, however, lie on the border between behaviour and opinion, for example, 'optimistic' or 'suspicious'. Usually if one is optimistic or suspicious one holds, or even expresses, a correlative opinion— for example, that things will turn out well, or that Brown is treacherous. Yet sometimes I merely act *as if* I thought this, without actually having thought so: 'Yes, I realize now that I *have* been rather optimistic'.

Behaviour-attitudes and intention-attitudes are very closely related. Indeed, if we wanted to distinguish them rigorously, we would have to change my original example of an intention-attitude or policy-attitude, which was:

'I'm supporting him in this, whatever people say.'

This would become:

'Though so far I have not helped him in this, I hereby pledge my support, whatever people say.'

Here the main clause, 'I hereby pledge my support', is a pure performative; it is a (Commissive) declaration of policy which includes no autobiographical report. However, it is not a natural reply to the question, 'What is your attitude to Smith?' The original example, 'I'm supporting him in this', is better; but it is not a pure performative; it combines the policy-declaring Commissive force with an autobiographical report of my behaviour. Hence the intention-attitude differs less sharply from a typical behaviour-attitude.

Indeed, where *I* report my attitude in the present tense, my utterance is rarely a mere report, equivalent to *your* report of my attitude. It tends to *commit* me to the pattern of behaviour to which I am referring; it has a forward reference to behaviour for which I am the responsible agent, not merely an observer. If I say, 'My attitude to Smith is condescending', this would usually be taken as an expression of intention to continue my behaviour as before, and not merely a report of what has been my behaviour up till now. There is a Prima-facie commitment to be disclaimed. I might say, 'My attitude to Smith is condescending, but I intend to change this'; but it would be more natural to say, in such a case, that my attitude 'has been condescending'. That is, both you and I may observe and report what my attitude *has been*; but if *I* say that my attitude *is* such-and-such, I am undertaking its continuation, unless I disclaim this.

There are important exceptions to this: (i) Some feeling-attitudes can hardly be undertaken, for one cannot bring them about directly: for example, jealousy or thankfulness, or indignation; (ii) some attitude-words carry unfavourable implications, so that it would be odd to say, for example, that one intends to be 'servile' or 'prudish' or 'hyper-critical'; such attitudes may be admitted, but they are not usually undertaken as such. Note also that some attitude-words carry a much stronger Commissive force than others: If I say, 'My attitude to Communists is uncompromising', it would be very odd to disclaim all policy-declaring, so that one's utterance is merely a report; the Commissive force is virtually Indefeasible. But if I say, 'My attitude to Smith is condescending', the Commissive force is weakly Prima-facie.

We should also notice one other feature of behaviour-attitudes. Consider these two examples:

(a) 'My public behaviour in relation to Smith has been condescending.'
(b) 'My attitude to Smith has been condescending.'

(a) is not equivalent to (b). My private way of feeling and

thinking about Smith may have been respectful, so that I might admit (a) but deny (b). On occasion, (a) and (b) may be equivalent: in the absence of any contrary thought and feeling, where I had not even noticed my behaviour and now have it drawn to my attention. But such pure behaviour-attitudes are not typical; indeed, it is debatable whether the word 'attitude' is applicable at all. We should consider behaviour-attitudes as attitudes in which a past pattern of behaviour is specially prominent in comparison with thought, feeling or intention. Where the latter three elements are absent, we scarcely have an attitude at all. Consider, for example, the following words, which describe various ways of behaving publicly in relation to someone else, but which are not usually attitude-words, since *only* behaviour is involved: 'courteous', 'supercilious', 'impertinent', 'rude'. The words 'haughty' and 'deferential' are border-line cases.

1.3. *Opinion-attitudes*

We noted that if I am asked, 'What is your attitude to Smith?', my reply may be an utterance which has the performative force of an expression of opinion: 'I think he's very clever, but unreliable on detail'. In some cases this reply may also be autobiographical; that is, it may report what I have been previously thinking about Smith. But it is not an expression of feeling, a report of past public behaviour, or an expression of intention. Note that many expressions of opinion are not attitudinal at all, or only in a minimal way:

'I think that the Alps are tougher than the Himalayas.'
'I think that the Americans are more pleasure-loving than the French.'
'I think that spaniels are less lively than terriers.'

If we remove the possibly-autobiographical words, 'I think', the minimal attitudinal element is further reduced. Why is our original example an appropriate answer to the question, 'What is your attitude to Smith?'

One answer is this: because the words 'clever' and 'unreliable' *imply* what my attitude is: respect, plus mild disapproval. That is, I have not told you directly what my attitude is; I have given you something from which to infer it. You do not know what my attitude to X is unless you know whether I am for

X or against X, or whether I regard X as important or unimportant. Thus my opinion of X, by itself, may provide a ground for my attitude, or evidence concerning my attitude; but it is not the attitude itself. The attitude itself is respect, plus mild disapproval.

Such an analysis is correct in its insistence on the fundamental core of attitudes (for/against, important/unimportant), but it is incorrect in so far as it abstracts the opinion-element from attitudes. My attitude to Smith is not merely one of vague respect-plus-mild-disapproval; it is one of respect for his cleverness plus mild disapproval of his unreliability in matters of detail. That is, the opinion is not merely a ground for the attitude; it is itself involved in the attitude. We should realize that my opinion of Smith, in the absence of the elements 'for/ against' or 'important/unimportant', is not an attitude. In expressing my opinion I do not express my attitude; I merely imply it. Yet my attitude to Smith is specific; it should not be abstracted from my opinion of Smith.

In opinion-attitudes, the element of opinion is specially prominent, in that opinion is what is referred to explicitly. Feeling, future behaviour and policy-commitment are in the background, weakly implied by what I say. By itself, the opinion as such does not constitute an attitude. But if it is a ground for an attitude, it is often nevertheless an inseparable part of the attitude.

1.4. *Intention-attitudes*

I hope that I have indicated fairly clearly what these are, as I compared them with other attitudes, but I shall add one comment. First, some examples:

'I am supporting him in this, whatever people say.'
'I submit to God's will in all things.'
'My attitude to Communists is uncompromising.'
'I am always friendly to Negroes.'

In saying what I say, I not only report that I am committed to a policy, I actually commit or re-commit myself to it. One could insert, before each example, the words 'As I said before'; this would bring out the force of the utterance as a policy-recommitment or redeclaration. The utterances obviously have a Commissive force.

The word 'policy' may suggest a degree of formality and self-consciousness which is absent from most attitudes. But declarations of policy shade off into expressions of intention, and the latter are involved wherever attitudes are explicitly adopted or continued. We have seen that the words, '*My* attitude to . . . *is* . . .' have this Commissive force in most cases, unless disclaimed. And the more formal and self-conscious the commitment, the more an attitude deserves the label 'policy-attitude'.

Not all declarations of policy are attitudinal, for example, 'I (shall) lock the door every night'. And a policy may arise *because* of an attitude (for example, door-locking because one does not trust the neighbours). But there is a Commissive element in many first-personal references to one's own attitudes, an element which is most obvious in policy-attitudes.

1.5. *Various elements in attitudes*

Our analysis of attitudes shows that it is not a *sufficient* condition for the presence of an attitude that there is a feeling (for example, joy), or a pattern of behaviour (for example, courtesy), or an opinion (for example, one concerning spaniels) or a policy (for example, one concerning door-locking). Nor is it *necessary* for an attitude to be a feeling (consider 'condescending'), a pattern of behaviour (consider 'resentful'), an opinion (consider 'conciliatory') or a policy (consider 'jealousy'). Yet in some attitudes all four elements are present as important aspects of the attitude; in many attitudes several of the elements are present and important; and in some attitudes one element is specially prominent, so that attitudes can be classified roughly as feeling-attitudes, behaviour-attitudes, opinion-attitudes and intention-attitudes.

What is essential to attitudes? Considering them very abstractly, we may say that attitudes are essentially 'relational'. For example, such dispositions as humility, pride and trustfulness are attitudes in so far as I am humble *towards* some definite person or group, proud *of* something definite or *towards* someone definite, and trustful *in relation* to someone definite. The unrelated disposition to particular attitudes is not itself an attitude.

Somewhat less abstractly, we can say that attitudes involve (a) being *for* or *against* someone or something, or (b) regarding someone or something as *important* or *unimportant*. Together, (a)-or-(b) forms a necessary condition: where neither (a) nor (b) apply, there is not an attitude. And each is a sufficient condition for the existence of an attitude: to say, 'I'm for x' or 'x is important' is to tell you what my attitude to x is. I tell you this, however, in an extremely vague way. The particular nature of an attitude depends on the particular feeling, behaviour, opinion or policy which are part of the attitude. Hence these four elements are more significant than (a) or (b) in any detailed analysis of attitudes, even though (a)-or-(b) forms a necessary and sufficient condition for the existence of an attitude and none of the four elements do this.

In saying, 'I'm for x', or 'I regard x as important', I *take up a position* in relation to x. The word 'attitude' originally had to do with a physical posture of the body, assumed by the agent so as to be in a state of readiness for certain actions in relation to something else—actions such as attacking, defending or embracing. This physical connotation is carried over metaphorically to cases where, in saying something, I dispose myself in a particular way in relation to something—hostility, suspicion, forgiveness, etc.

Sometimes this 'self-disposal' is related to Behabitive performatives. Sometimes when I tell you what my attitude is ('I am very grateful to you', 'I feel very apologetic about not having knocked') my utterance is like a Behabitive ('I thank you', 'I apologize'). Indeed, we might call it a 'non-explicit Behabitive', if we had not defined Behabitives as utterances in which an attitude is *implied*; for here I *report* my attitude. But my utterance performs the same social function as a Behabitive. And without the Behabitive social-conventional actions, there would not be the specific attitudes which correspond to these: gratitude, apologetic-attitude, reverence, forgiveness, blame, honour, rebellion, etc. Hence the nature of a particular attitude sometimes depends not only on feelings, behaviour, opinion, and intention, and not only on the abstract feature (a) or (b), but also on the specific Behabitive performance with which it is connected in meaning.

1.6. *Expressions of attitude*

We are now in a position to draw some conclusions concerning what it is to 'express an attitude': In so far as an attitude includes an intention and an opinion, an 'expression of attitude' is Commissive and Verdictive; we have also seen that an 'expression of attitude' has a Behabitive function. In so far as an attitude includes a pattern of behaviour, an 'expression of attitude' may be an autobiographical report.

Thus when p is an expression of attitude to x, we may find any or all of the following elements present:

(1) *Expressive:* In saying p, I express my feeling (Response or Mood) in relation to x.

(2) *Performative:* (i) *Commissive:* In saying p, I express an intention or declare a policy concerning my future conduct in relation to x; I *decide to* do something. (ii) *Verdictive:* in saying p, I express an opinion or register a verdict concerning x; I *decide that* such-and-such is the case. (iii) *Behabitive:* In saying p, I report a Behabitive 'posture' in relation to x (for example, gratitude, blame or reverence). The utterance has the same social function as a non-explicit Behabitive.

(3) *Autobiographical:* In saying p, I report my own behaviour in relation to x, up until now. In some cases I also report a disposition (for example, jealousy) which probably will continue in the future.

We have seen that the mere existence of a feeling, an intention, an opinion or a pattern of behaviour is neither a necessary condition nor a sufficient condition for the existence of an attitude. Similarly the presence of an expressive, Commissive, Verdictive, or autobiographical element in an utterance is neither a necessary nor a sufficient condition for the utterance's being an expression of attitude. We have seen that the necessary and sufficient condition for an attitude is (a) being for or against, or (b) regarding as important or unimportant. Similarly an utterance which is an autobiographical report of any such Behabitive 'posture' is an expression of attitude—for example, 'I'm for x' or 'I regard x as important.' Nevertheless, the expressive, Commissive, Verdictive and (non-Behabitive) autobiographical elements in many attitudes are more important. They are especially important in the sort of attitudes which we will now consider.

2. *'Onlooks'*

In section 1, we ignored something which is the core of many attitudes, and which is extremely important in the analysis of evaluative language generally, and of religious language in particular. (Indeed, it is fundamental in the biblical conception of Creation, as we shall see in Part II.) It is similar to opinion, but not identical with opinion. If I were to ask you, 'What is your attitude to death, or to your present illness, or to your work, or to sex?', your replies would not naturally be preceded by the phrase, 'In my opinion'. Rather, you would say something like:

'I look on death as the mockery of human hopes (or as the gateway to a higher form of life).'

'I look on my suffering as a wise discipline, imposed by God (or as an opportunity for self-discipline, or as something trivial compared with my growing inner wisdom, or as an annoying interference with my work).'

'I look on my work as a way of making money, no more (or as my one reason for living, or as my calling from God).'

'I look on sex as a sordid animal urge (or as an expression of a profoundly spiritual relation).'

I have coined the word 'onlook' as a substantive for what it is to 'look on x as y'. It is necessary to coin a word, for no existing word is quite appropriate. The word 'view' would be misleading, since it is so close to 'opinion', especially in its plural form, 'my views concerning x'. The word 'conception' is a little too intellectual; and like 'outlook' and 'perspective', it lacks the element of commitment, and is too vague.

Consider some other examples of onlooks:

'I look on Smith as a tool to be used by us till the Revolution (or as the cause of all our trouble, or as a future district manager, or as the leader of our new movement).'

'I look on God as an all-knowing Judge to be feared (or as a trustworthy Shepherd who guides me along life's way, or as a loving Father who yearns for the return of his children)."

'I look on the State as my father (or as the servant of the people, or as a machine, constructed by men to achieve certain limited ends, or as an organism with a functional unity).'

'I look on my life as a game (or as a struggle, a search, a voyage, a pilgrimage, a dream, or a drama).'

'I look on myself as a custodian of classical culture (or as a prodigal son seeking divine forgiveness, or as the mid-wife for a master race, or as a craftsman who builds with words, or as a steward of God's world).'

'I look on Smith as a person, in spite of his terrible psychosis.' (Cf. 'I look on the baby as a person, even before he can smile.' 'I

do not look on Jews as persons.' 'I do not look on other people as persons but as tools.')
'I look on all Tories as vermin.'
'I look on alcoholism as a disease.'
'I look on Adenauer as the architect of the new Germany.'
'I look on Henry as a brother.'
'I look on England as my mother.'
'I look on the vicar as my shepherd.'
'I look on students as parasites.'

2.1. *Some common features of onlooks*

These examples indicate the tremendous variety of onlooks. Yet a number of logical features are common to all of them:

(i) *Commissive.* There is a Commissive element, a declaration or redeclaration of policy; or, at least, there is an expression of intention, a minimal undertaking.

It is interesting to notice that one does not usually say, 'I look on *x* as *y*' if one is no longer personally involved with *x*. For example, let us suppose that I have fired Smith from his job in my office. I still express my present opinion of him: 'I think that Smith was the cause of the trouble'. But since I no longer have anything to do with Smith, I express my onlook as something which belongs to the past: 'I always looked on Smith as the cause of the trouble'. If I say, in the present tense, 'I look on Smith as the cause of the trouble', I imply that I am still involved with Smith in some way, and the natural question for someone to ask is, 'So what are you going to do about it?'

In some onlooks, the personal involvement is more profound and dramatic:

'I look on death as the mockery of human hopes.'
'I look on Smith as a person, in spite of his psychosis.'
'I look on my suffering as an opportunity for self-discipline.'
'I look on God as an all-knowing Judge, to be feared.'

(ii) *Autobiographical.* In so far as an expression of onlook is an autobiographical report, it refers both to behaviour and to a way of looking. Thus an onlook may be revealed or displayed in one's behaviour and it may also be formulated privately without being expressed. As a pattern of behaviour, an onlook resembles a behaviour-attitude. As a way of thinking, it is to be compared with an opinion-attitude.

(iii) *Expressive.* An onlook may involve various feelings.

But it is futile to try to analyse the onlook in terms of the feelings, rather than the feelings in terms of the onlook, for these feelings are logically connected to the words of the onlook. The meaning of, 'I have a brotherly feeling towards all men' involves the onlook, 'I look on all men as brothers'. Similarly the meaning of 'stoical feeling' involves a complex onlook or view of life. It is not as if such feelings came to us with their names attached, with intrinsic differences which are independent of our way of looking on the world. (Note that the words of an onlook may be used evocatively, so as to arouse in someone the total mental state in which one comes to 'look on x as y'. But if we try to say precisely what it is that is evoked, we must use the language of the onlook or very similar language.)

(iv) *Behabitive-postural.* Though saying, 'I look on x as y' often reveals that I am for or against x, I am not for or against in an unspecified way, as I am when I say, 'I'm against it'. (Consider, 'I look on sex as a sordid animal urge'.) Similarly when I express an onlook I may report that I think that x is important or unimportant, but I do not do so in a merely general way. (Consider, 'I look on my life as a drama'.) The Verdictive element in onlooks gives the Behabitive element particularity.[1]

(v) *Verdictive.* 'Looking on x as y' involves placing x within a structure, organization or scheme. This often involves the ascription of a status, function or role to x in my own mind, though I may have no official authority to do so in a public way. Thus the Verdictive element sometimes is a sort of private, unofficial Exercitive. Sometimes the conceptual framework is non-literal and highly imaginative: for example, death as a 'mockery'. Sometimes x is placed in a future structural context rather than a present one: for example, Smith as a 'future district manager'. The onlook sometimes expresses a world-view: for example, 'I look on matter as the ultimate reality' or 'I look on desire as the source of all evil'.

An onlook is not merely speculative, subjective or fanciful; in such cases we would not say, 'I look on x as y', but 'I picture x as y' (for example, atoms as billiard balls), or 'I *see* x as y' (for example, the trick drawing as a rabbit, and then as a duck),

---

[1] Cf. section 1.3, concerning opinion-attitudes.

or 'I *imagine x is y*' (for example, the clouds are warriors).
Onlooks are practical, putatively-objective and serious. They
are appraised in such terms as profound/superficial, reasonable/
unreasonable, true-to-reality/mistaken, adequate/inadequate,
coherent/inconsistent.

The formulation of an onlook resembles the forming of an
opinion in that it involves a decision that certain words are
most appropriate in the matter being considered. The words in
onlooks are sometimes not meant literally,—for example,
looking on God as a 'shepherd' or the State as a 'machine'—
but they are chosen in all seriousness. The decision that a
certain word applies is rather like the forming of a verdict,
for example, that a car accident was a case of 'negligence'.
At any rate, the formulation of an onlook is more like the
deliberative process leading to a Verdictive performative than
it is like applying the word 'cat' to a cat (where everyone would
agree that it is a cat). The onlook-decision that a word applies
is not made arbitrarily; reasons, and sometimes evidence,
provide a basis. Indeed, for onlooks as well as for expressions of
opinion and various Verdictives, only one of the alternatives
may appear to be at all reasonable. Often, of course, it is difficult to abstract and state the reasons or evidence, which are
embedded in an individual's total life-experience, an experience
which has already been permeated and shaped by various
interpretative onlooks.

The combination of Commissive and Verdictive aspects in
an expression of onlook is important. In saying, 'I look on *x*
as *y*', I commit myself to a policy of behaviour and thought and
I register my decision that *x* is appropriately described as *y*;
my utterance combines an undertaking with a judgment. One
cannot abstract what is undertaken (for example, in relation
to my suffering) from my view of it (for example, as God's
discipline); or rather, if one does abstract some action which is
interpreted in terms other than the onlook, (for example,
refraining from groans), this is at best only a part of what is
undertaken. One undertakes to do certain things, viewing
them or interpreting them in a certain way. Indeed, the commitment to public behaviour is sometimes much less definite than
the commitment to *thought* concerning one's behaviour and
concerning others. This is specially evident in some religious

onlooks, for example, 'I look on each man as a brother for whom Christ died'.

In this section we have considered some of the logical features which onlooks have in common. In the next section we shall note some of the important differences among onlooks. Before we do so, however, I should clarify one important matter: the relation between the formulae, 'look on x as y' and 'see x as y'. We found that we could not replace 'see the drawing as a rabbit' by 'look on the drawing as a rabbit'; a similar non-equivalence would occur in other cases of simple Gestalt perceptions, where 'see x as y' is logically parallel to 'hear x as y'. But there are many cases where we *can* replace 'see x as y' by 'look on x as y'; indeed, it is true of most of my examples of onlooks that, if they had been expressed in terms of 'see x as y', they could have been changed into 'look on x as y' with only a minimal change of meaning:

'I see death as the mockery of human hopes.'
'I look on death as the mockery of human hopes.'
'I see life as a game.'
'I look on life as a game.'
'I see myself as a prodigal son seeking divine forgiveness.'
'I look on myself as a prodigal son seeking divine forgiveness.'
'I see Adenauer as the architect of the new Germany.'
'I look on Adenauer as the architect of the new Germany.'

Hence onlooks are not restricted to the formula, 'look on x as y', though they are typically and reliably indicated by it. Other formulae which *may* indicate an onlook are, 'see x as y', 'regard x as y', and 'think of x as y'.

2.2. *Classification of onlooks*

Some onlooks are quite *literal* in their meaning:

'I look on Smith as a future district manager.'
'I look on Brown as the cause of all our trouble.'

When it is an established fact that 'x is y', we do not say, 'I look on x as y': we would not say, 'I look on Macmillan as Prime Minister' or 'I look on cars as a means of transport'. But Smith is not yet a district manager, and Brown's responsibility has not yet been demonstrated. For a literal factual onlook, x is not yet y, or x is not yet known to be y; but the procedure for verifying the content of the onlook, 'x is y', is straightforward.

Sometimes, however, an onlook is literal although the speaker and others would agree that 'x is y'. For example, if I say, 'I look on Jones as my friend', I imply that I think that he *is* my friend. My utterance contains a value-word, 'friend', however; the content, 'x is y', is not a statement of fact but a Verdictive (and Commissive) utterance. Hence I can in this case say, 'I look on x as y' and mean it literally, without implying that 'x is not y'. This can happen in another sort of case, which is illustrated by the following:

> 'I look on Smith as a means by which I may gain access to the President.'
> 'I look on my suffering as an opportunity for self-discipline.'

Here too, it would not be odd to say, and to mean literally, 'Smith *is* a means . . .' or 'My suffering *is* an opportunity . . .'. Such an utterance, however, would not be a flat Constative; it would be an abbreviated form of the expression of onlook, in which I undertake to make x *become* y. Whether or not 'x is y' is true (or becomes true) depends on whether or not I act in accordance with 'I look on x as y'.

Many onlooks, however, are non-literal. When I 'look on Henry as a brother', it is not that Henry happens not to be my brother *yet* though he will be some day; and it is not that he is not yet *known* to be my brother, though I suspect that he is. If I say, 'I look on Henry as a brother', I imply that Henry is not (strictly or literally) my brother at all. I am comparing Henry with someone who is, or who might be, my brother. Similarly I compare students with parasites, the State with an organism, the vicar with a shepherd. The formula, 'I look on x as y' is applicable in such cases, not because x is not yet y, or because x is not yet known to be y, but because x is not strictly or literally y at all.

Some non-literal comparisons, however, are not open to being expressed in an onlook-formula at all:

> 'Her cheeks are roses.'
> 'The sun is a sower of light.'
> 'Feelings are the eyes of the heart.'

Such metaphors tend to be called '*mere* metaphors', for there is no obviously appropriate attitude to roses, sowers or eyes. If I accept such a metaphor, I do not commit myself to any particular pattern of behaviour or thought. Other metaphors, nevertheless, do have an important attitudinal significance —as we have seen.[1]

When we use the formula 'look on x as y', we assume that there is an appropriate way of thinking and behaving in relation to y, so that we are committing ourselves to a similar way of behaving and thinking in relation to x. Consider these examples:

'I look on death as the gateway to a spiritual form of life.'
'I look on alcoholism as a disease.'
'I look on all Tories as vermin.'
'I look on my life as a game.'
'I look on the vicar as my shepherd.'
'I look on God as our father.'

It is of course possible that someone may dread a spiritual form of life, or regard disease with moral disapproval, or love vermin, or play all games in deadly earnest, or distrust shepherds, or despise fathers; but if he does, it would be eccentric and misleading to express one of these onlooks. An onlook depends for its communicable meaning on the fact that there is an obviously-appropriate way of behaving or thinking in relation to y: the speaker commits himself (though not Indefeasibly) to a similar attitude towards x. But there is no sharp dividing-line between onlook-comparisons and metaphors. For example, is 'The spider is an artist' an eligible candidate for the formula 'look on x as y'? And some literal onlooks may be ambiguous because we do not know what the speaker regards as the appropriate way of dealing with y: for example, a South African says, 'I look on Verwoerd as the champion of white supremacy in Africa'.

But let us set aside both mere-metaphors on the one hand and literal onlooks on the other, and focus our attention on two main kinds of non-literal onlooks. Consider these two examples:

(I) 'I look on all Tories as vermin.'
(II) 'I look on students as parasites.'

In (I), the only similarity between Tories and vermin which the

[1] Thomist accounts of metaphor as 'analogy of improper proportionality' tend to stress 'dynamic likeness' at the expense of the *attitudinal* significance. I shall argue that the latter is primary when metaphors are applied to God. For a Thomist account, see James F. Anderson, *The Bond of Being*, Herder, St Louis, 1949, ch. XIV.

speaker is suggesting is that the feelings and behaviour appropriate in relation to vermin are in some way like those appropriate in relation to Tories; the speaker may have reasons for alleging this similarity of appropriate response, but he does not indicate them. In (II), the speaker alleges a similarity of appropriate response, but his words suggest also an independent similarity as the basis of this: as parasites feed on useful, self-sustaining organisms, so students. . . . Consider some other examples, which illustrate the difference between (I) and (II):

    (I) 'I look on Henry as a brother.'
        'I look on Smith as a tool.'
        'I look on the vicar as my shepherd.'
    (II) 'I look on music as a language.'
        'I look on alcoholism as a disease.'
        'I look on Adenauer as the architect of the new Germany.'

In the (I)-examples, the similarity which is implied between x and y is mainly in terms of appropriate attitude: x is *such that* the attitude appropriate to y is similar to the attitude appropriate to x. Henry may or may not have brother-like qualities, Smith may or may not have tool-like qualities, the vicar may or may not have shepherd-like qualities. All we can gather from what the speaker says is that there is something or other about Henry, Smith and the vicar which makes a particular attitude appropriate. Indeed, one may say, 'I look on Henry as a brother, but he is *not*', and so on.

The speaker in the (II)-examples suggests a similarity which is independent of any similarity of appropriate attitude. The meaning of 'I look on x as y' can here be readily analysed by abstracting a content (for example, 'Alcoholism is a disease') and then adding autobiographical and Commissive elements. Such an analysis is scarcely feasible for the (I)-examples, since the comparison of x and y involves a reference to the speaker's attitudes. Note also that, for the (II)-examples, it would be odd to add, 'but it (he) is not'.

I propose that we call the (I)-examples 'parabolic onlooks', and the (II)-examples 'analogical onlooks'. I do not claim that all non-literal onlooks obviously belong to one or other of these classes. Some analogical onlooks are virtually literal, for example, 'I look on alcoholism as a disease'. And many non-literal onlooks combine analogical and parabolic features:

for example, 'I look on the State as an organism' suggests various similarities between the State and an organism which can be only *partially* explained without reference to a recommended way of behaving in relation to the State.

The examples of parabolic onlooks which have been given are not in any way bizarre or elusive. We may interpret them as '*x* is *such that* the attitude appropriate to *y* is similar to the attitude appropriate to *x*'; but the 'such that' can be filled in if required. The speaker has not said how *x* is similar to *y*, but he can do so on request; for example, 'I look on Henry as a brother because he has behaved in a brotherly way towards me'. The similarity, however, might be much less straightforward:

(a) 'Henry reminds me of my brother Jim. I can't say what the similarity is, but he does.'
(b) 'My friend John tells me that Henry has in fact behaved in a very brotherly way towards me. John says that he is in a position to know, though he can't explain it to me; and I trust John's word.'

These two answers bring us closer to a logical parallel with some parabolic onlooks in religion, where 'I look on God as *y*', but, (a) I cannot specify the similarity between God and *y*, or (b) I trust the testimony of someone else (for example, Jesus) that God *is* like *y*. In either case I can believe that 'God is like *y*' and act accordingly. This is not a matter of acting *as if* I believed that God is like *y*; for example, it is not a matter of acting as if I believed that God is like a father. Rather, I actually do believe that God is like a father; but what I mean by this is to be explained in terms of human attitudes: I believe that God is *such that* the attitude appropriate to Him is similar to that which is appropriate towards a human father. In the words of Edwyn Bevan:[1]

'The Theist or Christian does not merely say: "Act as if there were a God who is a loving Father, and you will find certain desirable results follow" (that is Pragmatism): he says, "Act as if there were God who is a loving Father, and you will, in so doing, be making the right response to that which God really is. God is really of such a character that, if any of us could know Him as He is (which we cannot do) and then had to describe in human language to men upon earth what we saw, he would have to say:

[1] *Symbolism and Belief*, London, 1938, pp. 335-6.

'What I see is undescribable, but if you think of God as a loving Father, I cannot put the reality to you in a better way than that: that is the nearest you can get.' " '

God *is* like a father, but the nature of the likeness is obscure, and I believe in it mainly because I accept the authoritative words of Jesus. In Part II we shall see that biblical talk about God as Creator involves similar parabolic onlooks.

But let us consider a secular example which is logically similar to religious parabolic onlooks. A father says to his small son: 'That bare wire is very hot'. The son is too young to understand about electricity and shocks, but he knows what a hot thing is, and he knows that it is foolish to touch it, that it causes sudden pain, etc. Hence what the father says is true for practical purposes; the word 'hot' serves to inculcate the appropriate attitude. The father accommodates his language to the boy's understanding. Later on, the boy will be able to understand language that is literally true. Similarly God accommodates His revelation to human language and understanding, and later on, after death, we will be able to understand in literal terms.

Now let us consider an example which carries us over the bridge from secular-moral to religious language:

'I look on every human being as a person. By "person" I do not mean merely "human being". What I mean is this: In every person there is something which claims my concern, reverence, personal involvement and acknowledgment of value—my "*agapē*", to use the New Testament word. This attitude does not depend on his particular, observable qualities. A person is a being *such that* "*agapē*" is the appropriate attitude. A person has something extra which makes this attitude appropriate, but I cannot specify this "something extra" except in terms of "*agapē*".'

Not everyone, of course, is willing to talk in this way.[1] Some philosophers may think that it is a crude mistake if one fills in the 'such that' by a metaphysical entity. What is important to notice here, however, is how such an onlook differs from analogical onlooks, for example, from 'I look on alcoholism as a disease'. Here the meaning of the onlook's content can be ascertained, and the legitimacy of the onlook can be debated,

---

[1] For a favourable presentation and discussion of this sort of talk, see A. Farrer, *The Freedom of the Will*, London, 1958, pp. 305-8, and *Faith and Logic* (ed. B. Mitchell), London, 1957, pp. 15-21.

without reference to attitudes. But in the 'person'-onlook, the comparison is an indirect one, involving a reference to attitudes: each human being has particular characteristics to which we respond with various attitudes; but to one attitude ('*agapē*') there is no correlative particular-characteristic; that to which this attitude is a correlative response is the man's 'person' or 'soul'. In ordinary parabolic onlooks there is a straightforward way of comparing x and y, which the speaker merely does not mention, though he could easily do so. But some religious or quasi-religious parabolic onlooks allow no such direct comparison at all; the comparison between x and y inherently involves a reference to attitudes; and the onlook is used to suggest some metaphysical entity in relationship with me. Such parabolic onlooks may be called 'metaphysical'.

2.3. *Onlooks and the 'autonomy of value'*

Let us set the peculiar metaphysical onlooks to one side, and consider ordinary onlooks in relation to the 'autonomy of value'. Obviously we can affirm the following slogans:

'No flat Constative entails an expression of onlook.'
'No flat Constative entails an utterance which implies an onlook.'

Hence a man might restrict his language to flat Constatives plus the simplest expressions of attitude: 'I'm for it', 'I'm against it', 'That's important' and 'That's unimportant'. Indeed, some modern philosophers seem to be recommending this as a paradigm of practical reasoning. For such people, there is no place for non-literal onlooks, except if these are reduced to 'picturing x as y' or 'imagining x is y' so as to stimulate oneself in being actively 'for' or 'against' x.

Such a programme is not made obligatory because of the 'autonomy of value'; it is merely made theoretically possible. Personally, I think the programme is of limited scope and applicability, though it is valuable as an antidote to the metaphysical dogmatism and sheer prejudice in moral matters which follow when the 'literal' and the 'factual' are ignored. But such a programme is very different from much moral reflection, which may be represented schematically as follows: I wonder what attitude to take up towards x, so I reflect on what is similar to x. I am fairly clear and definite concerning what attitude is appropriate to y, and I note that x and y are similar in such-and-such relevant respects (though they are dissimilar in other, irrelevant, respects). These similarities may, or may *not*, be of a sort which is relevant to a programme of scientific understanding, prediction or control; they *are* of a sort which is relevant in terms of appropriateness of attitudes.

Onlooks vary considerably, of course. When I compare alcoholism and disease, similarities which are of scientific relevance are dominant, and the attitude which is appropriate to alcoholism virtually 'follows' from the factual study (if we assume an attitude to disease). When I compare students and parasites, the attitudinal element gains in importance. When I compare the State and an organism, there is a further shift. And when the onlook is definitely parabolic rather than analogical, the *meaning* of 'I look on x as y' involves a reference to my attitude towards y; for example, 'I look on all Tories as vermin'. Finally, there are the metaphysical parabolic onlooks, where a direct comparison between x and y is not only omitted in the onlook-expression, but is not even possible.

Typical moral reasoning, where it is imaginative and reflective, deals with onlooks which are partly analogical and partly parabolic. For example, a man wonders whether to look on his life as a struggle, a game, a dream or a pilgrimage; whether to look on this possible disclosure of information as honesty or cruelty; whether to look on an unwanted foetus as an animal or a person; whether to look on his friendships as political opportunities or as private concerns; whether to look on his artistic ambition as integrity or self-centredness; whether to look on death as a friend or an enemy; whether to look on the threat of nuclear retaliation as a legitimate bluff or a commitment to mass murder. In each case, there is a Verdictive, judgmental aspect to the pondering: in what respect (scientific, imaginative or metaphysical) are x and y alike? And in each case, there is a Commissive, attitude-adopting aspect: to what thought and behaviour am I committing myself if I come to look on x as y; and is such thought and behaviour right?

There is a temptation in modern philosophy to reduce such hybrid reasoning to one of two simple forms:

(i) x and y are similar in having features a, b and c. I am for (against) whatever has features, a, b and c. Hence I am for (against) x.

This is a distorted account, because the first premise is overly-simplified. x has features similar to the features a, b and c which y possesses; but the decision *that* features a, b and c are relevant and that there is sufficient similarity for me to 'look on x as y' is not entirely independent of the decision *to* 'look on x as y'. That is, such judgments concerning relevance and similarity depend in part on a Commissive or intentional element.

In the second distorted account, it is claimed that the comparison between x and y is not a factual investigation at all, but is governed entirely by the personal decisions-*to* which the person has made already. That is:

(ii) I am for (against) x.
I am also for (against) y—even more definitely and clearly.
So I allege that there are some similarities between x and y.

This makes the judgmental, deciding-*that* element a mere epiphenomenon of the underlying deciding-*to* element.

Such misinterpretations of onlook-deliberation arise partly from a misunderstanding of the 'autonomy of value'. No flat Constative entails an expression-of-onlook; but this does not show that onlook-language can be reduced to 'x is like y and I'm for (against) y', or to 'I've decided to treat x like y'. For a typical onlook is a *fusion* of a decision-*that* x is like y with a decision-*to* treat x like y. It is true that I am under no logical compulsion to continue with my previous attitude to y, or with society's prevailing attitude to y ('I look on life as a game, but I play all games in deadly earnest'). But if I *do* deliberate concerning the formulation or acceptance of a typical onlook, it is misleading to depict the logical structure of this deliberation either in terms of a decision-*that* and a decision-*to* which are completely independent, or in terms of a decision-*that* which is totally dependent on a decision-*to*.

2.4. *Onlooks and actions*

A man may look on his own action in various ways. Suppose that Jones leaves his mistress and returns to his wife. He may look on this action as a surrender to bourgeois morality, or as a dole to the woman in greatest need, or as a repudiation of sexual passion, or as a second self-commitment to his marriage vows, or as a sacrificial self-offering to God, or as a punishment of his fickle mistress. Or, like a character in a modern French novel, he may find or impose no 'meaning' for his action: that is, his action has no performative meaning for him—it is not a 'surrender', a 'dole', a 'repudiation', a 'self-commitment', a 'self-offering' or a 'punishment'.

An action may also seem 'meaningless' to the agent if he does not look on himself as someone who has a *role*.[1] A role may be 'objective', that is, it may be officially and explicitly established by a social group; for example, a man is a magistrate or a policeman or a waiter or a doctor. But a role may be largely 'subjective' and non-literal: I look on myself as a 'custodian' of classical culture, or as a 'spectator' of the world stage, or as the 'locomotive' of history (Krushchev), or as the 'servant' of all men, or as a 'workhorse' at the disposal of superior men, or as a 'prodigal son' seeking divine forgiveness. Any such role-onlook would be part of one's interpretation of many different actions.

It is important to realize that an agent may view the 'same' action (for example, moving his arm) in various ways; the meaning or rationale which the action has for the agent often depends on the onlook which he adopts. It is true that he or anyone else can describe his action in an utterance which is a flat Constative, an utterance which lacks the Commissive force (deciding-*to*) which an expression of onlook has, and the Verdictive force (deciding-*that*). Thus when he says, 'I am moving my arm', he is reporting a fact, and other people would generally assent to his statement. But other people may not agree with the Verdictive element in the onlook which he applies to his action. He may look on his action as the noble gesture of an aristocrat, whereas you see a clumsy bear pawing the air. The meaning which an action has for the agent—the unofficial performative force which he ascribes to it and the unofficial role which he sees himself playing in it—depends on the onlook which he adopts.[2] If someone else wishes to under-

[1] Cf. p. 67.

[2] Note that in my analysis of action I am not *equating* this onlook-dependent 'meaning' with 'intention'. An action need not have any such 'meaning' for an agent, even though he has his own highly-personal interpretation of his 'intention'. When he interprets his intention, he may merely select one aspect of what happened rather than another; for example, he may say, 'My intention was to ward off a blow, not to hit him in the face'. This involves no onlooks, though the ascription or disclaiming of responsibility is more Verdictive than Constative, (cf. p. 219 n. 1). For an interesting discussion of intention 'in doing' something, see G. E. M. Anscombe, *Intention*, Oxford, 1958, sections 4, 22-7.

stand his action, he must understand the onlook, though he does not need to accept the onlook.[1]

Onlooks are sometimes self-verifying. That is, in so far as I actually look on x as y in my daily life, it becomes true that x is y. For example, if I look on my suffering as a means to moral growth, it is likely that my suffering will *be* a means of moral growth. If I look on life as a struggle, life is likely to *be* a struggle. If I look on myself as the servant of all men, it is likely that I will *be* the servant of all men. In general, people tend to conform to the roles which they see themselves as playing. In the words of a well-known hymn:

'What we choose is what we are,[2]
And what we love we yet shall be.'

(In Part II we shall see that belief in world-Creation includes looking on oneself as God's steward; in so far as one does this in daily life, one *is* God's steward.)

An onlook need not be expressed in the first-person *singular*. Jones may say, '*We* look on x as y'. Such an utterance involves him in the same way as '*I* look on x as y'; but it also involves him in a different way. Not only does he, as an individual, commit himself to a pattern of thought and behaviour; he also identifies himself with a particular group, committing himself to a group-loyalty, or at least implying such a loyalty. An adequate analysis of first-person plural onlooks is not possible here; their Commissive, Behabitive and Verdictive elements are elusive and complex. All that I wish to emphasize here is the fact that onlooks are not inherently individualistic. Indeed, we should note that performative language in general need not be individualistic; one can say, 'We promise . . .', 'We confess . . .', 'We praise . . .', 'We judge . . .' and so on. (In Part II I shall usually consider self-involving language in the first-person singular, but this is merely for the sake of simplicity. Philosophical analysis does not settle the theological question concerning how important the individual or the group should be in the Christian religion or in Christian religious discourse.)

When I adopt a parabolic onlook towards a particular action of mine, or towards my life as a whole, the Verdictive element

[1] Cf. pp. 111-12.
[2] W. de Witt Hyde, 'Creation's Lord, we give Thee thanks'.

may be interpreted as an *imposition* of meaning or as a *discovery*
of meaning. Modern existentialist atheism insists on the former;
religious belief is a conviction that it is the latter. Religious
belief is the conviction (or hope) that one's onlook conforms to
an authoritative onlook, a divine onlook. We shall see that
biblical belief in world-Creation includes the belief that God
has *prescribed* a role and status for men and has *appraised* human
existence positively.

The notion of a 'divine onlook' requires further elucidation.
We have seen that in so far as an onlook is Verdictive, it is a
matter of judgment. Where I have reason to rely on another
person's judgment concerning something (life, State, God)
more than I rely on my own judgment, I may accept his authority concerning what onlook is appropriate (looking on life
as a game, or the State as an organism, or God as a father).
This is not the same as accepting someone's authority concerning a pure matter of fact, which can be settled, in principle if
not in practice, without any reliance on an authority. The
matter of judgment which is involved in many onlooks is
'settled' for oneself either by deciding-*that* on one's own
authority, or by accepting someone else's decision-*that*. Usually
a mixture of these procedures is used. But Christians believe
that there is a divine onlook concerning certain matters, an
onlook which is authoritative: human onlooks are 'true' in so
far as they approximate to the divine onlook. Some Protestants
differ from Catholics in denying that any human onlook can
have divine authority; but even here the search for the true
onlook is based on the hope that one's onlook might conform
to the divine onlook, though one could never be sure that it does
conform. Christians also differ concerning the range of onlooks
for which it is feasible to seek, or to claim, a divine onlook. For
example, are political onlooks included in this range? All that I
wish to maintain here is that the notion of a divinely-authorized
onlook does make sense in relation to the judgmental element of
onlooks. In contrast to this element, matters of fact—virtually
by definition—are matters which can be settled without reference to God or to any other special authority. Religion finds
one of its linguistic homes in the Verdictive aspect of human
onlooks. It is interesting to notice how Herbert Butterfield has
used the language of onlooks in his account of religious faith:

'Nobody can pretend to *see* the meaning of this human drama *as a god might see it*. . . . What one acquires is a *vision for working purposes in the world*, and one gains it by *adopting* an *attitude*, assuming a certain *role* within the drama itself . . . a mission which, though *prescribed by God*, must be accepted as self-assumed. . . . Ultimately our interpretation of the whole human drama depends on an intimately personal decision concerning the part that we mean to play in it.'[1]

In Part II we shall see that the biblical conception of world-Creation is a 'vision for working purposes in the world'. It is a complex onlook-attitude which, the Christian believes, is 'prescribed by God'; that is, the divine onlook is authoritative.

[1] *Christianity and History*, London, 1949, p. 86, my italics; cf. p. 114. Cf. also the unnoticed use of 'see . . . as . . .' by O. R. Jones, *The Concept of Holiness*, pp. 86, 137, 189. (My study of 'onlooks' and 'divine onlook' was made independently of Jones' study of 'visions' and 'divine vision'; the main similarity lies in his *use* of onlook-language.)

II

SELF-INVOLVING ELEMENTS
IN THE BIBLICAL CONCEPTION
OF CREATION

4

CREATION AS A PERFORMATIVE ACTION

1. *The creation of Israel by miracle and covenant*

IN THE Old Testament, the conception of world-Creation was similar to the conception of Israel's creation, for the distinctive and fundamental religious ideas of the Old Testament arose as an interpretation of Israel's historical origin as a people rather than as an interpretation of nature.[1] Yahweh, the God of Israel, was identified[2] as the God who had brought the people of Israel into existence by miracle and covenant: He had miraculously rescued them from slavery in Egypt, bringing them safely to the promised land of Canaan; and He had authoritatively initiated a covenant with them, by which the institutions of a society were established.[3] Hence all Israelite thought about God tended to combine the ideas of miraculous power and society-producing authority, as these had been combined in the interpretation of God's creation of Israel as a

[1] Here I am reflecting the views of those Old Testament scholars and theologians who minimize the similarity between official or orthodox Israelite religion and the nature-religions of Israel's neighbours, for example: K. Barth, *Church Dogmatics*, III, 1, Eng. tr. Edinburgh, 1958, pp. 84ff.; W. Eichrodt, *Theology of the Old Testament*, Vol. I, tr. J. A. Baker, London, 1961, pp. 230-2, 413; W. Foerster, 'Ktizo', *Theologisches Wörterbuch zum Neuen Testament*, ed. G. Kittel, Band III, Stuttgart, 1938, pp. 1,004, 1,008; E. Jacob, *Theology of the Old Testament*, tr. A. W. Heathcote and P. J. Allcock, London, 1958, pp. 136-8; L. Koehler, *Old Testament Theology*, tr. A. Todd, London, 1957, pp. 29-30; G. A. F. Knight, *A Christian Theology of the Old Testament*, London, 1959, pp. 108-9; G. E. Wright, *The Old Testament Against its Environment*, London, 1950, *passim*, and *God Who Acts*, London, 1952, *passim*; Th. C. Vriezen, *An Outline of Old Testament Theology*, Oxford, 1958, pp. 183-9.

[2] Exod. 20.2; Deut. 5.6; 6.12; 8.14; 13.10.

[3] Cf. B. S. Childs: 'The Old Testament . . . explained this people's total existence in terms of an encounter with the covenant-God of Israel, who in the Exodus had created them into a people, who in the conquest of Palestine had provided them with a home, and who through the covenant had given them their institutions.' (*Myth and Reality in the Old Testament*, 1960, pp. 96-7.)

people. The Exodus-events provided the paradigm case or norm for the rest of religious thought.

Many contemporary biblical theologians stress the similarity between the biblical conception of Israel's creation and the biblical conception of world-Creation. Some of them would even claim that, as a matter of history, the Israelites did not believe in a world-Creator until *after* the events of the Exodus, and then believed *because* of these events. We need not consider here the various versions of this controversial claim,[1] or possible objections to it;[2] but the *conceptual* similarity can not be ignored. So before we examine the biblical conception of world-Creation we shall have a look at the biblical conception of Israel's creation.

(In this chapter and in subsequent chapters I shall not consider the historical reliability of the Exodus-story or the origin and growth of the story, for we are only interested in analysing the conception of Israel's creation which eventually emerged in the Old Testament.)

1.1. *Creation as miracle*

The idea of Israel's total dependence on Yahweh was focused on the miracle of the Exodus:

> 'Has any god ever attempted to go and take a nation for himself from the midst of another nation, by trials, by signs, by wonders, and by war, by a mighty hand and an outstretched arm, and by great terrors, according to all that the Lord your God did for you in Egypt before your eyes?'[3]

Though there had been a people before the Exodus,[4] it was thought of as having been in the 'womb',[5] dependent on Yahweh's initiative in order to emerge into existence. Had Yahweh not intervened in history with His 'out-stretched arm', Israel would have remained a rabble of slaves and never become a nation. Along with the Exodus, the conquest of

---

[1] See L. Koehler, *op. cit.*, pp. 70ff.; W. Foerster, *op. cit.*, p. 1,004; A. Richardson, 'The Biblical Knowledge of God', *A Theological Word Book of the Bible*, ed. A. Richardson, London, 1950, pp. 89-90; E. Brunner, *Dogmatics*, II, tr. O. Wyon, London, 1952, p. 8; B. W. Anderson, 'The Earth is the Lord's', *Interpretation*, Vol. IX, 1955, pp. 7-8.

[2] G. Lindeskog sees Hebrew religion as a fusion of two relatively-independent elements: the myth of creation and the story of the Exodus. See 'The Theology of Creation in the Old and New Testaments', *The Root of the Vine*, ed. A. Fridrichsen, London, 1953, p. 5.

[3] Deut. 4.34.   [4] Exod. 3.7-12.   [5] Isa. 44.2, 24; cf. Jer. 1.5.

Canaan was understood as God's action on behalf of His People. Israel was warned that her power in the conquest came from Yahweh; neither fear[1] before battle, nor self-glory[2] after victory, were appropriate. When Israel appeared as a nation in Canaan, it was Yahweh who was the cause of her existence. By His mighty power, He had 'formed'[3] Israel, like a potter moulding clay; He had planted Israel, like a husband-man planting a vineyard.[4]

1.2. *Creation as covenant*

Yahweh's creation of Israel, however, was an exercise not only of supernatural causal power but also of institutional authority; and it is the latter which concerns us in this chapter. Yahweh created Israel with a subordinate status, a role and a positive value; and He committed Himself to her. We shall consider each point in turn.

1.2.1. *Creation with subordinate status.*

The Exodus and conquest did not in themselves establish Israel as an organized and unified community. In order to accomplish this, Yahweh provided a covenant which bound the individual Israelites to each other and to Himself. This covenant arose, not because the Israelites decided to bargain an agreement with Him, but from Yahweh's own initiative and authority:

'The Lord spoke to you out of the midst of the fire. . . . He declared to you his covenant.'[5]

Now a covenant has no place where a natural kinship already exists.[6] This fact is of momentous significance in the theology of the Old Testament. It means that Yahweh was not bound to Israel by quasi-biological ties—as her eponymous ancestor, for example. The relation between them arose because Yahweh, independent and distinct from Israel, had initiated a covenant. And in so far as the relation was covenantal, it was understood, and God Himself was understood, in terms of a variety of institutional relations: lord/servant; king/subject; husband/wife;

---

[1] Deut. 3.22.   [2] Deut. 8.11-20.   [3] Isa. 43.1; cf. Jer. 18.2-6.
[4] Ps. 80.8-13; cf. Isa. 5.1-7; Jer. 2.21.   [5] Deut. 4.12-13.
[6] Cf. J. O. Cobham, 'Covenant', *A Theological Word Book of the Bible*, ed. A. Richardson, p. 55.

owner or redeemer/property; father/adopted child.[1] In each of these institutional relations Israel's subordinate status was stressed.

In saying, 'Yahweh is Lord', a man acknowledges his own subordinate status. This logical point is noted by W. Foerster in his discussion of *adhonai*, the Hebrew word for 'lord': 'Such a mode of address in this context involves the self-designation of the speaker as "servant" and expresses the dependence—even when not meant to be taken literally—of the speaker upon the person addressed; it is expressive of subjection.'[2]

1.2.2. *Creation with a role*

Israel depended on God not only for her status, but also for her role as an instrument in His wider purposes, which extend beyond Israel:

> 'Turn to me and be saved, all the ends of the earth! For I am God, and there is no other. By myself I have sworn, from my mouth has gone forth in righteousness a word that shall not return: "To me every knee shall bow, every tongue shall swear."'[3]

God's redemption and revelation were to be mediated[4] through the people of Israel, appointed to the role of prophet,[5] priest,[6] and (perhaps) expiatory sacrifice[7] for the nations. We should

---

1 Ezek. 16.4-6; perhaps also Hos. 11.1-4. Israel is not only an adopted child but also a 'first-born' son; see Exod. 4.22 and Jer. 31.9. But the latter image, and the father-image where adoption is not explicitly mentioned (for example, Deut. 32.6; Jer. 3.4; Isa. 63.16; 64.8; Mal. 1.6; 2.10) are primarily a way of depicting God's *attitude* to Israel, an attitude of loving regard like that of a father to his children, especially to his first-born son (cf. Knight, *A Christian Theology of the Old Testament*, pp. 170-2, and Vriezen, *An Outline of Old Testament Theology*, p. 145). The 'biological-father' image is nevertheless used as a metaphor for Israel's dependence on God as her Creator, yet not in such a way as to equate divine and human nature (cf. Knight, *op. cit.*, p. 173 and Vriezen, *op. cit.*, pp. 145-7). A thorough study of *Israel's* creation would include a detailed examination of the father-image in both its institutional and causal aspects; but in a study of *world*-Creation, the image needs little attention, for (i) in the Old Testament it is not used at all to refer to the relation between God and mankind in general (cf. Vriezen, *op. cit.*, p. 146), and (ii) in the New Testament the biological metaphor is used to distinguish Jesus from all other men who are mere creatures.

2 *Lord*, tr. from *Theologisches Wörterbuch zum Neuen Testament* (ed. G. Kittell) by H. P. Kingdon, London, 1958, p. 82.

3 Isa. 45.22-3; cf. Ps. 86.9; 148.11; 96.10; 66.8.

4 This is the theme of A. G. Hebert's *The Throne of David*, London, 1941; cf. H. H. Rowley. *The Biblical Doctrine of Election*, London, 1950, p. 68.

5 Cf. Isa. 2.1-4, according to C. R. North, *The Old Testament Interpretation of History*, London, 1946, p. 177; cf. Zech. 8.20-3.

6 Exod. 19.5-6; cf. G. A. Danell, 'The Idea of God's People in the Bible', *The Root of the Vine*, ed. A. Fridrichsen, London, 1953, pp. 27-8.

7 Isa. 53, interpreting the 'servant' as Israel.

note that this is mainly a matter of creating with a role (like appointing an ambassador) rather than creating with a function; a role is something a person accepts, whereas a function may be fulfilled voluntarily or *in*voluntarily by a man, and also fulfilled by a thing. It was the other nations that had functions,[1] as God's unwilling instruments in carrying out His purposes for Israel. These purposes were stressed as much as His purposes for the world. Indeed, there was a particularist element in Israelite thought which culminated in the view, not that God had created Israel for the sake of the world, but that He had created the world for the sake of Israel. But in either case, Israel was created as having a role, whether it be one of service or one of supremacy.

1.2.3. *Creation and valuation*

Israel's dependence on God included not only a status and role, but also a divinely-bestowed value. Yahweh's choice of Israel to be His 'own possession'[2] involved a creation of value, an unmerited ascription of value. For it was not because of any greatness,[3] or righteousness,[4] or beauty,[5] or obedience[6] that Yahweh chose Israel; it was because of His inexplicable love,[7] a love which was not a response to worth, but a creation of worth.[8] Israel was important, but only because God deemed her to be so, because she was 'precious'[9] to God. It is not that one could infer Israel's value-to-God from her inherent qualities, as one might look at a diamond and infer how much it is valued by its owner. Israel's value depended on God's evaluation, not human evaluation.

It was possible, however, to infer God's beneficence from His dealings with Israel; and such an inference would not depend on the fact that He Himself deemed the results of His actions to be good. According to any ordinary human judgment, the results of God's actions—or rather, some of the results—were obviously good. A rabble of slaves had been rescued, moulded

---

[1] E.g., Hab. 1.6; Zech. 11.16; Jer. 50.41; Isa. 45.1.
[2] Deut. 7.6; cf. Deut. 14.2; 26.18; Exod. 19.5; Isa. 43. 1, 4.
[3] Deut. 7.7. [4] Deut. 9.4-6. [5] Ezek. 16.4-6. [6] Jer. 7.25; Deut. 9.7.
[7] Deut. 7.7-8; Ezek. 16.1-4; cf. Deut. 4.37; 10.15, which trace God's love back to the patriarchs; cf. G. E. Wright, *God Who Acts*, pp. 50-1, and *The Old Testament Against its Environment*, pp. 50-1.
[8] Cf. Rowley, *op. cit.*, p. 19: 'Nowhere is it taught in the Old Testament that God chose Israel because of her inherent greatness; yet there are passages where it is held that Israel's greatness lies in the fact that God chose her.'
[9] Isa. 43.4.

into a nation, and showered with material abundance;[1] and the divine covenant-law had enabled the community to achieve a good, happy life.[2] Crises of faith arose, of course, when an ordinary evaluation of worldly troubles seemed to show that God was not benevolent. But the word of God which came through the prophets provided a deepening religious interpretation of Israel's troubles: as disciplines,[3] or punishment,[4] or even as vicarious suffering.[5] This word was believed to be God's authoritative evaluation of the historical processes which continued to reveal His beneficence.

Thus both the created people of Israel and God's creative dealings with Israel received an authoritative evaluation from God.

Let us summarize the outline which has been given so far: Yahweh created Israel with a subordinate status, with a role, and with a value. In the biblical context, to believe in God was to acknowledge Him as Lord, Appointer, and Evaluator, accepting His supreme authority. This is different from belief that God is Maker, if one is merely giving bare assent to some statement concerning supernatural causal dependence—a statement similar to, 'That cup was moved by a poltergeist'.

The idea of 'accepting His authority', however, is somewhat puzzling. On the one hand, since God had initiated and authoritatively established the institutional relation between Himself and Israel, it was for Israel merely to acknowledge it as a *fait accompli*. On the other hand, the relation was surely 'complete' only in so far as Israel did acknowledge it, accepting the status, role and value. As C. H. Dodd has said, 'God's covenant is a *diatheke*, not a *syntheke*; that is to say, God fixes the terms of the Covenant and offers it to man that he may accept it; the acceptance is also essential.'[6] This raises a difficult question, which we will consider later: Does God's institutional authority over men depend on human acknowledgment? That is, (recalling our 1641-decree example),[7] does the

---

[1] Deut. 26.5-10.   [2] Ps. 19.7-10.

[3] Deut. 8.3; cf. Ps. 119.71; Prov. 3.11-12; 13.24; Heb. 12.5ff; Wis. Sol. 16.11-15.

[4] Amos. 3.2.

[5] Isa. 53, interpreting the 'servant' as Israel.

[6] *Etudes théologiques et religeuses*, xxiii, 1948, 2-3, quoted by Rowley, *The Biblical Doctrine of Election*, p. 47, n.1.

[7] See p. 72.

Exercitive force of God's word depend on the recognition which is accorded it?

1.2.4. *Creation as Yahweh's self-commitment*

We have seen that Yahweh's covenantal word had Exercitive force as an authoritative decree of Israel's status, role and value. It also had commitment-making, Commissive force as a reliable promise in relation to Israel. For Yahweh's creation of Israel as a people was understood to be the fulfilment of a covenantal promise which He had made to the patriarchs.[1] And in His covenant at Sinai, He committed[2] Himself to go on preserving the newly-created people in existence, in its special relation to Himself. The continued existence of Israel, with its divinely-constituted status, value and role, was assured by the divine word of promise. Unlike man, God does not go back on His promises.[3] His covenant-loyalty (*hesed*) is strong[4] and everlasting.[5] Hence a devout Israelite should adopt an attitude of unlimited trust in God, whose unchanging word assures His faithfulness to the covenant.[6] As Israel's Creator, Yahweh was her Guarantor.[7]

We have seen that Yahweh was also her Lord, Appointer and Evaluator. Now we turn from Israel's creation to the conception of *world*-Creation, where similar institutional ideas are involved. (For the time being we shall set aside ideas of world-Creation which are causal: 'making', 'building', etc.)

2. *World-Creation by the word*

The institutional element in the Old Testament idea of world-Creation is most obvious in the idea of Creation by the word,[8] an idea which became prominent in intertestamental literature[9] and which was continued in the New Testament:[10]

---

[1] Exod. 6.2-4; 32.13; Deut. 7.8; Ps. 105.7-11.

[2] Exod. 19.3-6; 23.31; cf. Judg. 2.1; Ps. 94.14; cf. Jer. 31.35-7.

[3] Num. 23.19; Hos. 11.8-9.

[4] Cf. E. Jacob concerning *hesed* as 'strength' (*Theology of the Old Testament*, p. 103).

[5] Isa. 54.7-8.   [6] Ps. 89.33-5.   [7] See Isa. 43.1-7.

[8] Or by words; that is, creation by spoken utterance, in words or sentences.

[9] 2(IV) Esdras 6.38: 'O Lord, thou didst speak at the beginning of creation, and didst say on the first day, "Let heaven and earth be made", and thy word accomplished the work.' Cf. Apoc. Bar. 21.4 (tr. R. H. Charles, London, 1918): 'O Thou . . . that hast called from the beginning of the world that which did not yet exist.'

[10] Rom. 4.17; Heb. 11.3; II Peter 3.5.

'God said, "Let there be light"; and there was light.'[1]

We shall see that Creation by the word included the four institutional ideas with which we are now familiar: Creation with a subordinate status, Creation with a role, Creation with a value, and Creation as God's self-commitment.

2.1. *Creation with subordinate status*

The word which was used in Creation by the word was a peculiar sort of command:

'By the word of the Lord the heavens were made . . . for he spoke, and it came to be; he commanded, and it stood forth.'[2]

Here we should recall our distinction between two sorts of 'efficacy' which words may have: causal power and Exercitive force. In our prosaic example, the sergeant-major's utterance, 'On the double' brings about Private Smith's behaviour, but it also (unlike a swarm of bees round Smith's head), constitutes the behaviour as obedience, as having a particular institutional status. Similarly God's Creative word has a two-fold efficacy: it has causal power, bringing about the sheer existence of the creature; and as a command, it has Exercitive force, invoking a subordinate status of the creature so that the creature's very existence is 'obedience'.[3]

The subordinate status of creatures is evident in the idea of existence as obedience-to-command. It is also to be seen in the use of specific institutional terms:

'By thy appointment they stand this day; for all things are thy *servants*.'[4]

---

[1] Gen. 1.3.   [2] Ps. 33.6, 9.

[3] W. Foerster connects this dependence-for-existence-on-a-word-of-command with the choice of '*ktizo*' by *LXX* as one of the verbs to translate the Hebrew verb '*bara*', which was used only with reference to divine Creation. Foerster makes two claims which, if legitimate, provide further evidence for what I have called the 'institutional' elements in Creation: (i) The usual secular meaning of '*ktizo*' was 'found'; the characteristic object was a town, society or social event; and the typical subject was a ruler 'autocratic and almost godlike' (*Theologisches Wörterbuch zum Neuen Testament*, ed. G. Kittel, Band III, p. 1,024). (ii) the choice of *ktistes* rather than *demiourgos* to refer to the Creator is highly significant, and reflects the biblical belief that God created things out of nothing by word of command (*ibid.*, pp. 1,023-5). Both claims, however, have been challenged by James Barr: (i) in private correspondence, and (ii) in *The Semantics of Biblical Language*, pp. 224-5.

[4] Ps. 119.91. Cf. H. Fisch: 'To the Hebrew mind, the Law of Nature has an imperative character; like *torah* in the human sphere, it involves command and response' ('The Analogy of Nature', *Journal of Theological Studies*, 1955, p. 170).

'The heavens are thine, the earth also is *thine*; the world and all that is in it, thou hast founded them.'[1]
'Know that the Lord is God! It is he that made us, and we are *his*.'[2]

God's creatures are His servants and possessions. In the biblical context, to say, 'God is my Creator' is to acknowledge a subordinate status.

It seemed to some of the biblical writers that since *all* men are subordinate to the Creator, all men have *equal* status in relation to one another:[3]

'The rich and the poor meet together; the Lord is the maker of them all.'[4]
'If I have rejected the cause of my manservant or my maidservant, when they brought a complaint against me; what then shall I do when God rises up? When he makes inquiry, what shall I answer him? Did not he who made me in the womb make him? And did not one fashion us in the womb?'[5]
'He who oppresses a poor man insults his Maker.'[6]

2.2. *Creation with a role*

The Old Testament idea of Creation-by-the-word included not only an ascription or assumption of subordinate status for the creature, but also an appointment to a role or function. The Queen says, 'I create you Governor of Kenya', and in a logically-similar way the various parts of the universe were given their role or function as they were created by the word. Karl Barth[7] stresses this in his exposition of the creation-stories in Genesis. For example, God created the concrete time of human existence, the day, 'by giving to light the name "day" '.[8] According to Barth, God 'determined and appointed the light to be day'.[9] 'The fact that God calls the light day means formally that the day as our unit of time is not an arbitrary human invention or convention, but a divine work and institution. The day is thus given to the creature as the sphere of its existence.'[10] The function of the sun, moon and stars is to provide

---

[1] Ps. 89.11; cf. Ps. 24.1-2.   [2] Ps. 100.3.
[3] See G. Lindeskog, *The Root of the Vine*, ed. A. Fridrichsen, London, 1953, pp. 9-10.
[4] Prov. 22.2.   [5] Job 31.13-15.   [6] Prov. 14.31.
[7] *Church Dogmatics*, III, 1, pp. 98ff.   [8] *Ibid.*, p. 125.
[9] *Ibid.*, p. 124; cf. G. von Rad, *Genesis, A Commentary*, tr. J. H. Marks, London, 1961, p. 51: 'The precise translation, therefore, is, "And God *appointed* the light as day".'
[10] *Op. cit.*, p. 126.

'the objective possibility of a human awareness of time and place, thus making it possible for man as a creature to have a history with God'.[1] In general, nature's functions (or roles, for things are often personified) are decreed by God in view of His purposes for mankind. Man, on the other hand, is created with a superior role in relation to nature: man is God's appointed steward over nature,[2] God's representative (or 'image')[3] to whom He has delegated authority. 'Man's role—not just Israel's —is to perform the task which is given him by his Creator.'[4]

Alan Richardson gives a liturgical interpretation of biblical Creation-with-a-role in his commentary on Gen. 1. God is the builder and founder of a vast cosmic temple, in which all creatures form a religious community, and each has his appointed role in the glorification of God: 'Sun and moon and stars, day and night, trees and herbs and grass, beasts and birds and fishes,—everything performs its duly ordained liturgical office, like the priests and levites of the sanctuary in their appointed courses.'[5] According to Richardson, man is not only the steward but also the 'arch-priest'[6] of the whole created world. The word 'arch-priest' is perhaps inadequately warranted by the biblical evidence, but it is clear that man has a special role as the one creature who can worship God articulately.[7]

Some individual men—Jeremiah for example—are created with their own specific status and role in relation to God:

'Before I *formed* you in the womb I knew you; and before you were born I consecrated you; I *appointed* you a prophet to the nations.'[8]

---

[1] *Ibid.* p. 163. This is not a peculiarly Barthian interpretation; see also J. Marsh, *The Fulness of Time*, London, 1952, p. 33; or B. S. Childs, *Myth and Reality in the Old Testament*, London, 1960, p. 39.

[2] See Gen. 1.2-6; Ps. 115.16; Ps. 8.6-8; cf. Ecclus. 17.3-4; cf. Apoc. Baruch 14.18: 'Thou didst say that Thou wouldst make for Thy world man as the administrator of thy works, that it might be known that he was by no means made on account of the world, but the world on account of him' (tr. R. H. Charles, London, 1918).

[3] For this interpretation of the *imago dei* see G. von Rad, *op. cit.*, pp. 57-8.

[4] B. W. Anderson, 'The Earth is the Lord's', *Interpretation*, 1955, p. 15.

[5] *Genesis I-XI, Introduction and Commentary*, London, 1953, p. 43; cf. Ps. 148; cf. W. Vischer, 'Words and the Word', tr. J. Bright, *Interpretation*, January, 1949, p. 11; cf. F. Michaeli, *Le Livre de la Genèse*, Vol. I, Neuchâtel, 1960, p. 24.

[6] *Genesis I-XI, Introduction and Commentary*, p. 44.

[7] Cf. E. Stauffer, *New Testament Theology*, tr. J. Marsh, London, 1955, p. 61; and cf. Ecclus. 17.1ff.

[8] Jer. 1.5; cf. Stauffer, *op. cit.*, p. 52, who refers to Ass. Mos. 1.14 and 12.6ff.

The divinely-produced births of Samson[1] and Samuel[2] are similarly conjoined with special divinely-appointed tasks. These examples do not show that *every* man is created with some individual role or function, but there are hints of this in the Old Testament:

'The Lord has made everything for its purpose, even the wicked for the day of trouble.'[3]

And one scholar translates and interprets Psalm 139.13-16 (which is unfortunately obscure) so as to infer that 'there is an ideal plan of life providentially marked out for every individual',[4] along with his creation. This exegesis is debatable. The main point, however, is straightforward: man in general is created with a role as nature's steward and God's articulate worshipper. In the biblical context, to say, 'God is my Creator' is to acknowledge the *role* which God has assigned.

2.3. *Creation and valuation*

Creation by the word thus includes creation with a subordinate status and creation with a role. It also includes creation with a positive status or *value*.

'And God saw everything that he had made, and behold, it was very good.'[5]
'Everything created by God is good, and nothing is to be rejected if it is received with thanksgiving; for then it is consecrated by the word of God and prayer.'[6]

God gave His own authoritative appraisal of His handiwork; it is not for man to dispute it. But does this mean that there is little or nothing in God's creation which seems good or beautiful to us, from which we might legitimately infer its value to God? Some theologians expound Genesis 1.31 in such a way, interpreting world-Creation as if it were like Israel's creation[7] in this respect too. Karl Barth says, 'That it (the creature) was good when He created it does not mean the impartation and appropriation of an inherent goodness which no longer needs the divine discovery. As its becoming good is a matter of divine creation, so its being good is a matter of divine seeing.

---

[1] Judges 13.5.   [2] I Sam. 1-2, especially 2.35.   [3] Prov. 16.4.
[4] A. F. Kirkpatrick, *Commentary on Psalms*, Cambridge, 1902, p. 790; cf. R.S.V. translation.
[5] Gen. 1.31.   [6] I Tim. 4.4-5.   [7] Cf. p. 149.

But this seeing is grace.'[1] A similar interpretation is given by Dietrich Bonhoeffer: 'It is good only in the way that the creaturely can be good; because the Creator views it, acknowledges it as his own and says of it: "It is good". God views his work, and only this makes the work good. This means particularly that the work is good only because the Creator alone is good.'[2]

Austin Farrer's exegesis is very different: 'God looked on all that he had made, and found it very good, and it is in the light of the achieved goodness that we understand the wisdom which fabricated it. When I see the thrush . . . I do not ask whether it is good that such a creature should be. I am made in God's image and God's own praise of his creation finds an immediate echo in my mind. As I acknowledge the good of the thrush's being, I am furnished with a clue to the providence which has brought it about.'[3]

The view of Barth and Bonhoeffer has little direct scriptural support.[4] On the other hand, there is little scriptural support for any view which would make God's cosmic value-judgment merely a redundant confirmation of man's. Farrer's view perhaps goes a little too far in this direction, but it seems to me to be more biblical. The Bible leads us to say that God's act of world-Creation includes an authoritative positive evaluation of the results; but the relation of this to man's evaluation is extremely complex. It is everywhere assumed that creation is a benefit and a gift; God is good, and so whatever He does is good,[5] even that which may seem to harm man.[6] Yet ordinary human judgments concerning what is good are not irrelevant: obvious benefits, such as timely rain,[7] provide evidence for God's goodness. And in the Wisdom of Solomon we even read, 'By the greatness and beauty of the creatures proportionably ('analogōs') the maker of them is seen'.[8]

The relevance of these issues to the problem of evil and the argument from design is obvious. Here, however, I wish simply to stress the intrinsic connection, in the Bible, between Creation

---

[1] *Church Dogmatics*, III, 1, p. 122; cf. pp. 38-9, 212-13, 331-44, 366-78.
[2] *Creation and Fall*, London, 1959, p. 32.
[3] *Lord I Believe*, London, 1958, p. 27.
[4] Barth (*op. cit.*, p. 122) seems to be unable to find any biblical quotation to support his position except Mark 10.18: 'No one is good but God alone.'
[5] Cf.. Ps. 145.9.   [6] Cf. Job, *passim*.   [7] Jer. 5.24; Acts 14.17.
[8] Wis. 13.5 (A.V.).

and *giving*.[1] If I hand you something and say, 'This is a gift', I imply that what you are receiving is good for you. If you thank me and thus accept my total act, you imply that you accept my value-judgment too.[2] In a similar way, the biblical man's belief in a world-Creation is not just a bare assent to a flat Constative concerning a supernaturally-powerful act; it is a grateful response to an act which includes its Agent's own evaluation. It involves agreement with an authoritative Verdict concerning the goodness of existence. In the biblical context, to say, 'God is my Creator', is to acknowledge existence—one's own and the world's—as a gift.

2.4. *Creation as Yahweh's self-commitment*

We have seen that the word of God in Creation has Exercitive force, establishing the subordinate status and role of the creature, and Verdictive force, determining the value of the creature. It also has Commissive force, as a word of promise in which God commits Himself to the maintenance of the order which He has created. Thus for Israel the obvious regularities of nature, such as the succession of day and night or the stability of earth and sky, were signs of God's faithfulness to His covenant, both with Israel[3] and with nature.[4]

'For ever, O Lord, thy word is firmly fixed in the heavens. Thy faithfulness endures to all generations; thou hast established the earth, and it stands fast. By thy appointment they stand this day.'[5]

The orderly and beneficial processes of nature were thus not merely evidences of design, analogous to Paley's watch or to a garden in the desert; they were signs of a pledged word, especially of God's covenantal promises to Israel. As Thomas Chalmers once said, 'The uniformity of nature is but another name

[1] Cf. Gen. 1.29; Ps. 115.16; Acts 14.17; 17.25; James 1.17.

[2] Of course, you may be insincere. Or you may be graciously polite—for example, you thank me for the gift, though you value only the thought.

[3] Cf. Jer. 31.35-6; cf. Jer. 33.19-26.

[4] Cf. Jer. 33.25, where God speaks of His 'covenant with day and night'. Note that the Noachic covenant (Gen. 9.22) can be understood as God's pledge to all men after Noah that the world-order would be preserved. G. Östborn takes Gen. 1.1-2.3 as a description of a covenantal relationship (*Yahweh's Words and Deeds*, Uppsala Universitets Arsskrift, 1951, p. 23). He refers to Hos. 6.7: 'They, like *Adam*, have transgressed the covenant'; but both A.V. and R.S.V. give a different translation.

[5] Ps. 119.89-91.

for the faithfulness of God'.[1] Yahweh's strong covenant-loyalty (*hesed*) fills the earth[2] and extends to the heavens,[3] for He created the world by His self-committing word.[4] The devout believer would look up to the starry heavens and renew his confidence in the God who pledges His protection[5] and strength[6] to those who trust in him. Similarly in the New Testament Jesus points to the feeding of the ravens and the clothing of the lilies as signs of God's providential commitment to His people.[7] Unlimited trust in God's faithfulness precluded an attitude of fear, despair and anxiety in relation to the world.

The Commissive element in divine Creation-by-the-word is thus correlated with a fundamental human attitude towards God and towards the world. To say, 'God is my Creator' in the biblical context is to acknowledge Him as Guarantor of one's existence. Both the divine Creative word of promise and the correlative human word of acknowledgment are performative.

2.5. *Divine word and human word*

We have seen that the correlation between God's word *of* Creation and man's word *concerning* Creation holds more generally: The efficacious word of God in Creation has not only supernatural causal power but also Exercitive, Verdictive and Commissive force; and man's word concerning the Creator who is Lord, Appointer, Evaluator and Guarantor is a self-involving acknowledgment. In the biblical context, if I say, 'God is my Creator', I acknowledge my status as God's obedient servant and possession, I acknowledge my role as God's steward and worshipper, I acknowledge God's gift of existence, and I acknowledge God's self-commitment to me. This act of acknowledgment includes both Behabitive and Commissive elements. As in other cases of 'acknowledgment',[8] it is not perfectly clear whether I imply that I have certain attitudes or commit myself to these attitudes, or somehow do both. There is

[1] Quoted by J. Baillie, *The Idea of Revelation in Recent Thought*, London, 1956, p. 72. Cf. H. Wheeler Robinson, *Inspiration and Revelation in the Old Testament*, Oxford, 1946, pp. 9-10, 47.
[2] Ps. 33.5; cf. Ps. 119.64; cf. W. Eichrodt, *Theology of the Old Testament*, Vol. I, p. 239.
[3] Ps. 36.5; cf. Ps. 108.4.
[4] Ps. 33.4-6. In Ps. 136 God's *hesed* is seen as the source not only of Israel's sacred history but also of world-Creation.
[5] Isa. 51.12-13.   [6] Isa. 40.25-31.   [7] Luke 12.22-31.
[8] Cf. chapter 1, section 4.

nothing strange in this: I may imply that, so far, I have had a particular attitude, and also commit myself to continuing this attitude into the future. In any case the acknowledgment is clearly a self-involving performative utterance which is 'correlative'[1] to God's performative 'utterance'. In his utterance concerning Creation, biblical man implies that he takes the divine action to be a performative; that is, he *looks on* Creation *as* a performative action.

This is a parabolic onlook, the basis for other parabolic onlooks. In the biblical context, I look on the divine action of world-Creation as a verbal performative, and so:

I look on myself as God's servant, *commanded* to exist by His 'word'.

I look on myself as God's steward, *appointed* to this role by His 'word'.

I look on my existence as God's good gift, positively *evaluated* and *bestowed* by His 'word'.

I look on nature's beneficial regularities as God's *pledged* 'word' to man.[2]

It is true that, since world-Creation is not *literally* verbal, the usual distinction between verbal and non-verbal performatives does not strictly apply.[3] But the distinction does not matter in this case, for the point of the onlook is that Creation is viewed as an action which has various performative forces—forces which *can be made explicit verbally*, whether or not the action itself is verbal.[4] And the explicit performatives are obviously correlated with self-involving performatives in which men acknowledge God's action:

God's 'utterance':	*Man's reply:*
(1) 'I order you to exist as my servant.' (Exercitive)	(1) 'I belong to thee, O Lord.'
(2) 'I appoint you as my steward over nature.' (Exercitive)	(2) 'May I perform the tasks which thou dost assign.'

[1] Cf. chapter 1, section 11.2.

[2] The onlooks need not be expressed in the first-person *singular*. Indeed, in the biblical context I am more likely to say, '*We* look on *ourselves* as God's servants (stewards, etc.)'. In an analysis of self-involving language, it is simpler to deal with the first-person singular; but no theological individualism should be inferred from this procedure. Cf. p. 139.

[3] Cf. chapter 1, section 11.1.

[4] Cf. pp. 76-8.

	God's 'utterance':	*Man's reply:*

(3) (i) 'I judge creaturely existence to be good.' (Verdictive)

(3) (i) 'I accept thy judgments, O Lord.'

(ii) 'I give you existence as a blessing.' (Exercitive)

(ii) 'I thank thee for this and every good gift.'

(4) 'I pledge you my steadfast love.' (Commissive)

(4) 'I put my trust in thee.'

Thus, in various ways, the Creative 'word' of God is correlated with the self-involving word of man. The correlation occurs because of a basic onlook: in the biblical context, a man looks on Creation as an action which has various performative forces and which is correlated with various performative replies.

The parabolic comparison between world-Creation and human performative actions is not a matter of 'Let's pretend'; I do not merely *act as if* I believed that there is a God who is like a human agent who commands, appoints, judges, gives and pledges. I act in accordance with the positive belief that God *is* like a human agent in these respects; but I cannot describe this similarity except in terms of human attitudes, onlook-attitudes which I believe to be appropriate in relation to God.[1] In the biblical context, world-Creation is understood in terms of a parabolic onlook.[2] Thus, in the biblical context, the utterance 'God is my Creator' is profoundly self-involving.

What do I mean by 'in the biblical context'? I have used this phrase frequently and crucially without having given any explanation. In the next section I shall try to explain what I mean and to forestall several possible misinterpretations.

2.6. *The biblical context for man's word concerning Creation*

I have been saying that if the utterance, 'God is my Creator' occurs in the biblical context, it is self-involving in certain specific ways. When a man utters these words in some other context, his utterance may not be similarly self-involving—for example, if the words form the conclusion to a quasi-scientific argument from design.[3] If the self-involving implications of the utterance depend on their occurrence in the biblical

---

[1] Cf. pp. 133-4.

[2] Parabolic onlooks will be discussed more fully in chapter 6.

[3] The argument from design will be discussed in *Some Further Problems*, section 3.

context, these implications and commitments are Traditional-Contextual.[1] That is, the words have the meaning which is built up in the Bible as a whole, as the Bible is interpreted according to some theological tradition. Various connotations of the words as they occur throughout the Bible have been selected, combined and prescribed for the believer's use *today*. This does not involve any claim that *whenever* a word occurs in the Bible it actually had this modern-confessional meaning for the particular biblical writer; biblical theology should not be imposed on biblical exegesis where the latter is solely concerned with what a passage meant to the man who wrote it. On the other hand, the modern-confessional meaning is *dependent* on the various connotations which the word actually had in various biblical passages. There is, nevertheless, an unavoidable element of selection, combination and prescription in any biblical theology; indeed, the biblical material is usually interpreted in relation (positive or negative) to modern conceptual frameworks.[2]

There are three possible misunderstandings of the phrase 'in the biblical context' which should be avoided. First, a biblical historian might be misled because I am not using the phrase in a way which would seem natural to him. For him, the biblical context of a sentence is the particular passage in the Bible where the sentence actually occurs. In biblical theology, however, though such particular contexts provide the basis for the whole conceptual structure, (i) the sentence need not actually occur in the Bible—it may be a confession of faith—and (ii) the phrase, 'in the biblical context' means 'in the context of the whole Bible as interpreted by someone within a theological tradition'. Secondly, we should perhaps speak of '*a* biblical context' rather than '*the* biblical context', for various theological traditions exist; indeed, we can combine and modify theological traditions so that many subtly-varying 'biblical contexts' are possible. Nevertheless, I shall continue to speak of 'the biblical context', meaning by this 'the biblical context which *I* am expounding'. No Barthian dogmatism should be inferred from this procedure! Thirdly, my account of linguistic theory in

---

[1] Cf. pp. 51-2.

[2] Some biblical theologians may protest against such an account of their methodology; but I think it can be shown that even the *rejection* of a conceptual framework usually affects the positive interpretation of biblical material.

biblical theology[1] should be understood in relation to my own practice. To some readers, the theory may seem to treat historical matters with cavalier nonchalance; to others, it may seem to betray an atavistic biblicism. The only useful test is the way in which I actually use biblical material.

When Jones says, 'God is my Creator', his utterance is self-involving if it occurs in the biblical context. Whether or not it does occur in the biblical context depends on his decision; it depends on either his participation in an Occasional context (such as Christian worship) which involves this Traditional context, or his inner intention to speak within this Traditional context. Similarly he can decide whether or not to say, 'Trade-unions are *political*' in the Traditional context of Marxism, or 'The safe-period is a *natural* method' in the Traditional context of Thomism. More generally, he is free to decide whether or not to speak (and think) biblically, or as a Marxist, or as a Thomist. In somewhat the same way (this is a prosaic Wittgensteinean example) he is free to decide whether or not to use cards to play Solitaire; if he does, there are rules-of-use to be followed. Whether or not his utterance 'God is my Creator' has the self-involving meaning which has been outlined in this chapter depends on his decision. Indeed, the so-called 'leap of faith' is partly a decision to speak concerning God in the biblical context, involving oneself in the implications and commitments which this context gives to one's words.

We have been considering the performative force of *man's* word concerning Creation. At this point it is interesting to digress for a moment to look again at the *divine* word. We shall see that contemporary biblical theology and analytic philosophy have a similar interest in language as activity, words as deeds.

2.7. *Language as activity: interpretations in biblical theology and analytic philosophy*

In Part I we considered the Exercitive and causal uses of words to *bring about* results, and I referred to Austin's *How to*

---

[1] I do not wish to convey the impression (a) that *all* biblical theologians would accept this account, for some would not, or (b) that biblical theology *consists* entirely of word-studies, for it does not. For brief studies which open up this whole area, see Th. C. Vriezen, *An Outline of Old Testament Theology*, chapter 5; G. Ebeling, 'The meaning of "biblical theology" ', *Journal of Theological Studies*, VI, 1955; James Barr, *The Semantics of Biblical Language*, chapters 8-10, and *Biblical Words for Time* (London, 1962), chapters 6-7.

do Things with Words, which is edited from his lectures on 'Words and Deeds'. It is no mere coincidence that an important work in biblical theology should bear the title, 'Yahweh's Words and Deeds',[1] for a central theme in biblical theology is the conception of the divine word as an act which *brings about* results.[2] Consider the following biblical passages, where God's word is an efficacious utterance, a deed with performative force and causal power:

> 'As the rain cometh down, and the snow from heaven, and returneth not thither, but watereth the earth . . . so shall my word be that goeth forth out of my mouth: it shall not return unto me *void*, but it shall accomplish that which I please, and it shall prosper in the thing whereto I sent it.'[3]
> 'By myself I have sworn, from my mouth has gone forth in righteousness a word that shall not return: "To me every knee shall bow, every tongue shall swear." '[4]
> 'Know then that there shall fall to the earth nothing of the word of the Lord, which the Lord spoke concerning the house of Ahab; for the Lord has done what he said by his servant Elijah.'[5]
> 'He sends forth his command to the earth; his word runs swiftly. He gives snow like wool; he scatters hoarfrost like ashes. . . . He sends forth his word, and melts them.'[6]

God's word was thought to be 'living and active',[7] and inherently efficacious; but human words are deeds which often fail. According to G. B. Caird,[8] words in the Bible are like

> 'messengers, sent out to *perform the task of which they speak*; and as messengers they may be of two kinds, according as their task is performed or neglected. On the one hand there are "vain words" that do not profit (Job 16.3); they do not stand up (Isa. 8.10), but fall to the ground (I Sam. 3.19). In all probability they are the idle words of which Jesus said that men must give account in the day of judgement (Matt. 12.36). They are idle not because they are spoken in a thoughtless moment, but because they do not accomplish the things they talk about. On the other hand, there are

---

[1] G. Östborn, Uppsala Universitets Arsskrift, 1951.
[2] See, for example, Th. C. Vriezen, *op. cit.*, p. 94, and E. Jacob, *Theology of the Old Testament*, p. 128.
[3] Isa. 55.10-11 (A.V.), my italics.
[4] Isa. 45.23.
[5] II Kings 10.10; cf. Joshua 21.45.
[6] Ps. 147.15-18; cf. Ps. 107.20.
[7] Heb. 4.12; cf. Wis. Sol. 18.15-16.
[8] 'The Biblical Doctrine of the Word', unpublished paper, my italics; the last biblical passage which he quotes is from I Sam. 3.19; cf. Isa. 44.26 and II Kings 10.10.

words which produce results, which are established, verified or performed, words which go out and do not return empty-handed. In the belief of the pious such words could not reach their objective without the help of God . . . ."The Lord was with him and did let none of his words fall to the ground".'

This biblical conception of language as an activity, of words as dynamic instruments, is alien to philosophies in which words are only used to express inner thoughts or to state facts. Modern analytic philosophy helps to make the biblical conception seem less alien. It can do so, however, only to a limited extent, for the biblical conception includes an element of magic in its notion of how language has causal efficacy: biblical writers believed in the automatic efficacy of blessings and curses,[1] and in the continued, substantival existence of words after they have been uttered.[2] Perhaps some of the 'magical 'passages were meant to be interpreted as mere metaphoric or poetic imagery;[3] many modern thinkers, at any rate, could not accept a literal interpretation, even if they do view language as an activity.[4]

Some biblical theologians have tried to show that the conception of language as activity, of words as deeds, has an intrinsic connection with peculiarities of the Hebrew language.[5] One of these alleged peculiarities is the Hebrew word '*dabar*', which means 'word' or 'speech', but sometimes means 'thing' or 'matter'. Where it *means* 'thing' or 'matter' it may be used to refer to a deed or to an historical event.[6] From these linguistic facts it may seem plausible to argue that:

(a) Where '*dabar*' refers to a deed or an historical event, it means 'deed' or 'historical event'.

(b) Where '*dabar*' means primarily 'word', it also means 'deed'.

(c) Where (according to (a)) '*dabar*' means primarily 'deed', it also means 'word'.

[1] Cf. E. Jacob, *op. cit.*, pp. 127-8, and Th. C. Vriezen, *An Outline of Old Testament Theology*, p. 20.

[2] Cf. C. H. Dodd, *The Interpretation of the Fourth Gospel*, Cambridge, 1953, pp. 264, 269.

[3] Cf. J. Y. Campbell concerning Ps. 147.15, 'Word', *A Theological Word Book of the Bible*, ed. A. Richardson, p. 284.

[4] For an interesting study of various ways in which language has been thought to have 'power', see T. Izutsu, *Language and Magic*, Keio University Studies in the Humanities and Social Relations, Vol. I, Tokyo, 1956.

[5] For a detailed (and devastating) criticism of various arguments which derive biblical conceptions from alleged peculiarities of the Hebrew language, see James Barr, *The Semantics of Biblical Language*.

[6] *E.g.* Gen. 20.10; 22.16; 24.66; Judges 6.29.

It seems to me that conclusion (a) is occasionally[1] correct. The argument as a whole, however, has been severely and effectively criticized by James Barr.[2] Barr would not deny that when '*dabar Yahweh*' means 'word of the Lord', the phrase may sometimes bring to the particular context some associations with the idea of the divine word as a *deed*. But the association is not a universal and distinctive feature of the Hebrew word '*dabar*' as such (as in argument (b)); it reflects the biblical *conception* of the *divine* word, which is evident in the *English* translation of the passages quoted on page 163. One might also remark that if the general view of language as an activity, of words as deeds, depends on peculiarities of Hebrew lexical stock, it would be a miracle that Austinian linguistic analysis ever arose without reference to Hebrew!

If a biblical theologian wishes to release biblical exegesis from the 'static' conceptions of some traditional philosophy, he should turn, not to alleged peculiarities of the Hebrew language, but to the contemporary philosopher's analysis of everyday speech in any language.

3. *New Testament Ideas of Creation*

So far in this chapter we have considered Israel's creation and world-Creation, confining our attention mainly to the Old Testament. Now, after digressing briefly to consider 'biblical context' and 'biblical language', we turn to the New Testament. Here the main Old Testament ideas concerning world-Creation are continued; but something new and momentous is added, which many biblical theologians regard as central in the biblical conception of world-Creation.

3.1. *Jesus as the Creative Word of God*

The new claim in the New Testament is this: the man Jesus was the divine 'Word',[3] by whose power and authority the world was created and constituted.[4] As the Word, he had been

---

[1] See the R.S.V. translations of I Kings 11.41 and Ps. 145.5.
[2] *Op. cit.*, pp. 129-40.   [3] John 1.1ff.
[4] In this section I shall be stressing the Old Testament background of John 1.1ff.; I do not deny the validity of an exegesis which also interprets the 'word' with reference to its background in Greek philosophy, so that it suggests the 'purpose' or 'meaning' of the Creative act. The two backgrounds are compared by C. H. Dodd, *The Interpretation of the Fourth Gospel*, ch. 12, or *The Johannine Epistles*, London, 1946, pp. 3-4. See also J. Y. Campbell, *op. cit.*, pp. 283-4.

God's Creative[1] instrument or agent, so that when he was born as a human child, he entered a world which was his own property because it was his creation.[2]

Why was such a claim made? Any brief answer to this question is likely to be overly-simplified; but it is possible to say that, broadly speaking, there were two sorts of basis for the claim: the historical Jesus, and the experiences of the early Church. Jesus, in his earthly life, had been the agent or instrument of miraculous *power*; his followers believed that he healed the sick, stilled the sea and rose from the dead. He also claimed and exercised divine *authority*, for example, in his religious and moral teaching ('But I say unto you'), and in his otherwise-blasphemous forgiveness of sins.

In the early Church, Christians experienced a new inner *power*, the power of the Holy Spirit, the power to love God and man as never before. They also acknowledged a new status, as forgiven sinners in a new covenant, and as adopted sons in a divine family. This element of status is evident in what C. H. Dodd says concerning Jesus as the Creative 'Word' of John 1.12 (Dodd first translates and then comments): ' "Those who received the word, to them it gave the right to become children of God". It is *exousia*, "right" or "authority" that is given, not "power", and *exousia* is given by a competent legislative or judicial pronouncement; in this case by the authoritative "word" of the Ruler of the universe.'[3] The early Christians also accepted a new *role*, as Christ's agents[4] and representatives,[5] continuing His work in a community newly founded by Him. Indeed, they believed that God had chosen them in relation to Christ before the foundation of the world,[6] so that they could say:

'We are his workmanship, created in Christ Jesus for good works, which God prepared beforehand, that we should walk in them.'[7]

The new status and role included a new self-*evaluation* based on the love of God for man as revealed in Jesus. And Jesus' death on the Cross was interpreted by him as the new *covenant* initiated by God in which He commits Himself to man;

---

[1] Col. 1.16-17; Heb. 1.2; I Cor. 8.6; Rev. 3.14; cf. Heb. 1.10; concerning Christ's pre-existence see I John 1.1; 2.13.
[2] Cf. John 1.10-11.   [3] *The Interpretation of the Fourth Gospel*, p. 270.
[4] II Cor. 5.21; cf. Eph. 2.8-10.   [5] II Cor. 5.20.
[6] Eph. 1.4; cf. Rom. 8.29.   [7] Eph. 2.10.

Christians acknowledged and renewed this covenant in the sacrament of the Lord's Supper. (Note how similar all this is to the main elements in the conception of Israel's creation: power, status, role, evaluation and commitment.)

The individual Christian and the Christian fellowship were both regarded as a new creation, in which the original world-Creation was restored and paralleled and transcended.[1] The new creation and new covenant together could be summed up in the word 'reconciliation'[2]—of man to God, and man to man. That is, God in Christ brought about a new institutional relation together with the power to live up to it. The early Christians thought that the grace (that is, the condescending power, authority and self-commitment) behind the new creation must be the same as that behind the original Creation; in each case, Jesus Christ was the creative 'Word'. Similarly today, Christians view the grace of Jesus in history and in the Christian fellowship as grounds for linking him with world-Creation.

The idea of Jesus as the 'Word' of God is of special logical interest in that His life, passion, resurrection and ascension could be interpreted as actions which have a 'performative force' and 'causal power' like words. It is as if God in the deeds of Jesus, *said*, 'I hereby adopt you as sons and decree that you are brothers'; and *said*, 'Become like this man Jesus'. In each case the performative and causal efficacy of the 'utterance' depends on the response of men; it depends on whether men acknowledge the new institutional relation and word of command, and whether men allow themselves to be influenced by the divine power.

We should note that here the causal power of Jesus as the 'Word' is analogous to human moral influence, whereas in the case of world-Creation, the causal power of Jesus as the 'Word' is apparently analogous to human magic.[3] The association between Creative power and personal *influence* is also important in the biblical idea of the divine *spirit* as an agent of Creation. I shall now describe this briefly, so as to fill in our New Testament picture of the 'new creation'.

[1] Cf. N. A. Dahl, 'Christ, Creation and the Church', *The Background of the New Testament and its Eschatology*, ed. W. D. Davies and D. Daube, Cambridge, 1956. The relations between the original Creation and the new creation are very complex; they are considered in detail by such typological studies as L. S. Thornton's *Revelation and the Modern World*, London, 1950.

[2] II Cor. 5.14-18; Eph. 2.14-16; Gal. 6.14ff.   [3] Cf. pp. 73-4.

3.2. *The divine Spirit as Creator*

Creation by the spirit meant Creation by God's 'breath'.[1]
This image has two aspects:

(i) Breath is involved in the spoken *word*, the word of world-Creation:

> 'By the word of the Lord the heavens were made, and all their host by the breath of his mouth.'[2]

The spirit-image here merely supplements the causal element of the word-image.[3] It adds a suggestion of mysterious, incomprehensible power, through its association with 'wind'. As a causal instrument by itself, it differs from the word in that it does not specify the result to be brought about. This is a feature which is logically interesting: it reminds us of the causal power of human words as mere sounds.[4] In the New Testament, however, there is no reference to spirit as the instrument of *world*-Creation,[5] so I shall not consider this aspect further.

(ii) Breath and *life* begin and end together. The Creation of animate nature, especially man, was pictured in terms of God's giving His breath:

> 'When thou sendest forth thy Spirit, they (living creatures) are created; and thou renewest the face of the ground.'[6]
> 'The spirit of God has made me, and the breath of the Almighty gives me life.'[7]

When life ends, it is because the life-breath has been recalled to God:

> 'When thou takest away their breath, they die and return to their dust.'[8]

---

[1] The Hebrew *'ruach'* which means 'breath' also means 'wind'. But where *'ruach'* is linked with God's creative activity, the meaning of 'wind' is subordinate; (Gen. 1.2 and Job 26.13 may, however, be exceptions to this). For another parallel between word and breath as instruments of divine action see Isa. 11.4.

[2] Ps. 33.6.

[3] Cf. E. Jacob: 'This parallelism (between breath and word) is the result of a development: originally the spirit was a force more dynamic than moral, more destructive than constructive; so, to become a power serviceable in creation it had to be subjected to the word. Probably it is in this way that the reference to spirit at the beginning of the creation narrative must be understood' (*Theology of the Old Testament*, pp. 143-4).

[4] See p. 73.

[5] Cf. W. D. Davies, *Paul and Rabbinic Judaism*, London, 1948, p. 188. In later Christian thought, the personification of the Holy Spirit (and the doctrine of the Trinity) led to the concept that *He* too, like the Father and the Son, is active in world-Creation. But this does not raise any logically-interesting new point.

[6] Ps. 104.30.   [7] Job 33.4 (cf. Gen. 2.7).   [8] Ps. 104.29; cf. Job. 34.14-15.

'The dust returns to the earth as it was, and the spirit returns to God who gave it.'[1]

Thus a man is continuously dependent on God for his existence as a man, rather than as dust, as a dead body. But the spirit of an individual man was not only the biological life within him; it was also the 'dominant impulse or disposition',[2] the 'motive power of the soul'[3] which is given to him by God:

'The Lord, who stretched out the heavens and founded the earth and formed the spirit of man within him.'[4]

Man's spirit was a continuous gift from God. The divine spirit also enabled some individuals to perform supernatural or more-than-human acts.[5] What sort of act or state is 'supernatural'? In the Bible the emphasis gradually shifted[6] from feats of strength or ecstatic 'possession' to religious insight and moral power. (What we would call the 'creation' of works of art was not generally attributed to the divine spirit.[7]) In the New Testament, the primary supernatural power that comes from the divine spirit is love,[8] which is the most god-like or divine thing in man.[9] The Old Testament had raised the hope that where the spirit of the individual or the community has deteriorated, God will give a new spirit,[10] creating a new level of life. In the New Testament this hope was fulfilled: the Holy Spirit, though not associated directly with cosmic Creation, is the instrument in the creation of new men in a new community with a new power to love:

'God's love has been poured into our hearts through the Holy Spirit which has been given to us.'[11]

The New Testament refers to this Spirit equally as the Spirit of God and the Spirit of Jesus.

'Spirit' is thus used in relation to an idea of Creation where

---

[1] Eccles. 12.7; cf. Deut. 32.39 and I Sam. 2.6.
[2] N. H. Snaith, *The Distinctive Ideas of the Old Testament*, London, 1945, p. 146.
[3] J. Pedersen, *Israel*, I-II, London, 1926, p. 104.
[4] Zech. 12.1; cf. Job 10.12.
[5] Cf. N. H. Snaith, *op. cit.*, pp. 154-7.
[6] *Ibid.*; cf. G. Johnston, 'Spirit', *A Theological Word Book of the Bible*, ed. A. Richardson, pp. 235-6.
[7] Exod. 31.3-6 is an exception. Concerning the Israelite suspicion of human artistic creation, see A. Richardson, *The Biblical Doctrine of Work*, London, 1952, pp. 17-20.
[8] Rom. 5.5; I Cor. 12-14; Gal. 5.22-3.
[9] I John 4.16.   [10] Ezek. 36.26-7; 37.1-4.   [11] Rom. 5.5; cf. Gal. 5.22.

Creation is the giving of personal life, as this is contrasted with mere material existence; the gift is not only biological life and ordinary personal life but also supernatural or god-like personal life. In the latter case, the Creative action of the Spirit is clearly analogous to personal influence rather than magic.

A similar contrast arose in the discussion of Jesus as the Creative Word: His causal power may resemble either personal influence or magic. Personal influence differs from magic in that it requires the free response of agents who are influenced. In the next section I shall maintain that institutional authority is inherently limited in a similar way: it requires the free acknowledgment of agents who are under the authority.

4. *The authority of the Creator*

In chapter 1[1] we saw that the decree of a king 'takes effect' as a decree only if some people recognize or acknowledge it to be a decree. Suppose that a king goes into the jungle, encounters two half-animal savages, and shouts, 'I decree that you run away'; they run away, frightened by the noise. His utterance would have causal power, but it would not have Exercitive force in relation to the savages. It has Exercitive force only in relation to a community which has the appropriate linguistic and other conventions. The king has institutional authority over agents only in so far as these acknowledge his authority. His utterance succeeds in being a 'decree', and the movements of the savages are correctly called 'obedience', only within a recognized institutional context. The causal power of his utterance, however, is not similarly restricted.

Consider another case.[2] Let us suppose that the Queen has magical powers, so that her utterance, 'One Governor of Kenya' brings a man into existence. The utterance would also have Exercitive force only within an institutional context which involves some recognition of her authority. Similarly the divine word of Creation could conceivably[3] bring things and persons into existence without any responsive action by these things and persons. But as a word of authority over creatures, it *has* authority only in so far as this is acknowledged by creatures.

---

[1] See section 9.3.   [2] Chapter 1, section 9.4.
[3] In chapter 6 I shall maintain that the causal-magical notion of Creation *ex nihilo* is not incoherent.

The notion of 'absolute' *power* (Creation *ex nihilo*) is obscure but meaningful;[1] but the notion of 'absolute' *authority* is radically incoherent, if it postulates an authority which does not depend on recognition or acknowledgment by agents under the authority.

This necessary connection between authority and acknowledgment is stressed by Emil Brunner, who is not one to minimize the divine authority: 'Because in the full sense God can be Lord only of such a subject who in free personal decision acknowledges Him as Lord, He wills this independence of the creature. . . . He wills to be their Lord because only in His being *known* as Lord *is* He really Lord in the complete sense.'[2]

There are various reasons why we may fail to realize that the notion of 'absolute authority' is incoherent. In the first place, the Creation-story in Gen. I represents God as having not only power but also correlative *authority* over creatures which, to modern men, are not personal agents: for example, the sun and the moon. But the idea of authority makes sense in such cases only if the heavenly bodies are thought of as personal agents who acknowledge divine authority. It is true that modern men need not interpret this personification literally, even if the biblical writers did so.[3] One may *look on* the sun *as* God's servant, or even reduce this to mere metaphor. But whatever our interpretation, the idea of authority involves the correlative idea of acknowledgment by a free personal agent. A misconception may arise because heavenly bodies, unlike men, *do whatever the Creator says*; thus the idea of absolute divine power may be illegitimately transferred to the idea of divine authority.

A second reason for possible confusion concerning the idea of divine authority is the submissive attitude of the individual believer. For him the divine authority is not to be questioned; there are no theoretical limits to the degree of submission which is appropriate; hence there are no theoretical limits to the corresponding degree of authority ascribed to the Creator. This makes the divine authority 'unlimited', but not in a sense which

---

[1] In chapter 6 I shall maintain that the causal-magical notion of Creation *ex nihilo* is not incoherent.

[2] *The Divine-Human Encounter*, pp. 40, 44. Brunner seems to think that God is 'Lord' in some lesser sense where He is not acknowledged as Lord; this makes sense only in so far as 'Lord' has connotations of *power*, or of *deserving* authority.

[3] It is difficult to determine how literally the Israelites and early Christians interpreted cosmological ideas which they shared with their contemporaries.

eliminates the need for human acknowledgment. It is one thing to say that there are no limits to the degree of authority which is acknowledged; it is another thing to say that the authority is not limited by needing to be acknowledged.

A third reason for possible confusion is the individual believer's firm rejection of any suggestion that God's authority over men depends on his own individual act of acknowledgment. This is a realistic view of his own importance, but it does not undermine the truism that if *all* men ceased to acknowledge God's authority, God would cease to have authority over *men*. He would not necessarily cease to have *power* over men; if there are other creatures who are personal agents, He would not necessarily cease to have authority over these other creatures; and He would not necessarily cease to *deserve* authority over men. But He would no longer *have* authority over men.

A fourth factor in the conception of divine authority is suggested by the conviction that God *deserves* authority over men. God deserves supreme authority and is worthy of unlimited submission because of His nature, His holiness and glory. Whether or not all men acknowledge God's authority, they *ought* to do so in view of His holy and glorious character, which does not depend on men's acknowledgment of His authority. And His revealed nature does in fact move men to acknowledge His authority. All this, however, does not mean that the divine authority over men is logically independent of acknowledgment by men.

Some biblical theologians may find this conceptual truth repugnant. I should reassure them that in Part II it is neither typical nor fundamental. I should also concede that I have asked a question which is, in a sense, 'unbiblical'; that is, no biblical writer is likely to have asked this question: 'If no men acknowledged God's authority, though God still deserved authority over men and still exerted power on men, would He still *have* authority over men?' Once the question is posed, however, the answer is inescapable. Moreover, the fact that the Greek word '*exousia*'[1] is sometimes translated as 'authority' and sometimes as 'power' *may* indicate that biblical writers did

---

[1] See J. Y. Campbell, 'Authority', *A Theological Word Book of the Bible*, ed. A. Richardson, p. 26.

not distinguish sharply between authority and power; but it may not. In any case, once the distinction has been made, one is not justified in reverting to ambiguities—if one is writing theology or philosophy, that is.

In the next chapter we shall consider the revealed nature of God the Creator, the holiness and glory which rightly move men to acknowledge His authority. We have seen that, in the biblical context, belief in the Creator involves acceptance of a subordinate status, an assigned role, and an authoritative evaluation of existence; it also involves a trust in divine steadfastness. This acknowledgment of authority ought not to be based merely on the supernatural (magical) power of the Creator. What if the character of a Creator-ex-nihilo were despicable? There must be an adequate basis in the revealed nature of the Creator. We shall see that human authority provides an analogy to divine authority where it depends on a distinctive personal character which is expressed to others so as to evoke their reverent wonder and grateful joy.

5

CREATION AS AN IMPRESSIVE AND EXPRESSIVE ACTION

IN CHAPTER 4 we saw that divine Creation is a performative action, which men acknowledge in a correlative performative action. I began with a consideration of Israel's creation, for the performative elements in the biblical conception of world-Creation are very similar to those in the conception of Israel's creation. In this chapter we shall examine the impressive and expressive elements in the action of divine world-Creation, and the correlative human acknowledgment and response. We shall consider Israel's creation first, as we did in chapter 4.

1. *Israel's creation as a revelation of God's glory and holiness*

The impressive and expressive elements in the biblical conception of Israel's creation are most evident in the ideas of glory and holiness. We shall see that, in the biblical context, the theological meaning of the words 'glory' and 'holiness' involves a three-fold reference: An *inner divine quality* is expressed through certain impressive *observables*, evoking a correlative *human feeling-Response and acknowledgment*. The observables are 'impressive' in that they effectively evoke the feeling and acknowledgment; the words 'glorious' and 'holy' are Aptness-words.[1] The observables are 'expressive' in that they are connected with the inner divine quality in somewhat the same sort of way that an observable expression of feeling is connected with the feeling which it expresses.

My first task is to outline the triadic ideas of divine glory and divine holiness in relation to God's dealings with Israel. Then I shall show how divine glory and holiness are 'impressive' in that they evoke an expression of attitude from men. Next I shall

---

[1] Cf. chapter 2, section 4.1.

show how divine glory and holiness are themselves 'expressive'. Finally, I shall consider some differences between glory and holiness, differences which are relevant to the conception of *world*-Creation as an impressive-expressive act. In my discussion of glory and holiness as 'impressive' and 'expressive' I shall make use of the detailed analysis in chapter 2, so as to provide a logical framework for some of the insights of modern biblical theology.

1.1. *The biblical conceptions of divine glory and holiness*

I shall begin by outlining the biblical conception of divine glory.

1.1.1. *Glory*

Yahweh's creation of Israel was an expression of His glory: in the spectacular Red-Sea miracle,[1] in the fire of the covenant-making at Sinai,[2] in the tabernacle-presence[3] and gifts of manna[4] and water[5] during the wilderness period. God's glory was also related to other impressive events in nature, such as thunder.[6] Another important association was with light: the light from Moses' face as he descended from Sinai,[7] and the light in Ezekiel's vision of the 'appearance of the likeness of the glory of the Lord'.[8]

In the Septuagint, the Greek word '*doxa*' (glory) was used to translate the Hebrew '*kabod*' and several other similar words.[9] The word '*kabod*' is the most important.[10] When '*kabod*' was applied to men, it suggested three aspects of glory:[11] (i) Sometimes the 'glory' of a man was the man's inner personal nature

---

[1] Exod. 14.17, 31; Num. 14.22.   [2] Deut. 5.24; Exod. 24.16-17.
[3] Exod. 40.34.   [4] Exod. 16.7, 10.   [5] Num. 20.6-7.
[6] Ps. 29.1-5.   [7] Exod. 34.29-35; cf. II Cor. 3.7-4.6.
[8] Ezek. 1.28. Scholars disagree as to when the idea of light came to be associated with '*kabod*', whose root meaning was 'weight'. E. Jacob (*Theology of the Old Testament*, p. 80) suggests a pre-Exilic time, whereas L. H. Brockington credits it to Ezekiel ('Glory', *A Theological Word Book of the Bible*, ed. A. Richardson, p. 175). G. B. Caird presents a detailed argument in favour of the latter view in *The New Testament Conception of Doxa*, unpublished doctoral thesis, Oxford.
[9] See G. B. Caird, *op. cit.*, ch. 2.
[10] According to G. Kittel, the meaning of '*doxa*' in the Septuagint and in the New Testament depends on the meaning of '*kabod*' in the Old Testament (and on the meaning of other Hebrew words in so far as they closely resemble '*kabod*'); '*Doxa*', *Theologisches Wörterbuch zum Neuen Testament*, ed. G. Kittel, Band II, Stuttgart, 1935, pp. 245-6, 251.
[11] Each of the three aspects is mentioned by Pedersen (*Israel*, I-II, pp. 214-39), and E. Jacob distinguishes (ii) from (iii), *op. cit.*, p. 79. But I have not found any clear and systematic study of the three aspects and their relation to one another; this is true also of 'holiness'.

or self;[1] it was his innermost soul, with its dignity, majesty, strength, worth or beauty. (ii) More frequently, the 'glory' of a man was the external observables which made him distinctive and impressive: his wealth, robes, manner and bearing, his shining face and eyes; or his achievements and personal influence, his weight in the community. (iii) Often the 'glory' of a man was the acknowledgment and response of others: their honour and respect, or their opening of themselves to his influence and his morale-boosting power.[2]

Similarly the 'glory' of God was (i) the inner nature or self of God,[3] or (ii) the external, visible expression of this in impressive observables (events or things or persons), or (iii) the acknowledgment and response by men and by (personified) nature. These three aspects should be considered together if we are to understand what is meant by the 'glory of God'. We should note three distinct uses of the verb, 'glorify': (i) 'God is glorified' means 'God reveals Himself as glorious'.[4] (ii) 'God glorifies Israel' means 'God makes Israel glorious'.[5] (iii) 'Israel glorifies God' means 'Israel acknowledges God as glorious.'[6]

God's glory is both a mystery and a revelation: God, like light, distinguishes Himself as He reveals Himself; He wilfully differentiates Himself from all else by imposing His presence

[1] In several passages 'kabod' is a psychological term, equivalent to 'self' or 'soul': Gen. 49.6; Job 29.18-20; Ps. 7.5; Ps. 16.9; 30.12; perhaps Ps. 57.7-8 and Ps. 108.1-2. Pedersen (*Israel*, I-II, p. 239, n. 1) and Caird (*op. cit.*, pp. 66-7) reject the substitution of 'kabed' ('liver') for 'kabod' ('glory') in these passages. Pedersen, however, seems to claim that *whenever* 'kabod' refers to impressive observables or to honour from men, it *also* refers to a person's inner soul-power (see *op. cit.*, pp. 234-9); this is surely an exaggeration. Kittel's view is that in relation to man 'kabod' does not characteristically have a psychological meaning, whereas in relation to God, His inner nature is involved (*op. cit.*, pp. 240, 247, 250).

[2] Job says that, before he lost his glory, he had 'smiled to them when they were not confident, and the light of my countenance kept them from falling' (Job 29.24, tr. Pedersen, *Israel*, I-II, p. 214).

[3] According to K. Barth, the divine glory includes all God's perfections (*Church Dogmatics*, II, 1, pp. 643-4). Cf. Pedersen: ' "Honour" and "glory" in particular are terms frequently used of the soul of Yahweh, as it manifests itself and acts among mankind' (*Israel*, I-II, p. 239). 'The honour (*kabod*) of Yahweh is Yahweh himself, as he appears in all his greatness and might' (*ibid.*, p. 238). 'Yahweh's honour is the greatness of his soul as well as that in which it reveals itself' (*Israel*, III-IV, p. 649).

[4] Lev. 10.3; Ezek. 39.13; Exod. 14.4, 17, 18; Isa. 66.5; Hag. 1.8; cf. the Hebrew reflexive (Greek passive) in Isa. 44.23; 49.3; 60.21; 61.3.

[5] Isa. 55.5; cf. Isa. 43.4 (together with 'honour' in Isa. 43.23); Isa. 60.1-2; Wis. Sol. 18.8; 19.22; Jer. 2.11; Isa. 4.2 (LXX); perhaps Mic. 1.15; cf. also R. Martin-Achard, 'Glory', *Vocabulary of the Bible*, ed. J.-J. von Allmen, p. 138. God also glorifies individuals or groups: Exod. 34.29, 30, 35 (LXX); I Sam. 2.30; Ps. 91.15.

[6] Ps. 22.23; 50.15; 86.9, 12; Isa. 25.3.

on men. Thus, on the one hand, God's glory is unique and peculiarly His own; He is intolerant of any idolatrous worship directed elsewhere;[1] He alone has supreme and permanent glory, for the glory of men is transient and is under His control.[2] On the other hand, God's glory is His presence[3] among men, His appearance to them, His dwelling[4] among them, His bestowal[5] of glory upon them; it is His power to evoke worship from men, who recognize His worth and distinctiveness, His mysterious splendour.

Israel glorified Yahweh for creating and preserving her as a people. To glorify Him was to praise Him, in a spirit of awe and exultation:

(Yahweh said) 'I will get glory over Pharaoh and all his host. . . . And Israel saw the great work which the Lord did against the Egyptians, and the people feared the Lord. . . . Then Moses and the people of Israel sang this song to the Lord, saying, "I will sing to the Lord, for he has triumphed gloriously; the horse and his rider he has thrown into the sea." '[6]

Such worship is an expression of awe and wonder, and also of exultation and rejoicing.[7] It is analogous to the spontaneous applause of an audience which has been 'carried away' by a glorious performance of some great work of music; to respond to God's glory was to enjoy it vicariously oneself. Thus God's glory was communicated through observables in a process which culminates in human worship. Yet the glory remained His (like the glory of a performer); indeed, God's glory distinguishes Him from the worshipper who receives it.

The worship was typically expressed in music. When God expresses His glory in historical action, man expresses his response in song:

[1] Isa. 42.8; 48.9-11; Ps. 106.19-20; cf. E. Brunner, *Dogmatics*, I, p. 161.

[2] I Chron. 29.11-12; Ps. 37.20; 49.16-17; Isa. 16.14; 17.4; 21.16; perhaps Isa. 40.4-8; perhaps Job 29, together with 40.6-14.

[3] Cf. L. H. Brockington, 'The Presence of God, A study of the use of the term "Glory of Yahweh",' *Expository Times*, October, 1945.

[4] The use of '*doxa*' as the Greek translation for both '*kabod*' and the rabbinic '*shekinah*' led to a 'unified imagery of God's glory and God's dwelling or tabernacling with His people' (A. M. Ramsey, *The Glory of God and the Transfiguration of Christ*, London, 1949, p. 20). E. G. Selwyn notes two interpretations of '*shekinah*': (i) 'the inner source and cause of the outward, glorious manifestation', (ii) 'the visible part of the divine majesty' (*The First Epistle of Peter*, London, 1947, p. 223). These two interpretations correspond to two aspects of '*kabod*'.

[5] See p. 176, n. 5.   [6] Exod. 14.17, 31 and 15.1; cf. Isa. 63.12, 14.

[7] For the connection between 'glory' and exultant joy, see the next note and Ecclus. 1.11-12; I Peter 1.8; John 8.54, 56.

'Sing to him, sing praises to him, tell of all his wonderful works! Glory in his holy name; let the hearts of those who seek the Lord rejoice. . . . Remember the wonderful works that he has done, his miracles, and the judgments he uttered.'[1]

To glorify God is to express a feeling-attitude; it is to rejoice or 'glory in'[2] the deeds of the Lord. To glory in something other than God (except as the expression of God's own glory) is idolatry.[3]

The glory of God includes beauty,[4] especially the attractive[5] aspect of beauty. Whether the divine glory is expressed in a shining light[6] or a Cross,[7] it attracts and fascinates men.[8] As Karl Barth says, 'Where it is really recognized, it is recognized . . . with its peculiar power and characteristic of giving pleasure, awaking desire, and creating enjoyment'.[9]

The acknowledgment of God's glory involves a declaration[10] of God's glory to others. This declaration is required because it is God's avowed purpose[11] that all men should respond to His glory.[12] As men respond to Him and acknowledge His true nature, they will receive salvation;[13] and they, like the Psalmist, will presumably find 'fulness of joy'[14] in His presence. However, this universally-successful revelation of God's glory lies in the future. And meanwhile, as men turn away from Yahweh and do not glorify Him, they incur His wrath.[15] Men become worthless, false and detestable, like the idols which they glorify.[16] For Paul in Romans 1.18-32, this moral nemesis is itself the expression of the divine wrath.[17]

The Old Testament usually kept two things fairly separate: God's revelation of His glory and man's acknowledgment of

[1] Ps. 105.2, 3, 5 (cf. Ps. 106); Job 38.7; Luke 2.9-10; Rev. 19.6-7.

[2] Ps. 63.11; 64.10; 106.5; Isa. 41.16; 45.25; Jer. 4.2; 9.23-4.

[3] Jer. 2.11; 9.23-4; Ps. 106.19-22; 115.1-8; Isa. 10.12-15. See also pp. 190-1.

[4] In LXX '*doxa*' is used to translate various Hebrew words which connote beauty; cf. G. B. Caird, *The New Testament Conception of Doxa*, ch. 2.

[5] Cf. A. M. Ramsey, *op. cit.*, p. 14.   [6] Isa. 60.1-3.   [7] John 12.27-32.

[8] Cf. R. Otto's 'element of fascination' (*The Idea of the Holy*, pp. 31-40), which he links with holiness rather than glory.

[9] *Church Dogmatics*, II, 1, p. 653.   [10] Ps. 96.3; cf. Ps. 19.1.

[11] Isa. 45.22-3.   [12] Isa. 59.19; 40.5; Ps. 86.8-10; 102.15; Hab. 2.14.

[13] Isa. 45.22; Ps. 85.9-10.   [14] Ps. 16.11; cf. Ps. 34.2, 8.

[15] Jer. 13.16; Mal. 2.2; Ps. 106.20-3; cf. Lev. 10.1-3; Num. 14.10-12; 16.19, 35; 16.42-6.

[16] Jer. 2.5, 11; II Kings 17.15; Hos. 9.10; cf. Ps. 135.15-18.

[17] Cf. C. H. Dodd, *The Epistle of Paul to the Romans*, London, 1932, pp. 20-4. We shall consider Rom. 1.18-32 later, in section 2.3.2.

glory. But there are hints[1] of the New Testament ideal: a way of life which is both a revelation and an acknowledgment of divine glory, so that 'God is glorified' means both 'God's glory is revealed' and 'God's glory is acknowledged'.[2] On the one hand, prophets looked forward to an Israel which would acknowledge or 'declare' God's glory by exhibiting such attractive righteousness that God's glory would thereby be *revealed* to others.[3] Israel would model her way of life on God's ways[4] with men, which reveal His glory. On the other hand, the glorification of God in the Old Testament was intimately connected with offerings and sacrifice,[5] that is, with gifts to God. Where a man gives, not a sheep or a goat, but himself and his daily life, this could be the supreme *acknowledgment* of God's glory. Later we shall see that the ideas of acknowledgment and revelation came together in the New Testament portrayal of Christ, and, derivatively, of His followers. As A. M. Ramsey says, 'The godward act of glorifying the Father includes the manward act of revealing Him to men'.[6]

1.1.2. *Holiness*

The events by which Israel was created were impressive observables evoking a feeling-Response of awe and fear,[7] and they were interpreted as revelations of God's holiness:

'He sent redemption to his people; he has commanded his covenant for ever. Holy and terrible is his name! The fear of the Lord is the beginning of wisdom.'[8]
'For when he (Jacob) sees his children, the work of my hands, in his midst, they will sanctify my name; they will sanctify the Holy One of Jacob, and will stand in awe of the God of Israel.'[9]

---

[1] Cf. A. M. Ramsey, *op. cit.*, p. 92.   [2] Contrast p. 176 and see p. 181.
[3] Isa. 60.21; 61.3; also Isa. 49.3-6 if it is linked with Isa. 52.13-53.12; also Isa. 60.1-3 if it is linked with Isa. 58.6-10; cf. Dan. 12.3 and Matt. 13.43; cf. G. B. Caird, *op. cit.*, pp. 98-9.
[4] Ps. 138.5; cf. Ezek. 39.21; Isa. 62.2; Ps. 97.6.
[5] *E.g.* Ps. 96.8; I Sam. 6.4-5; Isa. 43.23; Dan. 11.38; Mal. 2.2; Ps. 50.23.
[6] *Op. cit.*, p. 77.
[7] Cf. E. Jacob: 'To recognize the holiness of God . . . is above all to fear him' (*Theology of the Old Testament*, p. 88). Cf. N. H. Snaith, *The Distinctive Ideas of the Old Testament*, pp. 49-50. Note Isa. 8.13 especially.
[8] Ps. 111.9-10. The words 'holy' and 'terrible' are closely associated with each other; cf. Th. C. Vriezen, *An Outline of Old Testament Theology*, p. 151. Also, the word 'terrible', 'like 'holy', was closely associated with the Exodus-and-Conquest, for example in Deut. 10.17-21; Exod. 34.10; II Sam. 7.23; Ps. 66.1-6; Ps. 106.21-2.
[9] Isa. 29.23.

Yahweh as 'holy' is utterly separate[1] and distinct and different[2] from other beings, whether these be gods or men:

> 'Who is like thee, O Lord, among the gods? Who is like thee, majestic in holiness, terrible in glorious deeds, doing wonders? Thou didst stretch out thy right hand, the earth swallowed them.'[3]
> 'I will not execute my fierce anger, I will not again destroy Ephraim; for I am God and not man, the Holy One in your midst.'[4]

Indeed, His holiness is a jealous insistence that men recognize and acknowledge His incomparable nature. As Brunner says, 'The Holiness of God is therefore not only an absolute difference of nature, . . . it is an active self-differentiation, the willed energy with which God asserts and maintains the fact that He is Wholly Other against all else.'[5] Since God cares[6] that man should acknowledge Him as He really is, He impressively reveals Himself as One who is mysteriously different. His holy presence in observables is uniquely imposing and effectual, moving Israel to 'sanctify' Him—that is, to respond to His holiness and acknowledge it. This holiness is His innermost and incomparable nature[7] expressed through impressive observables (events, things and persons) for human response and acknowledgment. Like God's glory, God's holiness has three aspects:[8] (i) God's hidden self, (ii) revelatory observables and (iii) the impression evoked in men.

The verb 'sanctify' or 'hallow' has three distinct uses[9]

---

[1] Some scholars hold that the earliest traceable meaning of the Hebrew 'qadosh' ('holy') is 'separate' or 'separated'; see N. H. Snaith, *op. cit.*, pp. 24-31; O. S. Rankin, 'Saint', *A Theological Word Book of the Bible*, ed. A. Richardson, p. 215; and P. Bonnard, 'Holy', *Vocabulary of the Bible*, ed. J.-J. von Allmen, p. 166.

[2] Cf. Ps. 77.11-15; I Sam. 2.2.   [3] Exod. 15.11-12.   [4] Hos. 11.9.

[5] E. Brunner, *Dogmatics*, I, p. 160; cf. pp. 157, 159-60: 'In the Biblical revelation, however, we are concerned not with "the Holy" (as an abstract conception), but with the Holy One (as personal).' 'The concept of "the Holy" contains the element of Will. . . . The border-line which separates the Nature of God from all other forms of existence, from that which has been created, is not only a frontier line, it is a *closed* frontier. . . . He actively maintains it, and defends it.' Cf. Vriezen, *op. cit.*, p. 153.

[6] Cf. Brunner, *op. cit.*, pp. 160-5.

[7] Cf. E. Jacob, *op. cit.*, pp. 87-8. God swears by himself (Gen. 22.16) or by His holiness (Ps. 89.35; Amos 4.2). His name is holy (Lev. 20.3; Amos 2.7; Isa. 57.15; Ezek. 20.39).

[8] Three similar aspects of holiness may have been present in early Israelite conceptions of *human* holiness (cf. the three aspects of human glory); but the theological view that all holiness comes from God was imposed at a very early stage.

[9] Cf. A. Plummer, *Exegetical Commentary on St Matthew's Gospel*, London, 1917, pp. 97-8.

which correspond to the three uses of 'glorify':[1] (i) 'God is
sanctified' often means 'God reveals Himself as holy.'[2] (ii) 'God
sanctifies Israel' means 'God makes Israel holy'.[3] (iii) 'Israel
sanctifies God' means 'Israel acknowledges God as holy';[4]
similarly 'God is sanctified' sometimes means 'God is acknowledged as holy'.[5]

The idea of holiness had associations in the Bible with both
salvation and judgment, and with the corresponding feeling-
Responses. On the one hand, God as the Holy One of Israel
was her Redeemer and Saviour,[6] as He acted in the midst of
her.[7] P. Bonnard even says, 'Yahweh is holy inasmuch as He
imparts Himself, inasmuch as He wishes men to share in His
own divine life'.[8] According to A. D. Martin, however, 'Even
though God in giving of his Spirit imparts some measure of
Holiness to men, Holiness remains that quality of the Divine
nature which distinguishes him from all his creatures'.[9] Indeed,
God's holiness was expressed not only in salvation, but also in
judgment, as jealous wrath;[10] the holy God opposes and destroys
men who commit idolatry, which is the refusal to acknowledge
the distinctiveness of the one true God. To these aspects of
holiness as salvation and judgment there were corresponding
feeling-Responses: grateful wonder[11] and self-repudiating fear.[12]

---

[1] For the three uses of 'glorify', see p. 176. There is one difference: sometimes
'God is sanctified' means 'God is acknowledged as holy' (cf. note 5); but I have not
found any passage in the Old Testament where 'God is glorified' means 'God is
acknowledged as glorious'.

[2] See the R.S.V. translation of Lev. 10.3; Num. 20.13; Isa. 5.16; Ezek. 20.41;
28.22, 25; 36.23; 38.16, 23; 39.27; (cf. Ecclus. 36.4). The R.S.V. translates the
Hebrew passive (A.V., 'is sanctified') in these cases as 'manifests his holiness' or
'shows himself holy' or 'vindicates his holiness'.

[3] Cf. Lev. 22.32; cf. also Lev. 21.8; Exod. 19.6; Deut. 7.6.

[4] Cf. Num. 20.12; Deut. 32.51; Isa. 8.13; 29.23; I Pet. 3.15.

[5] Cf. R.S.V. translation of Lev. 22.32: 'I will be hallowed', not 'I will show my
holiness'. Where God is the subject the context determines whether the use is (i)
or (iii).

[6] Cf. Ps. 111.9-10; Ps. 77.11-15. In II Isa. the 'Holy One of Israel' is the Saviour
or Redeemer of Israel; see Isa. 41.14; 43.3, 14; 47.4; etc.; cf. K. Barth, *Church
Dogmatics*, II, 1, pp. 360-1.

[7] Cf. Hos. 11.9.   [8] *Op. cit.*, p. 166.

[9] *The Holiness of Jesus*, London, 1934, p. 30. Cf. K. Barth, *Church Dogmatics*, II,
1, p. 364.

[10] Vriezen says that God's wrath is a 'manifestation of God's holiness as directed
against man' (*op. cit.*, p. 155). Cf. E. Jacob, *op. cit.*, p. 90: 'The holy one, in spite of
his distance . . . enters into a relationship intimate to the point of jealousy'.

[11] Cf. Ps. 77.11-15; I Sam. 2.1-2; perhaps Ps. 130.4.

[12] Cf. M. Foster, *Mystery and Philosophy*, London, 1957, p. 46, concerning Isa.
6.3-5: ' "To say: God is holy, is the same thing as to say: I am a man of unclean
lips." To recognize the holiness of God *is* to repent and *vice versa*.' (Foster's

The conception of holiness which I have been outlining depends on a *selection* of biblical material. There are some passages in which we detect ideas of holiness which are rather similar to the 'mana' of primitive man: a dangerous amoral power,[1] or a contagious, quasi-material stuff.[2] It is also possible to interpret various passages in terms of an uncanny, spooky or weird entity which evokes primitive shudderings.[3] But in so far as holiness is viewed as a wilfully-maintained divine prerogative and as an ethical quality linked with salvation and judgment, a new conception emerges, which has only tenuous links with 'mana' and 'numinous'.[4]

The acknowledgment of God's holiness included a commitment to a way of life, the way of holiness, following the commandments of God. God's holiness is intrinsically a standard for the holiness towards which Israel should aspire; 'you shall be holy; for I the Lord your God am holy'.[5] Israel will become[6] holy in a process which involves both divine influence and human co-operation:

'You shall keep my commandments and do them: I am the Lord. And you shall not profane my holy name, but I will be hallowed among the people of Israel; I am the Lord who *sanctify you.*'[7]

'*Consecrate yourselves* therefore, and be holy, for I am holy.'[8]

As Pedersen says, 'It is Yahweh who makes the people holy, but it is achieved through fulfilment of the law'.[9]

---

quotation is from J. Zink, *Sontagsblatt*, no date given.) Note that Gen. 18.27 and Job 42.6 are often interpreted as responses to holiness, though this is not explicit in the texts themselves.

[1] I Sam. 6.19-20; II Sam. 6.7.

[2] Exod. 29.37; 30.29; Lev. 6.27-8; Ezek. 44.19; but note Hag. 2.11-13.

[3] R. Otto, *The Idea of the Holy*, pp. 13-19, 28-9.

[4] Cf. E. Jacob: 'Holiness in the Old Testament has a character *sui generis* which is only very partially explained by etymology and extra-Israelite analogies' (*op. cit.*, p. 87). Cf. M. Foster, *op. cit.*, pp. 44-6, and K. Barth, *Church Dogmatics*, II, 1, pp. 360-1.

[5] Lev. 19.2.

[6] Israel already *is* holy in the sense that God has appointed Israel to a special *status* as his peculiar possession. This institutional element in the conception of holiness should not be confused with the impressive and expressive elements which I have chosen to emphasize here. For a more detailed discussion, see my 'Three Philosophers Discuss Christianity', *Scottish Journal of Theology*, June, 1960, and N. H. Snaith, *The Distinctive Ideas of the Old Testament*, pp. 46-7. Note that I have also ignored the fact that God's bestowal of *glory* on Israel includes the ascription of a status.

[7] Lev. 22.31-2; cf. Num. 15.40.   [8] Lev. 11.44.

[9] J. Pedersen, *Israel*, III-IV, London, 1959, p. 294; he refers to Deut. 28.9. Cf. Phil. 2.12-13.

Israel acknowledges God's holiness by being holy; and her holiness is a way of life which is modelled on His ways. For example, the holy God loved Israel when the people were strangers in Egypt, so holy Israel similarly should love the strangers in Canaan.[1] Since 'the holy God shows himself holy in righteousness',[2] He requires righteousness in Israel.[3] Ezekiel's hope was that one day God would so transform Israel's way of life that He would thereby reveal His holiness to all the nations.[4] Thus there are hints in the Old Testament that the Israelite way of life might 'sanctify' God in two ways, just as it might 'glorify' God in two ways: as an *acknowledgment* of God's holiness and glory, and as a *revelation* of God's holiness and glory.[5]

1.2. *Glory and holiness as impressive qualities*

We are now in a position to apply some of the analysis in Part I to the biblical conceptions of glory and holiness. In the biblical context, to say, 'God is glorious', or 'God is holy' is to worship God; it is to express an attitude.[6] As an expression of attitude, the utterance is both performative and expressive: (a) We have seen that the personal God of the Bible evokes and demands a human acknowledgment of His glory and holiness; 'glorious' and 'holy' are Behabitive-Commissive words of acknowledgment. The words are used performatively, to perform an act of praise and to commit oneself to various attitudes of supreme and exclusive devotion to God. (b) 'Glorious' and 'holy' are also Exclamatory-words;[7] they are used to express various feeling-Responses in the presence of God. (To speak in the biblical context is to speak in the presence of God.)

But 'glorious' and 'holy' are also Aptness-words;[8] they are used to refer to God's power of impressing men. To say, 'God is glorious' or 'God is holy' is to report that God is apt to evoke a particular acknowledgment and feeling-Response in some people. Note that the performative force and the expressiveness are speaker-dependent:[9] it is up to the speaker to decide the

---

[1] Lev. 19.2, 34; cf. Deut. 10.18-19; 15.14-15; 24.17-22.   [2] Isa. 5.16.
[3] Cf. Th. C. Vriezen, *An Outline of Old Testament Theology*, p. 159.
[4] Ezek. 36.22-7.
[5] In this section I have mentioned only a few elements in the biblical conception of divine holiness; see O. R. Jones, *The Concept of Holiness*, for an interpretation of creaturely holiness in relation to life and blessing (pp. 62-7), divine possession (pp. 90-7), cleanness and health (pp. 100-6) and separatedness (pp. 107-12).
[6] Cf. chapter 3, section 3.   [7] Cf. chapter 2, section 4.1.
[8] *Ibid.*   [9] Cf. chapter 4, section 2.5.

context for his words, 'God is glorious' or 'God is holy'. There are two main alternatives to the biblical context: (i) Instead of speaking in the biblical context, I may decide that my utterance should occur in a descriptive context; thus I set aside any self-involving elements, and my utterance becomes a flat Constative (neither Behabitive nor Commissive) which is impersonal (non-expressive). Only the descriptive meaning of 'glory' or 'holy' as an Aptness-word remains; in saying, 'God is glorious' or 'God is holy' I mean no more than, 'God is apt to evoke a particular acknowledgment and feeling-Response in some people'; I report the impressiveness of God without even implying that *I* am impressed. (ii) Instead of speaking in the biblical context, I may decide that my utterance should occur in the context of another religious tradition; in this context it will have self-involving elements which may differ considerably from those in the biblical context, and which can similarly be set aside in a descriptive context.

We should realize that the meaning of the utterance in a descriptive context is parasitic on its meaning in the biblical (or other religious) context. That is, if I am to understand the meaning where my utterance is not Behabitive-Commissive and not expressive, I must understand the Behabitive-Commissive act which is performed and the feeling-Response which is expressed in the biblical (or other religious) context. Both God's (glorious and holy) inner nature and the observables through which he expresses this are objective; but without the acknowledgment and the feeling-Response, the 'glorious' or 'holy' observables do not help me to understand what is meant by 'glorious' or 'holy', for they seem to be merely neutral constituents of the ordinary world—things, events and people; and the 'glorious' or 'holy' divine nature is itself unobservable and can only be understood indirectly, in terms of the acknowledgment and the feeling-Response. Hence in so far as one does not understand the acknowledgment and the feeling-Response, to that extent one does not understand the meaning of the word 'glorious' or 'holy' in the biblical (or other religious) context. And the understanding of the acknowledgment and the feeling-Response depends, to a great extent, on one's active participation in worship. Moreover, since the acknowledgment of God's glory and holiness is extended to include a whole way of life, one must participate in this way of life in order to gain an adequate understanding of this acknowledgment. In short, God's glory and holiness are impressive qualities, which I understand in so far as I am impressed.

When the words 'glorious' and 'holy' are applied to God, their meaning involves a reference to the impression which God evokes in man. God is called 'glorious' and 'holy' because His actions evoke an attitude which is expressed by the words 'glorious' and 'holy'. The words thus refer to the inner self of God indirectly, as a power to create impressions in men. Here Whitehead's dictum applies: 'The power of God is the worship He inspires'.[1]

At the end of chapter 4 I raised the question of the basis for God's *authority*. We now see that the justification for a man's acceptance of God's authority is God's glory and holiness, in so far as these are impressive qualities. We should also note the relation between glory and the authority which God delegated to *man*, when He created man with the role of a 'steward':[2] God crowned man with glory and honour[3] and made man in His own image,[4] thus establishing man's authority over the rest of the world.[5]

We have seen that in so far as God's action in creating Israel and revealing Himself to Israel is glorious and holy, His action is impressive; the meaning of God's 'glory' and 'holiness' involves a reference to the impression made on man. We shall soon see that His action is also expressive; the meaning of God's 'glory' and 'holiness' involves a reference to the particular observables through which God expresses His inner nature.

1.3. *Glory and holiness as expressive qualities*

God expresses His inner nature through observables in somewhat the same way that man expresses his inner feelings through observable behaviour.

In chapter 2 we saw, in relation to feelings, that Jones' action (or the result of Jones' action) may be both impressive and

---

[1] A. N. Whitehead, *Science and the Modern World*, New York, 1927, p. 276.
[2] Ch. 4, section 2.2.   [3] Ps. 8.5; cf. I Cor. 11.7.
[4] Gen. 1.27; cf. I Cor. 11.7; Ecclus. 17.3.
[5] F. Horst discusses the relation between 'glory', 'image' and 'dominion' in 'Face to Face, the Biblical Doctrine of the Image of God', tr. J. Bright, *Interpretation*, July, 1950, p. 262. G. von Rad discusses 'image' and 'dominion' in *Genesis, A Commentary*, tr. J. H. Marks, pp. 57-8.

expressive: it may evoke feelings in me and it may also express his feelings. For example, his gesture or his landscape-painting may be 'sad', where 'sad' is both an Aptness-word (describing an *occasion* of feeling) and a Feeling-word (describing an *expression* of feeling). The feeling in me and in him may be a feeling-Response (horror or amazement) or a feeling-Mood (sadness or joy) or a feeling-attitude (courage or love). Human behaviour which is impressive, evoking awe and inspiration in me, may also express something which is beyond the range of feelings and feeling-attitudes. Sometimes it expresses the 'inner nature' of a man: his inner dignity, integrity, nobility, moral power, spiritual power or will-power. In primitive societies, such impressive-expressive behaviour was correlated with the idea of 'soul'. Such a correlation does not seem implausible to me, even in the modern world.

In chapter 2 we considered FRB, feeling-revealing behaviour. Now I shall suggest a new term: SRB, *soul*-revealing behaviour. Where SRB is expressive, it has various logical similarities with expressive FRB. We recall[1] that expressive FRB is generally part of the meaning of the Feeling-word ('F') which is used to report the feeling; for example, behaviour which expresses sadness is part of the meaning of the word 'sad'. Similarly, expressive SRB is part of the meaning of the word ('S') which is used to describe a quality of soul; for example, behaviour which expresses dignity and integrity is part of the meaning of the words 'dignity' and 'integrity'; in Hebrew thought, behaviour which expresses divine glory and holiness is part of the meaning of the words 'glory' and 'holiness'. The external observable behaviour has this intrinsic logical connection with the 'inner' quality, power or nature.

Thus if we speak of expressive SRB as *evidence* for the existence of S (the soul-quality), we must realize that it is not 'evidence' in the way that Johnny's bulging cheek is evidence for an object in his mouth, or Jones' courteous door-opening is evidence for his courtesy, or a watch is evidence for a hidden watch-maker (in Paley's argument from design). Expressive SRB, like expressive FRB, differs from such evidence in two closely-related ways: (i) S is *in principle unobservable* (except perhaps, in some way, after death). I do not observe a correlation between

[1] Ch. 2, section 3.1.

cases of S and cases of expressive SRB (for example, between God's inner glory and His expressions of glory), and then infer S from SRB on some other occasion when I happen not to be in a position to observe S. I have never observed S, and I cannot do so. (ii) The *meaning* of 'S' (for example, 'glory') as applied to God is not abstractable from the observables in which God expresses S (for example, the Exodus, the starry heavens, or the Cross).

It is clear that God's deliberate, active self-revelation of holiness and glory is not *symptomatic* SRB. Men do not 'detect' God in spite of Himself. But why do I speak of *expressions* of God's holiness and glory rather than *manifestations*? In the discussion of FRB (chapter 2) we noticed how surprisingly difficult it is to distinguish expressions of feeling from manifestations of feeling. Several of the differences which we noted there are relevant here, however: (a) Manifestive FRB is usually associated with feelings which lack thought-content since they are not feelings *about* such-and-such.[1] God's self-revelation of His impressive qualities clearly involves a good deal of thought-content,[2] like much expressive FRB. (b) Expressive FRB varies not merely in intensity, but in the adequacy or appropriateness of its 'correspondence' with the feeling which is expressed;[3] hence special insight is often required for both the creation and appreciation of expressive FRB. God's expression of His holiness and glory is similar in this respect, too. (c) Expressive FRB is open to understanding and misunderstanding in so far as it typically has a reportive meaning.[4] In section 2.2. we shall see that divine SRB has a similar link with reportive meaning. (d) The same expressive FRB may have very different expressive meaning for different people, depending on their personal life-experience, outlook and affinity with the agent; we can speak of *the* expressive meaning only if we acknowledge one man's view as authoritative.[5] Similarly divine SRB has different meaning for different people, and God's own view of it provides *the* meaning in that men acknowledge it as authoritative. (This will be considered further in section 2.2.)

In the discussion of FRB[6] we noted that a man does not *have* to express the (expressible) feeling which is within him; the feeling may in fact occur without being expressed; but the

[1] Ch. 2, section 3.5.3.   [2] See pp. 176-7, 180.   [3] Ch. 2, section 3.5.4.
[4] *Ibid.*   [5] Ch. 2, section 3.5.4.   [6] Ch. 2, section 3.1.

nature of the particular feeling is logically connected with the ways in which he *would* express it if he did express it. Similarly God does not *have* to express His holiness and glory; and God's holiness and glory *exist* whether or not they are expressed. But the nature of God's holiness and glory is logically connected with the ways in which God has actually expressed his holiness and glory, or *would* express them (for example, in the final revelation at the end of history). The Bible does not attempt to describe a divine soul-quality as it is 'in itself',[1] completely apart from expressive observables in the past or future. But this logical connection between inner divine quality and outward observable expression does not restrict God's freedom in any way, and it does not make the existence of the inner quality dependent on the existence of the outward expression.[2] Nor does this logical connection rule out the possibility that inner divine qualities exist which could never be expressed in anything which man can observe in this life.[3] The connection does, however, rule out the possibility of saying anything positively meaningful about such qualities.

The earlier discussion of expressive FRB alongside *reportive* FRB is important in understanding divine SRB. Reportive FRB differs from expressive FRB in that it is not part of the meaning of the Feeling-word 'F'. Thus we can *replace* one item of reportive FRB by another: 'I am sad' and 'Je suis triste' are virtually equivalent. But we cannot similarly replace one item of expressive FRB by some item which depends on arbitrary conventions; and if we substitute another item of expressive FRB, these are not equivalent *qua* expressive—each item of expressive FRB expresses a particular, specific feeling.[4] Similarly in biblical thought the Exodus (or the starry heavens

[1] Cf. G. A. F. Knight, *A Christian Theology of the Old Testament*, p. 19; cf. F. Michaeli, *Dieu à l'Image de l'Homme*, Paris, 1950, pp. 154-5.

[2] E. Brunner wrongly holds that God's glory differs from His holiness in that it is dependent on the existence of the world and man (see *Dogmatics*, I, p. 287). There is little biblical evidence in support of such a distinction, and there is evidence to the contrary, for example, Jesus' words in John 17.5: 'Father, glorify thou me . . . with the glory which I had with thee before the world was made.' Cf. A. M. Ramsey, *The Glory of God and the Transfiguration of Christ*, p. 83: 'It is not that the existence of creatures is necessary to His glory, but that His creating them is the utterance or overflowing of a glory which eternally lacks nothing.'

[3] According to traditional theology, these qualities could not differ radically from that which has been revealed in the man Jesus; the doctrines of the Incarnation and the Trinity preclude this.

[4] See pp. 91-3.

or the Cross) is not merely a code-sign which *reports* God's inner glory and which could be replaced by another code-sign. The divine self-revelation has an intrinsic connection with specific things, events and persons; these are not replaceable by others. We shall see later that Christian claims concerning the uniqueness of the divine self-revelation in Jesus depend on the expressive character of this self-revelation, rather than the reportive (or other performative) elements.

1.4. *Differences between 'glory' and 'holiness'*

In this study of Israel's creation as a revelation of God's glory and holiness, we have seen that the words 'glory' and 'holiness' are logically similar in many important respects. But there are important differences, which make 'glory' more applicable to *world*-Creation; nevertheless the words are so closely connected with each other when applied to God that 'holiness' cannot be ignored in relation to world-Creation.

Let us consider the differences first. When 'holy' was applied to creatures, it was used to distinguish some creatures from others, from the 'common'; the latter do not reveal the holiness of God. This use of 'holy', to contrast some creatures with others, is specially prominent in the case of Israel, the holy people created by separation from all other peoples. The word 'glory', on the other hand, could be applied to some observables—the events of the Exodus, the people of Israel—without excluding its application to others; hence 'the heavens are telling the glory of God'[1] and 'his glory is the fulness of the whole earth'.[2]

Nevertheless the 'fulness of the whole earth' reveals God's *holiness*: 'Holy, holy, holy, Lord God of hosts; his glory is the fulness of the whole earth.'[3] The inner divine glory and holiness are very closely related. As E. Jacob says, 'Each individual has his *kabod* . . . but Yahweh has a quality of soul superior to any that can be imagined and it is this quality which in his case is called holiness. Thus there is no clear distinction between holiness and glory.'[4] Moreover, the two words are often

---

[1] Ps. 19.1.   [2] Isa. 6.3 (A.V. margin).   [3] *Ibid.*

[4] *Theology of the Old Testament*, p. 88; cf. N. H. Snaith, *The Distinctive Ideas of the Old Testament*, p. 48; cf. P. Bonnard, 'Holy', *Vocabulary of the Bible*, ed. J.-J. von Allmen, p. 166; cf. E. F. Scott, *The New Testament Idea of Revelation*, London, 1935, pp. 48-9. According to G. B. Caird (*The New Testament Conception of Doxa*, ch. 2), the passive forms which are translated as 'is glorified' and 'is sanctified' are frequently synonymous, especially in Ezekiel (see *op. cit.*, p. 92).

used as virtual equivalents in Hebrew parallelism,[1] or in very close logical relation.[2] (Indeed, the relation is so close that Otto fails to distinguish them: his book, *The Idea of the Holy* is really a study of both holiness and glory.)[3] According to Isa. 40.25-31, the created heavens reveal the holiness of God, His unique and saving power, in a cosmic revelation which is similar to the historical revelation in His dealings with Israel. But, apart from Isa. 6.3, I can find no other passage which explicitly associates the created world or the act of Creation with divine holiness. There may be an implicit connection in Ps. 89.5-13 or Job 28.25-28, but this is disputable. Otto interprets Job 38-40 in this way,[4] but here Creation is associated with glory rather than holiness. Thus it seems wise to focus our attention mainly on 'glory' as we consider world-Creation, though I shall refer occasionally to 'holiness'.

2. *World-Creation as a revelation of God's glory*

The biblical connection between world-Creation and glory is clearly stated by E. Stauffer: 'What is it that is revealed in creation? It is God's divinity. It is the quality by reason of which he, and he alone, is called God: his glory. Consequently, the revelation of the divine glory in creation contains a demand within itself. It is intended to quicken men's hearts to glorify God in thanksgiving and praise.'[5]

The glory of God as revealed in world-Creation evokes and requires an exultant proclamation of His wondrous works:

'Sing to the Lord, bless his name; tell of his salvation from day to day. Declare his glory among the nations, his marvellous works among all the peoples! For great is the Lord, and greatly to be praised; he is to be feared above all gods. For all the gods of the peoples are idols; but the Lord made the heavens.'[6]

(Similarly in Isa. 40.25-31 the *holiness* of God as revealed in

---

[1] *E.g.* Lev. 10.3; Ezek. 28.22. LXX even translates forms of the Hebrew '*qadosh*' by forms of the Greek '*doxa*' in Isa. 5.16 and Jer. 23.9.

[2] Exod. 15.11; 29.43; Rev. 15.4.

[3] Otto's 'numinous' is an impressive quality which evokes various feelings; Otto examines these aspects of divine holiness and glory. But he does not deal adequately with holiness and glory as *expressive* divine actions and *performative* human acknowledgments.

[4] *Op. cit.*, pp. 78-9.

[5] *New Testament Theology*, tr. J. Marsh, London, 1955, p. 88.

[6] Ps. 96.2-5; cf. Job 38.4-7; Ecclus. 43.28-33; cf. also Ps. 72.18-19; 86.8-10; 145.1-13; I. Chron. 29.10-13; Ps. 92.1-4.

world-Creation evokes and requires a confident trust in His saving grace.) God has revealed His unobservable inner nature (His 'deity', Rom. 1.20) in His observable works; men should respond to this revelation by acknowledging His glory.[1] Since God alone is the Creator, it is foolish and sinful to glorify any creature, especially an idol which is the work of men's hands, lacking life and reality and power:[2]

> 'The heavens proclaim his righteousness; and all the peoples behold his glory. All worshippers of images are put to shame.'[3]
> 'Every goldsmith is put to shame by his idols; for his images are false, and there is no breath in them. They are worthless, a work of delusion.' 'They have to be carried, for they cannot walk.' 'Not like these is he who is the portion of Jacob, for he is the one who formed all things.'[4]

God's revelation of His glory in Creation is sufficient, positively to call forth worship, and negatively to make idolatry inexcusable.[5]

In section 1 we saw that divine glory is an impressive quality which I understand in so far as I am impressed, and an expressive quality which has an inherent connection with the observables through which it is expressed. All this applies to the divine glory which is revealed in *world*-Creation, and I shall not repeat the detailed analysis which has already been given. But special problems arise in the case of world-Creation. To these we now turn.

2.1. *World-Creation as a continuous action*

When we say that God's glory is revealed in 'creation', do we mean the divine *action* of world-Creation in the beginning, or the resultant *world* which goes on existing for man to observe? Since there were no human eye-witnesses for the initial action,[6] it could not reveal anything to men. Hence one might conclude that God's glory is revealed to men only by the created world, and not by a divine action at all.

[1] Rom. 1.19-21; cf. Ecclus. 17.7-9; cf. section 2.3.
[2] Concerning this three-fold attack on idols, see B. Gärtner, *The Areopagus Speech and Natural Revelation*, tr. C. H. King, Uppsala, 1955, pp. 219-23.
[3] Ps. 97.6-7.
[4] Jer. 10.14-15, 5, 16; cf. Isa. 40.12-20; 42.5-8; 45.18-21; Wis. Sol. 13-14; 15.11-17; Rom. 1.18-32; Acts 17.22-30; cf. Isa. 44.9-20, 24-5; Ps. 135.5-7, 15-18; cf. Gärtner, *op. cit.*, chapters V-VII.
[5] Rom. 1.20; Wis. Sol. 13.8; 2(IV) Esdras 7 (cf. Gärtner, *op. cit.*, pp. 100-1); cf. section 2.3.
[6] Cf. Job 38.4.

This is not the biblical emphasis, however, for world-Creation is a continuous action,[1] and God's glory is continuously revealed in this action. It is true that nature and man are regarded as the product of an initial divine action, but they are also thought to be continuously dependent on God; and the initial action is not usually associated with the revelation of divine glory (or holiness) unless it is considered alongside the continuous and contemporary action:

'To whom then will you compare me, that I should be like him? says the Holy One. Lift up your eyes on high and see: who created these? He who brings out their host by number, calling them all by name.'[2]
'The Lord, who created the heavens and stretched them out, who spread forth the earth and what comes from it, who gives breath to the people upon it and spirit to those who walk in it. . . . I am the Lord, that is my name; my glory I give to no other, nor my praise to graven images.'[3]

These two quotations illustrate the two main ways[4] in which Creation is continuous: (i) God's initial action in creating the physical universe is somehow repeated or continued. As in Genesis 1, God calls forth the heavenly host, and as in Genesis 2, He 'makes the mist rise from the ends of the earth'.[5] God also controls the physical universe in ways which are not linked explicitly with the Creation-stories—for example, in storms.[6] The divine *control* of stars and storms is not a continuous Creation (or preservation) *ex nihilo*; but one passage suggests that the continued *existence* of heaven and earth depends on God:

'Of old thou didst lay the foundation of the earth, and the heavens are the work of thy hands. They will perish, but thou dost endure; they will all wear out like a garment. Thou changest them like raiment, and they pass away; but thou art the same, and thy years have no end.'[7]

[1] Cf. E. Jacob, *Theology of the Old Testament*, pp. 139-41; H. Wh. Robinson, *Inspiration and Revelation in the Old Testament*, Oxford, 1946, pp. 23-8; G. A. F. Knight, *A Christian Theology of the Old Testament*, p. 103; G. Wingren, *Creation and Law*, tr. R. Mackenzie, Edinburgh, 1961, p. 85; G. Pidoux (concerning Isa. 44.24), 'Creation', *Vocabulary of the Bible*, ed. J.-J. von Allmen, p. 73.
[2] Isa. 40.25-6; cf. Ps. 97.1-7; 104.1-13; Rom. 1.20; Ecclus. 43.28-33; cf. Ps. 135.5-7, 15-18; 145.1-13; Jer. 10.11-13; Amos 5.8.
[3] Isa. 42.5, 8; cf. Ps. 104.29-31; Acts 17.24-8.
[4] There is a third way, Creation as 'conflict', which will be considered in chapter 6.
[5] Jer. 10.13.   [6] Ps. 97.1-7; cf. Ps. 135.5-7.   [7] Ps. 102.25-7.

(ii) God's initial action in creating man is somehow repeated every time a man is born. This dependence of each man on the Creator was sometimes depicted in terms drawn from the story in Gen. 2 (God moulds clay and breathes life)[1] and sometimes in other terms (God forms the infant in the womb).[2] Often we are told that man, like all animate nature, depends on God for the continuous gift of life from the time of his birth until his death:

'If he should take back his spirit to himself, and gather to himself his breath, all flesh would perish together, and man would return to dust.'[3]

This passage implies that if the divine preservation of life should cease, the dust would remain. But this imagery for continuous Creation does not differ from the imagery of Gen. 2 concerning the initial Creation of man, for this too presupposes the existence of dust.

The imagery concerning continuous Creation is extremely complex. I shall examine it again in Chapter 6, in relation to other images or parables of Creation. Here I have simply tried to show that *some* form of continuous Creation is the vehicle for God's continuous revelation of His glory to men.

2.2. *God's glory and human onlooks*

There are passages in the Old Testament which imply that the revelation of God's glory in world-Creation is not obvious in ordinary circumstances, or that it is not yet full or complete. Isaiah,[4] Ezekiel[5] and the author of Hab. 3.3 had peculiar experiences, special *visions*, in which the revelation came to them. And in Num. 14.21 we read, 'All the earth shall be filled with the glory of the Lord'; here the sort of revelation which came to Isaiah is something which lies in the *future*. If we ask why the revelation of divine glory in world-Creation needs to be visionary or eschatological, two answers seem to be provided in the Bible. On the one hand, there are limitations imposed by the world as a *vehicle* of revelation. The existing world and its human inhabitants must be transformed[6] if the earth is

---

[1] Job 33.4, 6 (cf. Wingren, *op. cit.*, p. 86); Job 10.8-12; cf. Ps. 119.73; Eccles. 12.7.

[2] Ps. 139.13; Job 31.15; Jer. 1.5; cf. Isa. 44.24 concerning personified Israel.

[3] Job 34.14-15; cf. Job 12.10; Neh. 9.6; Ps. 66.9; Zech. 12.1; Wis. Sol. 15.11; I Tim. 6.13; cf. references on p. 192, n. 3; cf. ch. 4, section 3.2.

[4] Isa. 6.3.   [5] Ezek. 1.1-28.   [6] Rom. 8.18-22; cf. Isa. 60.19-20.

to be 'filled with the glory of God'. On the other hand, there are limitations imposed by the *recipients* of revelation. The earth will not be filled with the glory of God until it is 'filled with the *knowledge* of the glory of God':[1] until all the nations recognize God's glory in world-Creation.[2]

In some cases, however, neither a special vision nor an eschatological hope is implied. The revelation comes to mankind here and now, continuously:

> 'The heavens are telling the glory of God; and the firmament proclaims his handiwork.'[3]

God's glory is sufficiently evident in His handiwork for men to be held responsible if they do not acknowledge it,[4] even though this handiwork, as it now exists, imposes limitations on the revelation. Why then do some men fail to recognize this revelation?

The Bible suggests various reasons for this, three of which we shall consider later: man's suppression of his knowledge of God because of sin,[5] man's need for likeness with God if he is to understand God's actions[6] and the inadequacy of the natural world as an expression of God's glory.[7] Here I wish to suggest another reason: The recognition of God's glory in world-Creation depends on the onlook which a man adopts; and *various* onlooks are possible. As W. A. Whitehouse says, 'I want to look at the world and see glory already displayed and further glory as a task to be achieved; but I can *see* it all too clearly *as* a "glory-hole", which the dictionary defines as "a receptacle in which things of no permanent value are heaped together without order or tidiness" '.[8] The biblical believer looks on the impressive features of the world as expressions of God's glory. In saying, 'God reveals His glory in His creation', I do not merely assent to a flat statement of fact; I express an attitude which involves an onlook. This expression of onlook includes not only Behabitive and Commissive elements, but also a Verdictive element.[9] In deciding *to* glorify Him, I decide *that*

---

[1] Hab. 2.14.   [2] Ps. 86.8-10; Ps. 102.15; Isa. 66.18-22.
[3] Ps. 19.1; cf. Rom. 1.19-21; Ps. 97.6-7; 104.24 (A.V.); Ecclus. 42.16; 43.28-33.
[4] Cf. p. 191, nn. 4, 5.   [5] See section 2.3.
[6] See sections 3.2.4 and 4.2.   [7] See section 3.2.2.
[8] *Order, Goodness and Glory*, Oxford, 1960, p. 77 (my italics). Cf. p. 24: 'God is preserving a creation which does not bring to him the credit he deserves.'
[9] Cf. ch. 3, section 2.1.

He is glorious. My utterance is an unofficial Verdictive; it is
an agreement with what I take to be an official Verdictive:
the verdict of God Himself, expressed by men of religious
authority.

I look on the impressive features of the world as God's
expressions of His glory only if I believe that these features
have been given this *reportive* meaning by God; that is, God
uses them to 'say', 'I am glorious'. In chapter 2 we saw that a
minimal understanding of the reportive meaning which an
agent's FRB has for him is required if I am to begin to understand the expressive meaning which the FRB has for him.[1]
Similarly, a minimal understanding of the reportive meaning
of divine SRB is required if one is to understand the expressive
meaning. I need to believe (or hope) that my onlook-framework
conforms to the divine onlook, to God's own 'conventions'
of reportive (and expressive) meaning.

The world as it is provides some basis for thinking that God
is glorious, so that it is not unreasonable to accept religious
authority in this matter.[2] But I may very well contrast the world
as it appears in ordinary circumstances with the glorious world
which I see (or others apparently see) in moments of special
vision, or with a more glorious world of the future. The world,
as it appears in ordinary circumstances now, is sufficiently
like a 'glory-hole' for a different onlook to be quite reasonable:
I might well look on the stars as expressions, not of divine
glory, but of divine indifference; or I might not look on them as
expressions of anything at all. If my faith were not an onlook
to which there are alternatives, if my faith were an assent to a
brute fact, then questions of decision and responsibility could
hardly arise; unbelief would be *merely* stupidity. Indeed, the
Old Testament conception of the world as a revelation of God's
glory includes imaginative pictures which a man is surely
free to ignore or reject. For example, in Ps. 104.1-2, the heavens
are compared with the impressive garments of a king;[3] in
Ps. 19.1-2, inanimate nature 'speaks' to God and to man,
acknowledging and revealing the glory of God;[4] and in

---

[1] Ch. 2, section 3.5.4.

[2] The relation between observable evidence and religious authority as bases for
onlooks will be discussed more fully in ch. 6, section 1.2 and in *Some Further Problems*,
section 3.

[3] Cf. Ps. 93.1; cf. Job 40.10-19.   [4] Cf. Ps. 145.10-11 and perhaps Job 12.7-12.

Ezekiel's vision[1] the universe is viewed as the counterpart of the temple, with God's glorious throne beyond the visible firmament.[2]

2.3. World-Creation, glory and man's knowledge of God

We have seen that men have a knowledge of God which comes from His revelation in world-Creation. In Rom. 1.19, Paul writes, 'What can be known (or 'what is known')[3] about God is plain to them. . . . Although they knew God they did not honour him'. But in I Cor. 1.21, he says, 'The world did not know God through wisdom'; and there are similar passages elsewhere in the New Testament in which the non-Christian (the Gentile and even the Jew) is alleged to be ignorant of God.[4] This apparent contradiction may move us to ask, 'Do the scriptures tell us that men have *any* knowledge of God which comes solely from His revelation in world-Creation?' But when the question is posed in such a way, it is fruitless. For the biblical and intertestamental evidence makes a negative answer quite unplausible,[5] yet a positive answer seems to be contradicted by many passages. Moreover, different answers arise mainly from differences concerning what is meant by 'knowledge of God'. The important question to ask is, 'What *sort* of knowledge is involved here?'

I shall deal with this question in two stages; in each case I shall use some of the philosophical tools of Part I to open up the structure of biblical theology. First, I shall outline the general biblical conception of the 'knowledge of God', with its three elements of 'acknowledgment', 'acquaintance' and 'knowledge-that'. Then I shall examine Paul's crucial argument in Rom. 1.18-32, which conforms to what was by his time the normal Jewish conception of the extent and relevance of God's

---

[1] Ezek. 1.1-28; cf. Ps. 8.1; 113.4; 148.13. (In Ps. 57.10-11 and 108.4-5 the phrase 'above the heavens' may reflect Ezekiel's vision, or it may be merely a metaphor suggesting exceeding greatness.)

[2] In this section, onlooks have been presented once again in terms of the first-person *singular*; and once again we should note that this is a methodological convenience rather than an indication of theological individualism; cf. p. 139 and p. 159, n. 2. In the biblical context, one most likely would say, '*We* look on the impressive features of the world as expressions of God's glory'.

[3] Cf. B. Gärtner, *The Areopagus Speech and Natural Revelation*, p. 74, n. 1, and J. Knox, *The Interpreter's Bible*, Vol. 9, New York, 1954, p. 398.

[4] *E.g.*, John 8.54-5; 17.25; Gal. 4.8; Matt. 11.27; Eph. 2.12; I Cor. 2.14.

[5] See B. Gärtner, *op. cit.*, pp. 73-169. In the Old Testament, the focus of interest was on God's revelation to the Jews; but this was later extended to the Gentiles (*op. cit.*, pp. 96, 103).

revelation through world-Creation: men are enabled to know God sufficiently well to glorify Him and to avoid idolatry.

2.3.1. *The biblical conception of the knowledge of God*[1]

In the biblical context, religious knowledge is a sort of *doing*. When a man 'knows' God, he acknowledges God; and when God 'knows' a man, He acknowledges the man.

To know God is to acknowledge Him. It is to be loyal to Him in the covenant-relationship,[2] or to obey His moral law,[3] or to recognize His personal authority,[4] or to take note of His actions,[5] or to act with due regard for Him,[6] or to call upon His name in worship,[7] or to glorify Him for His beneficence,[8] or to fear His holiness.[9] In short, to know God is to acknowledge His actions, which are performative (authoritative) or expressive (glorious and holy).[10] This acknowledgment is not only in word but also in deed; it includes a righteous way of living:

> 'He judged the cause of the poor and needy; . . . Is not this to know me? says the Lord.'[11]

Those who fail to know the Lord are not only ungodly[12] but also unrighteous.[13] As B. Gärtner says, 'In the Old Testament, knowledge of God, worship and ethics are fused, and become *one* expression of the God-fearing man's acknowledgment of the One God'.[14]

Knowing God is a sort of doing, so it makes sense to issue the imperative: 'Know the Lord'.[15] Ignorance of God is an active

---

[1] See C. H. Dodd, *The Interpretation of the Fourth Gospel*, Cambridge, 1953, pp. 152-69; B. Gärtner, *op. cit.*, pp. 90-5; A. Richardson, *An Introduction to the Theology of the New Testament*, London, 1958, ch. 2; J.-L. Leuba, 'Know', *Vocabulary of the Bible*, ed. J.-J. von Allmen, pp. 221-2; R. Bultmann, '*Gnosis*', tr. from *Theologisches Wörterbuch zum Neuen Testament* (ed. G. Kittel) by J. R. Coates, London, 1952; C. F. D. Moule, *The Epistles of Paul the Apostle to the Colossians and to Philemon*, Cambridge, 1957, pp. 159-64.

[2] Hos. 6.6; cf. Hos. 4.1 and Th. C. Vriezen, *An Outline of Old Testament Theology*, p. 129.

[3] Jer. 22.15-16; cf. Jer. 4.22; 31.34; Hos. 4.1, 6; Isa. 11.9; cf. I John 2.3-5.

[4] Isa. 1.3ff.; cf. C. H. Dodd, *The Interpretation of the Fourth Gospel*, p. 157.

[5] Deut. 11.2; Mic. 6.5; Isa. 41.20; cf. Gärtner, *op. cit.*, p. 92, n. 1.

[6] I Sam. 2.12ff.   [7] Ps. 79.6; Jer. 10.25; cf. Dodd, *op. cit.*, p. 156.

[8] Jer. 9.23-4.   [9] Prov. 9.10; Isa. 11.2; Ps. 119.79.

[10] Cf. Dodd, *op. cit.*, p. 152: 'To know God is to acknowledge Him in His works and to respond to His claims.'

[11] Jer. 22.16; cf. Isa. 11.9; cf. C. Tresmontant, *Essai sur la Connaissance de Dieu*, Paris, 1959, p. 169.

[12] Job 18.21.   [13] Hos. 4.1-6; 5.4; Ps. 36.10; I John 4.7-8.

[14] *Op. cit.*, p. 116; cf. p. 95.   [15] Jer. 31.34; cf. I Chron. 28.9.

ignoring of Him, a refusal[1] to know Him—that is, a refusal
to be loyal to Him, to obey Him, to glorify Him, etc. The
so-called 'atheist' in the Bible is someone who ignores God,
someone who pretends that God is not there, someone who
refuses to acknowledge Him in worship and way of life;[2] to
say, 'There is no God', is to express an attitude.[3] Since knowing
God is an action from which I may refrain, my lack of knowledge of God is 'an offence as well as a mistake'.[4]

To know God is to acknowledge Him in word, Behabitively
and Commissively, implying that one has a particular attitude
to God and committing oneself to a way of life. And to know
God is to carry out this performative act without Infelicities
IIa or IIb:[5] the attitude which I imply is one which I genuinely
have, and the way of life to which I commit myself is actually
exemplified in my conduct. Thus Vriezen can say, 'The knowledge of God does not imply a theory about the nature of God,
it is not ontological, but existential: it is a life in the true
relationship to God'.[6] (And thus religious truth is something
one 'knows' by doing[7] it, by living in an appropriate relation
to God.)

God's knowledge of men is similarly a deed. If He 'knows' a
righteous man,[8] this means that He concerns Himself personally[9] with the man. The divine utterance, 'I know this man' is
Behabitive and Commissive: the opposite would be to ignore
the man. When God 'knows'[10] or 'foreknows'[11] Israel, this means
that He acknowledges her, granting her a special status in
relation to Himself. His utterance, 'I know Israel' is Exercitive;
the opposite action would be to reject Israel. (Similarly when
Jesus says, 'I never knew you; depart from me, you evil-doers',[12]
it is not that he lacks factual knowledge concerning them,

---

[1] Jer. 9.6; Hos. 4.6; Wis. Sol. 12.27.   [2] Ps. 10.4-11; Ps. 14.1-4; cf. Ps. 94.4-7.
[3] Cf. G. Wingren, *Creation and Law*, p. 22, n. 45; and B. Gärtner, *The Areopagus
Speech and Natural Revelation*, p. 100, n. 1.
[4] R. Bultmann, *Gnosis*, p. 17.   [5] Cf. chapter 1, section 1.
[6] *Op. cit.*, p. 129.   [7] John 3.21; I John 1.6.
[8] Ps. 1.6; cf. Ps. 101.4 (A.V.); 144.3; cf. Jer. 1.5; Deut. 34.10; Nahum 1.7.
[9] Cf. N. H. Snaith, *The Distinctive Ideas of the Old Testament*, p. 135; also R. H.
Fuller, *The Mission and Achievement of Jesus*, London, 1954, p. 92.
[10] Amos 3.2; Hos. 5.3; cf. C. H. Dodd, *The Interpretation of the Fourth Gospel*,
p. 154.
[11] Rom. 11.2; cf. Rom. 8.29, where divine foreknowledge of Christians does not
imply any lack of information concerning non-Christians, but does imply choice or
appointment.
[12] Matt. 7.23.

or even that he lacks acquaintance with them; rather, he refuses to acknowledge them, he rejects them.)[1] When God knows a man, He acknowledges the man; hence a man's knowledge of God includes the realization that God 'knows' Him in this way.[2] A man is in a position to acknowledge God (thus avoiding Infelicity I) because God has already acknowledged him. (This link between knowing and acknowledging does not depend on any alleged peculiarities of the Hebrew language. In modern English, where the verb 'know' has a person as its direct object, its meaning is often linked with acknowledgments. If I should say, 'I know Churchill', I would claim not merely that I possess information concerning him, but that he acknowledges me—which is false. If Churchill should say, 'I know Evans', he would be acknowledging me, and placing me in a position to acknowledge him.)

Man's knowledge of God is not only an acknowledgment. Ideally it includes a personal *acquaintance* or encounter with Him. To know God is to know Him in one's own experience,[3] responding to Him within a personal relationship. In some secular contexts,[4] the Hebrew '*yada*' ('know') meant 'to have sexual intercourse with'; in Hosea 2.20, Israel's future knowledge of God is compared with the carnal[5] knowledge which a wife has of her husband.[6] For Paul, the Christian's knowledge of God arises 'in Christ'; it is a personal experience of His presence and power in one's own life as a part of the Christian fellowship;[7] it is knowledge of the 'mystery which is Christ in you, the hope of glory'.[8] Such knowledge is to be contrasted with intellectual speculation or second-hand information. Only a partial knowledge is possible now, but when love is perfected in men, the knowledge of God will be 'face to face'.[9]

---

[1] Cf. Deut. 33.9; similarly the utterance, 'If one loves God, one is known by him' (I Cor. 8.3) does not imply that God lacks information concerning men who do not love Him.

[2] Gal. 4.9; cf. I Cor. 8.3; 13.12; cf. A. Richardson, *An Introduction to the Theology of the New Testament*, p. 48.

[3] Cf. J.-L. Leuba, 'Know', *Vocabulary of the Bible*, ed. J.-J. von Allmen, p. 221; cf. Dodd, *op. cit.*, p. 152; cf. A. Richardson, *op. cit.*, pp. 40-1.

[4] Gen. 4.1, 17, 25; Num. 31.18, 35; cf. Matt. 1.25; Luke 1.34.

[5] Cf. Hos. 2.14, where God 'woos' Israel (cf. Gen. 34.2-3) and Ezek. 16.7-8; cf. G. A. F. Knight, *A Christian Theology of the Old Testament*, pp. 177-84; F. Michaeli, *Dieu à l'Image de l'Homme*, p. 37.

[6] Yahweh is Israel's husband in Jer. 3.14 (A.V.); Isa. 54.5-6.

[7] Eph. 3.17-9; Phil. 3.8-10; Col. 2.2-3; I Cor. 2.7-16; Philem. 6; Gal. 2.20.

[8] Col. 1.27.   [9] I Cor. 13.12.

Then men will know God as He knows them,[1] with profound personal intimacy and understanding.[2]

The knowledge of God which is an 'acquaintance' is not possible without a knowledge of God which is an acknowledgment. The acknowledgment itself, however, presupposes[3] a 'knowledge-that' (or a 'belief-that'): in acknowledging God I imply that I know (or believe) that God exists, or that God has acted. Such an acknowledgment, moreover, is not the same thing as my 'knowledge-that'. Consider some secular examples: It is one thing to know that Jones is present in the room, and another to acknowledge his presence; the latter presupposes the former. It is one thing not to know that Jones has helped me, and another to ignore his help. A minimal 'knowledge-that' is *presupposed* by an acknowledgment and is distinct from an acknowledgment. (Indeed, 'He acknowledged that p' obviously differs from 'He knew that p' in that the first statement is ordinarily true only if he *said*, 'p'. In this respect 'acknowledge' is like 'assert' or 'admit', whereas 'know' is like 'believe'.)

Thus we need to distinguish three sorts of knowledge of God:

(a) A minimal 'knowledge-that' God has done such-and-such.
(b) An acknowledgment of God's action, in worship and way of life.
(c) An 'acquaintance' with God as God acts.

In the biblical context, (a) and (b) are different, but they are closely related in various ways.

(1) A refusal to acknowledge God's action in one's worship and way of life results in a suppression of one's knowledge-that He exists. In particular, if I refuse to acknowledge *to myself* what He has done, I repress this knowledge: I do not realize that I actually know what He has done. (Here modern psychoanalytic terminology is relevant). Conversely, a godly and righteous acknowledgment of God makes possible a change of mere 'knowledge-that' into 'acquaintance'.

(2) We have seen that in so far as an action of God is expressive and impressive (glorious and holy), I understand it in so far as I acknowledge it. Thus where my acknowledgment is minimal, my understanding of what I acknowledge is minimal, and my 'knowledge-that' is minimal.

[1] I Cor. 13.12.   [2] Ps. 139.1-6.   [3] Cf. chapter 1, section 2.4.

(3) In chapter 6 we shall consider the interpretation of God's action in causal terms which express an onlook, for example, looking on God as a Potter. We shall see that in such cases my 'knowledge-that' (cf. 'decision-that') and acknowledgment (cf. 'decision-to') are inseparable.

2.3.2. *Paul's argument in Rom. 1. 18-32*

We are now in a position to understand what Paul says in Rom. 1.18-32 concerning man's knowledge of God through world-Creation. This passage has given rise to considerable theological controversy;[1] but Paul's argument is not difficult to interpret, if we bear in mind the general biblical conception of religious knowledge and the impressive-expressive elements in the act of world-Creation. I shall deal with the main exegetical questions in turn.

First, is Paul himself presenting an argument for the existence of God the Creator? No. It is surely obvious that the conclusion of his argument is not that God exists, but that men (or the Gentiles)[2] are without excuse before God.[3] Here, as in Jewish appeals to world-Creation,[4] the point at issue is not the existence of God, but the nature of God as revealed to men.

What is being revealed to men concerning God? Paul speaks of God's 'invisible nature, namely his eternal power and deity',[5] and he says that what is revealed should move men to glorify God[6] and should show men that idolatry is folly.[7] In other words, God is revealing His inner *glory*,[8] which differs utterly from idols in being invisible, eternal and powerful.

How is God's glory revealed? Paul's '*tois poiēmasin*' may be translated either as 'in His creatures' (things made) or as 'in

---

[1] E. Brunner finds a 'natural revelation', distinct from the revelation in Christ, in Rom. 1.18-32; K. Barth does not. For Brunner's view, see *The Letter to the Romans, A Commentary*, London, 1959, pp. 17-18, and *Dogmatics*, I, pp. 132-6; cf. A. Nygren, *Commentary on Romans*, tr. C. C. Rasmussen, London, 1952, p. 106. For Barth's view, see *A Shorter Commentary on Romans*, tr. D. H. van Daalen, London, 1959, pp. 24-30, *Church Dogmatics*, I, 2, pp. 304-7, and *Church Dogmatics*, II, 1, pp. 119-23. Barth and Brunner agree in finding no 'natural theology' (philosophical argument for God's existence) in Rom. 1.18-32; but other scholars have found this—for example, W. Sanday and A. C. Headlam, *A Critical and Exegetical Commentary on the Epistle to the Romans*, 5th ed., Edinburgh, 1902, p. 43.
[2] Nygren says that Paul is referring to the Gentiles (*op. cit.*, p. 101); but Gärtner maintains that Paul is referring to all men (*The Areopagus Speech and Natural Revelation*, p. 74, n. 2).
[3] Cf. G. Wingren, *Creation and Law*, p. 53.
[4] Cf. Gärtner, *op. cit.*, pp. 90, 104, 129, 136, 146, 167.
[5] Rom. 1.20.   [6] Rom. 1.21.   [7] Rom. 1.22-5.
[8] Cf. Gärtner, *op. cit.*, p. 137, n. 1; cf. Sanday and Headlam, *op. cit.*, pp. 43-4.

His works' (things done).[1] In either case, the reference is to the continuous Creative action of God and not merely the initial act of world-Creation. The invisible glory of God is 'seen with the understanding'[2] by men who see His self-revelatory[3] Creative activity in the visible world. That is, world-Creation is an expressive action, by which God enables man to know His inner glory; and it is an impressive action, which man understands in so far as he is impressed. Since His action is deliberately and continuously expressive, man's knowledge is not acquired by detecting or inferring God from His finished artefacts, as if the world were like a watch or a footprint inadvertently left on a beach. Since His action is impressive, it is not discerned as such by someone whose attitude is neutral and aloof; His impressive action does not bring knowledge unless one has already responded to it, to some extent at least.

Are philosophical arguments for the existence of God relevant to the interpretation of Rom. 1.18-32? This question is partly an historical one, concerning the background of Paul's thought; Gärtner's detailed *contrast*[4] between Paul's Jewish 'natural revelation' and Stoic philosophers' 'natural theology' is very persuasive as an answer to the historical question. But the question may also be answered in more general terms: If by a philosophical argument men come to see and understand the divine glory as it is impressively expressed in world-Creation, then such an argument is relevant to Rom. 1.18-32. In so far as a philosophical argument for the existence of God is likely to be an attempt to detect Him from a neutral standpoint, it is not likely to bring such an understanding of the divine glory. But particular philosophical arguments should be examined individually by Christian theologians; they should not all be dismissed, *a priori*, as being irrelevant to the God of the Bible.

Do men know God apart from the revelation of God in Jesus Christ? Paul says that they do, but that they suppress His truth and so their minds are darkened and their thinking becomes futile;[5] that is, they no longer realize what they actually know concerning God. They suppress their 'knowledge-that' God is

---

[1] Gärtner (*op. cit.*, p. 138) favours 'works'; he notes that '*poiēma*' is not used in LXX with specific reference to things made. The verb '*poiō*', however, is often used with reference to Creation, and most translations seem to favour 'things made'.

[2] '*nooúmena kathorâtai*'; see Gärtner, *op. cit.*, pp. 133-7.

[3] Rom. 1.19.   [4] *Op. cit.*, chapter V.   [5] Rom. 1.21.

glorious by refusing to acknowledge Him,[1] that is, by being ungodly and unrighteous. Their ungodliness consists in their failure to glorify God in worship, and in their glorification of creatures—indeed, of idols—instead of God.[2] Their unrighteousness consists in various sensual and social vices; these carry a moral nemesis to which God 'gives them up',[3] thereby[4] revealing His wrath. (Paul also claims that men know their unrighteousness to be contrary to the decree[5] or law[6] of God; I do not stress this here because it is not directly relevant to the knowledge of God through world-Creation.)

What then does Paul mean when he says that non-Christians do not know God (for example, in I Cor. 1.21)? He may be interpreted as meaning any one, or all, of the following: (a) Their minimal 'knowledge-that', which is made possible by God's self-revelation in world-Creation, has been suppressed; they have made themselves ignorant, though an act of repentance, a conversion, could bring their knowledge back into consciousness.[7] (b) They do not acknowledge God's glory in their worship and their way of life. (c) They lack the knowledge as 'acquaintance' which Christians enjoy 'in Christ'.

In this section I have tried to interpret Paul fairly, without interjecting my own views. I should make it clear, however, that I disagree with him in two important ways: (i) Paul's depreciation of all non-Christian religious knowledge seems to me to be both uncharitable and false. (ii) Paul claims that all men are 'without excuse' if they fail to recognize and acknowledge God's glory as revealed in Creation; in section 2.2., however, I argued that such recognition depends in part on a man's onlook, and I claimed that alternative onlooks are reasonable. These two disagreements would be crucial in the context

---

[1] Rom. 1.28; cf. G. S. Hendry: 'Our apprehension of God the Creator must be carefully distinguished from the ordinary process of acquiring knowledge; it is not so much an act of knowing as an act of acknowledgment.' *God the Creator*, p. 178; cf. p. 149.

[2] Rom. 1.21-5.   [3] Rom. 1.24, 26, 28.

[4] Cf. C. H. Dodd, *The Epistle of Paul to the Romans*, London, 1932, p. 29; A. Nygren, *Commentary on Romans*, pp. 109-10; G. Wingren, *Creation and Law*, p. 54.

[5] Rom. 1.32.

[6] Rom. 2.14-15. Gärtner (*op. cit.*, pp. 77-8) points out that the four broken commandments to which Paul refers in Rom. 2.17ff. (stealing, adultery, idolatry and blasphemy) are included in the six commandments which Jews had come to associate with Adam, and the seven associated with Noah—in each case the representative of all mankind.

[7] Cf. Eph. 4.17-19; Acts 17.23, 30, 31; cf. Gärtner, *op. cit.*, chapters VI-VIII.

of a theological controversy concerning Christian attitudes in missionary work; but in the context of this thesis they are not of fundamental importance. I do not reject Paul's conception of the knowledge of God or his conception of God's self-revelation in Creation. I accept these conceptions, but I reject his answers to the questions, '*Who* knows God?' and 'How *obvious* is God's self-revelation in Creation?'

My disagreements with Paul do not depend on philosophical analysis: (i) Obviously a Christian's appraisal of non-Christian religions is a matter of theological judgment combined with empirical study. (ii) The notion of onlooks does not in itself exclude the claim that men are 'without excuse', for someone could argue that the various non-biblical onlooks only seem to be reasonable to men who are sinners. (Indeed, the extreme dogmatist should find that onlooks are not only compatible with his convictions but also highly useful in interpreting them: 'There is only one true onlook, the divinely-authorized one, and I know it in detail.' When one is dealing with onlooks rather than (scientific) facts, it becomes at least plausible to appeal to a supreme Authority concerning the truth.)[1]

3. *Jesus as the revelation of God's glory*

According to the New Testament, the glory of the world-Creator is revealed in Jesus Christ. Our next step is to consider this revelation. First I will outline the New Testament account, mentioning divine holiness as well. Then I will examine this account in relation to what I have said concerning revelation as an impressive-expressive action (sections 1.2; 1.3), and concerning the revelation of God's glory through world-Creation (section 2).

3.1. *The New Testament account of Jesus as the revelation of God's glory*

Jesus is related to the glory of God in a three-fold way: (i) The inner glory of Jesus is equated with the *inner glory* of God.[2] Christians refer to Jesus in terms which previously were reserved

---

[1] Cf. p. 227; also p. 256.
[2] See John 12.41 in relation to John 1.14 and 2.11; cf. A. M. Ramsey, *The Glory of God and the Transfiguration of Christ*, p. 28: 'Such is the place of Jesus Christ in relation to the divine glory that it is possible to speak of *the glory of Christ*, and by those words to mean no less than the glory of God Himself.'

for God alone; he is 'the Lord of glory'[1] and 'the glory of thy people Israel'.[2] Christians glorify Jesus in the same way that Jews glorify God.[3] The glory of Jesus is commensurate with his activity as the agent or instrument of world-Creation.[4] (ii) Jesus is in some unique way the *observable expression* of God's inner glory, the divine 'effulgence'[5] by which men are enabled to 'know'[6] this glory. As Th. H. Robinson says, this effulgence is 'something of His own essence, so transformed as to be perceptible by the ordinary human eye. . . . God translated into terms of human life, maintaining His oneness with His source'.[7] (iii) Jesus is also the man who renders the perfect *acknowledgment* of God's glory, the 'perfect obedience which alone is perfect worship'.[8] His glorification of God is a representative act of worship in which men may participate, uttering 'the Amen through him to the glory of God'.[9]

Why were such convictions held concerning Jesus? We may refer again[10] to two main bases: the historical Jesus and the experience of the early Church. Since today we know the historical Jesus only through the interpretation which the early Church gave in the light of its religious experience, it is notoriously difficult to isolate the first basis from the second.[11] But there seems to be no reason to doubt that the works[12] and teaching[13] and presence[14] of Jesus moved men to glorify God; and since whatever moves men to glorify God reveals God to them, the Fourth Evangelist's interpretation in terms of revelation[15] is legitimate. Also, it is highly probable that the Transfiguration was an historical event in the life of Jesus:[16] three of his disciples had a vision in which he was identified with the glorious presence of God.[17]

---

[1] I Cor. 2.8 and perhaps James 2.1; cf. Ps. 24.7 and Acts 7.2.
[2] Luke 2.32 (A.V.); cf. Jer. 2.11; Deut. 10.21; Ps. 106.19-20.
[3] Heb. 13.21; Rev. 5.12; 1.6.   [4] Heb. 3.3-4; cf. Heb. 1.2-3; John 1.3, 14.
[5] Heb. 1.3; cf. V. Taylor, *The Names of Jesus*, London, 1953, pp. 129-30.
[6] II Cor. 4.6.   [7] *Commentary on Hebrews*, London, 1933, p. 3.
[8] E. G. Selwyn, *The First Epistle of Peter*, p. 255; see John 12.23-8.
[9] II Cor. 1.20; cf. John 14.13.   [10] Cf. chapter 4, section 3.1.
[11] See E. Hoskyns and N. Davey, *The Riddle of the New Testament*, London, 1931, and James M. Robinson, *A New Quest of the Historical Jesus*, London, 1959.
[12] Luke 2.20; 5.25; 7.16; 13.13; 17.15; 18.43; cf. the Birth Story in Luke 2.4-20, which may be largely legendary.
[13] Luke 4.15.   [14] Luke 19.38.   [15] *E.g.*, John 11.40.
[16] Rather than a post-Resurrection experience projected back into pre-Resurrection history.
[17] Luke 9.28-36.

The experience and reflection of the early Church gradually produced a complex conception of Jesus as the glory of God. For the early Church, the Resurrection was an act which revealed God's own glorious power[1] and indicated God's bestowal of glory upon Jesus.[2] Also, the appearance of the risen Christ to Paul was a revelation of glory which closely resembled previous revelations of God's glory.[3] The Crucifixion came to be interpreted in relation to the divine glory: as men became convinced that it had brought salvation, they were moved to glorify God.[4] Hence Jesus' voluntary submission to Crucifixion came to be viewed as itself the *revelation* of God's glory, even apart from the Resurrection.[5] This revelation was a human *acknowledgment* of God's glory: on the Cross, and in his whole ministry as it culminated in the Cross, Jesus 'glorified'[6] God by his obedience to God's will, his accomplishment of God's work. The revelation was also a divine *bestowal* of glory: God bestowed glory on Jesus not only in the Resurrection as a consequence of the Crucifixion, but also in the Crucifixion itself.[7] Thus glory is revealed and acknowledged and bestowed in one event.[8]

The early Christians found that they participated[9] in Christ's glory in three similar ways, through their union with Him: (i) They were challenged and enabled to live according to his example, so that their way of life (both individual and corporate) might move men to glorify God[10] and thus might be a *revelation* of God's glory.[11] Mere external behaviour will not

---

[1] Rom. 6.4.

[2] I Peter 1.21; Acts 7.55; I Tim. 3.16; Acts 3.13-15; Phil. 2.9-11; Heb. 2.9.

[3] Acts 9.3; cf. Acts 22.6; 26.13.

[4] Gal. 1.5; 6.14; I Cor. 6.20; I Tim. 1.15-17; Rom. 15.9; Acts 11.18; 13.48.

[5] John 12.23-8; 13.31-2; 17.1.

[6] John 12.23-8 (cf. E. Hoskyns, *The Fourth Gospel*, London, 1940, p. 497: 'This obedience is the glorification of the Father's name'); John 17.4; cf. A. M. Ramsey, *op. cit.*, pp. 93-4.

[7] John 8.54; 12.23; 13.31; 17.1, 5; cf. 12.32.

[8] Cf. C. H. Dodd, *The Interpretation of the Fourth Gospel*, p. 208.

[9] The idea of participation in eschatological glory was prominent in later Jewish apocalyptic writings; see G. Kittel, '*Doxa*', *Theologisches Wörterbuch zum Neuen Testament*, ed. G. Kittel, Band II, pp. 249-50; and G. B. Caird, *The New Testament Conception of Doxa*, pp. 165-9.

[10] Matt. 5.16; I Peter 2.12 (cf. I Cor. 10.24-33); II Cor. 9.11-13.

[11] John 17.10; II Thess. 1.10-2. See especially II Cor. 3.18, R.S.V. margin, '*reflecting* the glory of the Lord'; in support of this translation, see A. Plummer, *A Critical and Exegetical Commentary on the Second Epistle of St Paul to the Corinthians*, Edinburgh, 1915, pp. 105-6; Selwyn agrees (*op. cit.*, p. 224). In II Cor. 3-4, Paul's ministry and the ministry of Christians generally are contrasted with the work of Moses: whereas the glory of God revealed through Moses was veiled by Moses,

bring this about; it requires a spirit of humble dependence on God and of loving service to others,[1] a deliberate seeking of God's glory rather than one's own glory.[2] Men must see that the transcendent power, the glory, belongs to God and not to the Christians who reveal it; hence Christians have the treasure of God's glory in 'earthen vessels'—in what looks like death and dishonour.[3] Suffering or death for Jesus' sake is a special means of glorifying God,[4] a means of revealing the hidden life of the risen Christ.[5] (ii) The Christian's way of life is itself an *acknowledgment* of God's glory, an act of worship. God is glorified by the 'fruits of righteousness'[6] in the lives of Christians: by abounding love,[7] generosity[8] and chastity.[9] (iii) The Christian way of life is a life made possible because God has already *bestowed* His glory, or Christ's glory, on His followers:

'We all, with unveiled face, reflecting the glory of the Lord, are being changed into his likeness from one degree of glory to another; for this comes from the Lord who is the Spirit.'[10]

Paul also speaks of 'the glory of this mystery, which is Christ in you, the *hope* of glory';[11] participation in divine glory is both a present reality and a future hope. The early Christians expected to be the recipients of further revelation of God's glory in Jesus' final 'appearance',[12] and also to be the vehicles of this future revelation,[13] through fuller participation in the divine glory.[14] Whether the gift of participation in Christ's glory is in the present or in the future, it is both a restoration and a new creation: it is a restoration of man to the glory (and the image) with which God originally endowed him at Creation and from

---

the glory of God revealed through Christ and then through Christians is open for all to see, though some are blind to it.

[1] I Peter 4.8-11.
[2] John 7.18; cf. John 5.44; I Cor. 1.29-31; 3.21; 4.7; II Cor. 10.17-18; Gal. 6.14.
[3] II Cor. 4.7; cf. A. Plummer, *op. cit.*, p. 127, and R. H. Strachan, *The Second Epistle of Paul to the Corinthians*, London, 1935, p. 93.
[4] I Peter 4.16; John 21.19; Rom. 8.17.   [5] II Cor. 4.10-11.
[6] Phil. 1.11; cf. John 15.8, where, however, the 'fruit' may be converts rather than righteous deeds in general.
[7] Phil. 1.9; cf. Rom. 15.5-9, where love and unity are preconditions for a proper acknowledgment of God's glory in verbal worship.
[8] II Cor. 9.13.   [9] I Cor. 6.20.
[10] II Cor. 3.18, R.S.V. margin; cf. John 17.22; Rom. 8.30; Heb. 2.10; II Cor. 8.23; cf. p. 206, n.
[11] Col. 1.27; cf. Eph. 1.18; Rom. 5.2; II Thess. 2.14.
[12] Col. 3.4; I Peter 1.7; 4.13; Titus 2.13; cf. Mark 8.38; 13.26; Matt. 25.31.
[13] Rom. 8.17-19 (A.V.).   [14] II Thess. 1.10-12.

which man has fallen;[1] and it is a new creation, endowing
man with the glory (and the image) which was God's inner
nature before the Creation of the world.[2] Modern Christians
who do not believe in a historical 'fall' of man from an earlier
glory will interpret the 'restoration' as the fulfilment of a divine
ideal for man *qua* man; the ideal then coincides with the
divinization of man. In any case, we may say that Christians
experience a transformation into the glory (and the image) of
Christ, by the power of the Spirit.[3]

We have been considering the glory of God in relation to
Jesus. The *holiness* of God is related to Jesus in somewhat similar
ways, though there are important differences. Jesus is called
'the Holy One of God',[4] but this title merely designates a man
set apart and consecrated to the service of God;[5] no worship of
the man is implied. Nevertheless Jesus was thought to be specially consecrated by the Holy Spirit at his Baptism[6] and His
Resurrection;[7] and Jesus accepted worship,[8] evoking the response which is typically evoked by divine holiness.[9] After the
Resurrection and Pentecost, the Holy Spirit or Spirit of Jesus
not only glorified his followers, but also *sanctified* them in a new
way of life as 'partakers of his holiness';[10] this sanctification,
like glorification, is both a present reality and a future hope.[11]
Christians acknowledge God's holiness, as they acknowledge
His glory, in their worship[12] and conduct.[13] The New Testament,
however, does not connect the *revelation* of God's holiness
explicitly with the holiness of Christians. Since holiness and
glory are so closely related (Selwyn even says, 'The holiness of

[1] Ps. 8.5-6; Rom. 3.23; I Cor. 11.7; Heb. 2.5-11.
[2] John 17.4, 21-4; concerning the divine image, see Col. 1.15; 3.10; cf. II Peter
1.4: 'partakers of the divine nature', and Eph. 3.19: 'filled with all the fullness of
God'; cf. C. Tresmontant, *Essai sur la Connaissance de Dieu*, pp. 153-7.
[3] II Cor. 3.8, 17-8; I Peter 4.14.
[4] Mark 1.24; John 6.69; Rev. 3.7; cf. Acts 3.14; 4.27, 30.
[5] *E.g.*, Aaron (Ps. 106.16) and Elisha (II Kings 4.9); cf. V. Taylor, *The Names of
Jesus*, p. 80.
[6] Luke 3.21-2.   [7] Rom. 1.3-4.
[8] Matt. 21.15-6; Luke 5.8-10; contrast Peter in Acts 10.25-6.
[9] Luke 5.8 (cf. Isa. 6.5); Mark 10.32 (cf. R. Otto, *The Idea of the Holy*, p. 158).
[10] Heb. 12.10-11 (A.V.); Rom. 6.22; cf. I Cor. 3.16-7; 6.11; Eph. 2.21-2; 5.26-7;
I Thess. 4.3; II Thess. 2.13; cf. Gal. 5.22.
[11] Cf. J. K. S. Reid, 'Sanctify', *A Theological Word Book of the Bible*, ed. A. Richardson, pp. 217-18.
[12] Matt. 6.9; I Peter 3.15.
[13] Rom. 12.1; cf. II Cor. 1.12; 7.1; Rom. 6.19; I Peter 1.15.

Christians is styled glory'),[1] such a connection may legitimately be surmised; but it certainly is not emphasized.[2]

3.2. *The revelation of God's glory in Jesus: an expressive and impressive action*

If we interpret God's glory as expressive SRB, we are in a better position to understand the meaning of three fundamental claims which Christians make concerning Jesus: that he is irreplaceable, that he is unique, and that he is divine.

3.2.1. *Jesus is irreplaceable*

Since Jesus is an *expression* of divine glory, he is not replaceable by a mere *report* of divine glory; he is not merely a code-sign, an item of reportive SRB, which is connected with divine glory by arbitrary conventions. Just as particular expressions of feeling-F have an intrinsic connection with feeling-F so that they are part of what is meant by 'F', so particular expressions of divine glory are connected with divine glory.[3] Just as particular expressions of feeling-F may be given a peculiarly self-referring reportive use,[4] so with particular expressions of divine glory; it is as if God said to men, 'I am like *this*'.

Expressions of feeling are not replaceable by reports of feeling. But it is possible to substitute one *expression* of feeling for another; though the two are not equivalent, the feelings which are expressed are sufficiently similar for the same feeling-word to be applied.[5] Similarly it would seem that it is possible to substitute one expression of divine glory by another. But Jesus is irreplaceable in relation to other expressions of glory; he is not merely *an* expression of divine glory, he is *the* expression. Thus Christians make a second claim concerning Jesus, that He is in some sense 'unique'.

3.2.2. *Jesus is unique*

Jesus is unique because he is the standard expression of divine glory. He provides the standard by which all other expressions of divine glory are to be appraised. An analogy to

---

[1] *The First Epistle of Peter*, p. 257; he refers to John Lightfoot, *Works*, V, p. 330.
[2] There are hints of such a connection: 'hallowed be thy name' (Matt. 6.9) may be interpreted both as an acknowledgment of God's holiness and as a request that God's holiness be revealed to men (cf. Ezek. 36.23); and in I Pet. 2.9 it is the 'holy nation' which is commissioned to *declare* God's wonderful deeds.
[3] See chapter 5, section 1.3.   [4] See pp. 92-3.
[5] See pp. 91-2 and chapter 5, section 1.3.

this may be found in the realm of expressive FRB: when an artistic school develops, a particular work of art sometimes becomes the *standard* by which other expressions of the same (or similar) feelings must be appraised. In art the appeal to such a standard may or may not be a good thing; but we do have here the closest logical analogy to the Christian claim that the revelation of God in Jesus is unique. Jesus provides the standard because the *correspondence* between him and God's inner glory is perfect; that is, no other observable event, thing or person could be a more adequate expression. Just as we may compare two expressions of a feeling in terms of their adequacy,[1] so we may compare two expressions of divine glory (or holiness). In each case the notion of 'correspondence' is involved, though there is no duplication, reproduction or repetition; and in each case two different expressions may differ in their adequacy, so that one is 'perfect' and the other is 'imperfect'. Such a difference is neither a 'difference in degree' nor a 'difference in kind'; the degree/kind distinction is not satisfactory as a way of interpreting the uniqueness of Jesus. Jesus is unique in that he is the perfect expression, the normative expression, of God's glory.

Jesus is irreplaceable and unique as the expression of God's glory. World-Creation, by comparison, is a very inadequate expression of God's glory, for two reasons. In the first place, since all things are continuously created, no particular glory is expressed unless one selects particular creatures as being specially revelatory. If the meaning of 'glory' as applied to God has an intrinsic and equal connection with *all* observables, so that each observable is *replaceable* by another as an expression of divine glory, then nothing concrete or particular is revealed at all. One needs a standard by which one can select and appraise observables as revelations of glory. In the second place, the natural world as a whole or in its parts is inadequate in its degree of correspondence to the inner glory of God. Indeed, Rom. 8.18-22 suggests that the natural world needs to be transformed by God, working through men, if its futility is to become glory.

3.2.3. *Jesus is divine*

If a Christian says, 'Jesus is divine', he may be confronted by

---

[1] See pp. 104-5.

a dilemma: 'When you judge that Jesus is divine, either you already have an idea of divinity (for example, an idea drawn from revelation through Creation) or you do not. If you already have such an idea, and merely find that Jesus conforms to it, then Jesus is not necessary as a revelation of God, for you already know what divinity is.[1] If you do not already have an idea of divinity, then you are not in a position to make the judgment, "Jesus is divine".'

This dilemma is seen to be false once we think of 'divinity' in terms of glory and holiness, and once we realize that these are expressive qualities, logically-similar to artistic expressions of feeling. When I understand a new expression of feeling-F, what I mean by 'F' is slightly changed. Previously I had not thought of this particular expression of F; and my understanding of the inner feeling-F had not been extended to include the specific feeling which now has been expressed. The particular expression of feeling is not unnecessary, yet my previous understanding of 'F' is not irrelevant. Similarly, when I begin to understand the expression of God's glory and holiness in Jesus, and come to believe that it is the (standard) expression, I say, 'He is divine'. This judgment involves a new and definitive meaning for the word 'divine': observables are 'divine' in so far as they resemble Jesus as the *expression* of God's glory and holiness, and thus correspond to some extent to this inner glory and holiness. The specific revelation of divinity in Jesus is not unnecessary; yet other revelations are not irrelevant.

3.2.4. *'Like knows like'*

We now turn to a rather different point: Since glory is an *impressive* and *expressive* quality, the revelation of God's glory in Jesus is understood only in so far as one becomes *like* Jesus, and thus *like* God. Here is a case of 'like knows like'.

Since glory is an *impressive* quality, the divine glory revealed in Jesus is understood in so far as one is impressed. We have seen that when I am genuinely 'impressed', I do not merely have a feeling-Response; like Jesus, I acknowledge God's glory in a way of life which reveals God's glory to others. That is, I

---

[1] Of course, someone might claim that a Christian could deny that Jesus *revealed* anything new about God, insisting only that Jesus is necessary as the *salvation* of God; but such a radical dissociation of the soteriological work of Christ from the revelatory work would be difficult to defend; I shall not consider it here, in any case.

need to become like Jesus in order to understand the revelation of God's glory in Jesus. I must allow myself to be transformed by the spirit of Jesus (or the Holy Spirit). (In this chapter,[1] I said that the authority of Jesus is based on the impression he makes. In chapter 4,[2] I said that the authority of Jesus is based on his transformation of those who respond to him. Now we can see that the two bases of authority are really the same.)[3]

Since the revelation of God's glory in Jesus is an *expressive* action, we would expect that there would need to be some analogy between the inner glory expressed by God and the inner glory of the man who understands it. We recall that there needs to be some analogy between the inner feelings which a man expresses and the feeling-experience of another man, if the first man is to communicate his feelings to the second man.[4] In a somewhat similar way, the inner glory of God is understood to the degree that one's own inner nature has been transformed into His likeness.

Since glory is impressive and expressive, only those who are 'being changed into his (Jesus') likeness from one degree of glory to another'[5] have the 'light of the knowledge of the glory of God in the face of Christ'.[6] Christians have 'put on the new nature, which is being constantly renewed in the image of its Creator and brought to know God'.[7] This idea, that only like knows or understands like, is evident in John's first Epistle:

'Beloved, we are God's children now; it does not yet appear what we shall be, but we know that when he appears, we shall be like him, for we shall see him as he is.'[8]
'He who loves is born of God and knows God. He who does not love does not know God; for God is love.'[9]

In so far as world-Creation is a revelation of divine glory, an impressive and expressive action, here too I need to become like the Agent in order to understand His action. A need for likeness also arises in so far as I try to understand the *intention* or

---

[1] Section 1.2.   [2] Chapter 4, section 3.

[3] Note that the impressiveness and transforming power of Jesus provide a 'basis' in two distinct ways: (i) His glory does in fact move men to acknowledge His authority and (ii) these men think that His glory ought to move them to acknowledge His authority. This does not violate the 'autonomy of value': even if I do not feel psychologically free to reject His authority and even if I judge it morally right that I should allow myself to be influenced in this way, I am *logically* free to say, 'Jesus is glorious but I reject His authority' (cf. chapter 1, section 7.3).

[4] See pp. 104-5, 110-11.   [5] II Cor. 3.18.   [6] II Cor. 4.6.
[7] Col. 3.10 (N.E.B.).   [8] I John 3.2.   [9] I John 4.7-8.

rationale of world-Creation. We shall now digress a little, to examine this second way in which an utterance concerning world-Creation is rapportive.[1] We shall see that the two ways are very similar, and that they are closely connected.

4. *The mystery of God's intention in world-Creation*

What reason did God have for creating the world? For what purpose did God create the world? How did God interpret His action of world-Creation? In short, what was the intention or rationale of world-Creation? (Or, since world-Creation is a continuous action, we may ask, 'What *is* its intention or rationale?')

We shall consider this question in two stages. First, I will sketch the Old Testament view concerning the rationale of the divine action. Second, I will examine the revelation of God's intention in Jesus, showing how this is connected with the revelation of God's glory and with the principle that 'like knows like'.

4.1. *The Old Testament and the rationale of world-Creation*

The Old Testament insists that a man's understanding of human actions (his own actions and other people's actions) is grossly inadequate for understanding divine actions.[2] Hence the beginning of human wisdom in such things is 'the fear of the Lord',[3] which includes the admission that one can not 'find out the deep things of God'[4] unless He reveals Himself. If a man has some glimmer of understanding, this brings him only to the 'outskirts of His ways'.[5] When an Israelite contemplated the vastness and complexity of the universe, it seemed to him that the divine wisdom—the meaning and purpose of world-Creation[6]—must be without measure[7] and unsearchable;[8] the rationale of God's action is beyond human understanding.

It is true that the prophets were able to discern some of the secret purposes[9] of God in His historical dealings with men. They 'overheard' what God said to the heavenly council[10] or

---

[1] See chapter 2, section 5.
[2] Isa. 29.14 (also 28.21, 29); 55.8-9; cf. I Cor. 1.18-2.16.
[3] Job 28.28; cf. Prov. 1.7; 9.10; Ps. 111.10.
[4] Job 11.7; cf. I Cor. 2.9-10.   [5] Job 26.14.
[6] Prov. 3.19; cf. C. H. Dodd, *The Interpretation of the Fourth Gospel*, pp. 274-8.
[7] Ps. 147.5.   [8] Job 11.7-8; 9.8-10; 38.4ff.   [9] Amos 3.7; cf. Ecclus. 49.25.
[10] Jer. 23.18; cf. Job 15.8; concerning this imagery of the council, see Job 1, Ps. 82.1; 89.7; cf. Gen. 1.26 and G. von Rad, *Genesis, A Commentary*, p. 57.

they were drawn into the personal intimacy of friendship with God,[1] and so they came to know some of the divine mysteries. (The Hebrew word '*sod*'[2] refers sometimes to God's secret purposes or mysteries,[3] sometimes to the heavenly council, and sometimes to divine friendship.) But the ultimate purpose of world-Creation remained hidden; it would be revealed in the future, at the End.

World-Creation is the extreme case of an action whose rationale is obscure to men. Suppose that we construct an imaginary scale of human actions which starts with the obvious and ends with the enigmatic. We start with an action which I easily understand by comparison with my own actions, and move to an action which is so different from mine that I will not understand it at all unless the agent tells me what he intended —and even then his words scarcely help at all because I am so unlike him. Such a scale of human actions points toward the divine action in world-Creation.

Another scale of human actions would be in terms of the *technique* of actions rather than their *rationale*. We would start with men making wheels and gradually increase the technical complexity of human manufacturing until we get to computers and imaginary devices of the future. Such a scale would be largely inappropriate to the Old Testament problem concerning world-Creation. There, the perplexity arises mainly from the Agent's peculiar and profound way of interpreting His own actions rather than His esoteric technical skill—though the latter is not ignored.

(In any discussion of the relations between religion and science, it is useful to remember this distinction between rationale and technique—between the agent's reasons, purpose and onlook, and the causal means which he employs. We then realize that modern scientific discoveries of the (causal) 'secrets'

---

[1] Ps. 25.14; Job 29.4; Prov. 3.32.
[2] See R. E. Brown, 'The Pre-Christian Conception of Mystery', *The Catholic Biblical Quarterly*, Vol. XX, No. 4, pp. 417-21.
[3] The Greek word '*mysterion*' is not used in LXX to translate '*sod*', but in the New Testament its meaning is usually continuous with the meaning of '*sod*' in the Old Testament, where this is 'secret purpose'; see R. E. Brown, *op. cit.*, and 'The Semitic Background of the New Testament *Mysterion*', *Biblica*, Vol. 39, Fasc. 4, and Vol. 40, Fasc. 1. According to L. Bouyer, the word '*mysterion*' in Paul's writings means 'the secret of God's plan for the unfolding of the world's history' ('*Mysterion*', *Mystery and Mysticism, a Symposium*, no editor, Blackfriars, London, 1956, p. 21).

of nature shed little light on the mystery or rationale of God's creative action. It is true that modern science provides a way of 'thinking God's thoughts after Him', for presumably no human theory is news to God; and the modern sense of the *unlimited* possibility of further scientific discoveries, all of which are anticipated by God, does suggest the transcendence of God's scientific knowledge, which is unlimited. Such transcendence, however, is not of the sort which is stressed in the Old Testament. There, God the Creator is mysterious, not because He is a superscientist, but because His purpose, thought and intention are hidden from man and strange to man.)

4.2. *Jesus, the mystery of God*

In the New Testament, we find the claim that God's intention in creating the world has been revealed in Jesus. The apostles proclaim that Jesus is the mystery[1] of God, in whom the Creator's purpose has been revealed.[2] 'Mystery' is closely associated with 'wisdom':[3] as the 'wisdom of God',[4] Jesus shows men what God had in mind when He created the world. The Fourth Evangelist's description of Jesus as the 'word of God' includes a similar idea:[5] Jesus is not only the performative-causal instrument in world-Creation; he is also the meaning and purpose of this action. If we ask, 'What reason did God have for creating the world?' and 'How did God interpret His action of world-Creation?', the answer is to be seen in Jesus. Jesus reveals the intention and rationale of world-Creation, for he is God's 'mystery' and 'wisdom' and 'word'.

Let us examine the notion of 'mystery' more closely,[6] for it is central. The divine mystery is not like a human secret which, once divulged, is a secret no longer and becomes public

[1] Col. 2.2.

[2] Eph. 1.7-10; 3.3-12; cf. I Cor. 2.7-10; cf. E. F. Scott, *The New Testament Idea of Revelation*, London, 1935, pp. 150-1; cf. J. Armitage Robinson, *St Paul's Epistle to the Ephesians*, 2nd ed., London, 1922, pp. 79-81, 171.

[3] I Cor. 2.7 (cf. I Cor. 2.1, R.S.V. margin); Eph. 1.9; Col. 1.27-8; 2.2-3; cf. Wis. Sol. 6.22; 7.21; Ecclus. 4.18; 14.20-1; cf. D. Deden, 'Le "mystère" Paulinien', *Ephemerides Theologicae Lovanienses*, Vol. XIII, 1936, pp. 411-13.

[4] I Cor. 1.24.

[5] See C. H. Dodd, *The Interpretation of the Fourth Gospel*, pp. 274-8; cf. Wis. Sol. 9.1-2.

[6] This paragraph is based on I Cor. 2.6-16 (cf. 1.18-25). Cf. W. Stählin, *The Mystery of God*, tr. R. B. Hoyle, London, 1937, pp. 13-28; G. S. Hendry, 'Mystery', *A Theological Word Book of the Bible*, ed. A. Richardson, p. 156; E. F. Scott, *op. cit.*, pp. 147-51; A. Richardson, *An Introduction to the Theology of the New Testament*, pp. 58-60.

information. God's mystery is revealed in Jesus only to those who
share to some extent in his life and mind, being inspired by the
Spirit.[1] To others, who depend on ordinary human wisdom and
insight, it is unintelligible. The profound thoughts of God are
only understood by the Spirit of God, and by men who are
spiritually mature, having received the gift of the Spirit and of
divine wisdom.[2] St Paul quotes[3] Isaiah's question concerning
world-Creation: 'Who has known the mind of the Lord so as to
instruct Him?';[4] and he answers, 'We have the mind of Christ'.
Only those who are like-minded can understand the divine
mystery in world-Creation.

The mystery which has been revealed through Jesus is the
mystery of God's intention in creating the world: the inclusion
of the Gentiles in His salvation, reconciling them with the Jews
in Christ by means of the Cross;[5] and the unity of all things
under the authority of Jesus as representative man.[6] But this
divine intention also includes the glorification[7] of men through
Jesus, the bestowal of glory on those who respond to the Gospel.
This glory is a gift which requires an affinity with the Giver if it
is to be received and understood.[8] To know the mystery of
God is to know 'His glorious grace',[9] 'the unsearchable riches of
Christ',[10] 'the love of Christ';[11] it is to know 'Christ in you, the
hope of glory'.[12] Jesus is the mystery of God because He is the
expression of God's glory and the means by which this glory is
bestowed upon men. Thus we return to our earlier version of
'like knows like'.[13]

We now can see that world-Creation is mysterious in two
ways: (1) The rationale or intention of the action (the divine
reason and purpose and onlook) is not intelligible to men unless

---

1 The need for such inspiration in order to know a divine mystery is suggested in
Dan. 4.9 (cf. 2.27-8); Wis. Sol. 9.13-17 and 1 QH 12.11-13; concerning the Qumran
reference, see R. E. Brown, *The Catholic Biblical Quarterly*, October, 1958, p. 441,
and *Biblica*, Vol. 39, Fasc. 4, p. 438.

2 Cf. Eph. 1.9.   3 I Cor. 2.16.   4 Isa. 40.13.

5 Eph. 2.13-14; 3.3-7; Col. 1.26-7; Rom. 11.25; cf. I Cor. 1.18-24.

6 Eph. 1.7-10; cf. Col. 1.16, 27 and R. E. Brown, 'The Semitic Background of
the New Testament *Mysterion* (II)', *Biblica*, Vol. 40, Fasc. 1, 1959, pp. 76-7; cf.
Heb. 2.6-10; cf. Rom. 8.18-21.

7 I Cor. 2.7-9, 12, 14; Eph. 1.6-9 (cf. 3.8); Col. 1.27.   8 I Cor. 2.12, 14.

9 Eph. 1.6; cf. Wis. Sol. 2.22-3, where men's failure to know God's mysteries is
their failure to understand His purpose, which is to bestow spiritual blessings upon
them.

10 Eph. 3.8.   11 Eph. 3.19.   12 Col. 1.27.

13 Cf. section 3.2.3; cf. also p. 113 concerning the limitations of the theory that
only like knows like.

they become like-minded, for divine thoughts are remote from men. The wisdom of God is not to be comprehended by mere analogy with ordinary human wisdom. (2) The divine intention includes the revelation of glory and the bestowal of glory through Jesus. This is an action which is impressive and expressive, and so it is understood only by those who have some affinity with God because they have been transformed by God. The transfiguration of man is both a condition and a result of the total action in which God reveals His glory.

Note that a man's utterance concerning the rationale or the expressiveness of God's creative action is rapportive[1] and self-revealing, whether or not it is also self-involving (Commissive, Behabitive or expressive).

The two aspects of mystery—wisdom and glory—are similar in three respects. First, the necessary likeness in each case is brought about by the Spirit of God, to whom men freely respond. Second, the knowledge of God which is involved is the sort which I have called 'acquaintance'.[2] We now see that such knowledge depends on one's affinity and rapport with the Agent. In so far as a man's likeness to God depends on his responsiveness to the Spirit, he is responsible for his lack of knowledge of God's mystery. Third, the two aspects of mystery both have a threefold logical pattern. We have seen that 'glory' may refer to God's inner self which is revealed, or to the observables through which He reveals Himself, or to the response of man to this revelation. Similarly 'wisdom' in the New Testament[3] may refer to a divine attribute which is revealed,[4] or to Christ the concrete revelation,[5] or to the human ability which is both a condition and a result of this revelation.[6] This triadic pattern seems to me to be fundamental in the biblical conception of revelation.

---

[1] See chapter 2, section 5.   [2] See section 2.3.1.
[3] Cf. D. Deden, 'Le "mystère" Paulinien', *Ephemerides Theologicae Lovanienses*, Vol. XIII, 1936, pp. 412-13.
[4] Eph. 3.10-11.   [5] I Cor. 1.24.   [6] Eph. 1.8-9 (A.V. or N.E.B.).

6

CREATION AS A CAUSAL ACTION

WE HAVE seen that, in the biblical context, the utterance, 'God is the Creator of the world' is *self-involving*. It is a Behabitive-Commissive and expressive utterance, for I acknowledge the Creator as Lord, Appointer, Evaluator and Guarantor,[1] and I express an attitude to the Creator's glory, an attitude which includes both a feeling-Response and a way of life.[2] The utterance is self-involving because world-Creation is viewed as a performative action (command, appointment, evaluation, pledge) and an impressive-expressive action. We have also seen that, in the biblical context, the utterance is *rapportive*; that is, an understanding of the utterance requires a way of life and an inner personal nature which has a rapport and affinity with God. There are, we saw, two reasons why the utterance is rapportive. First, world-Creation has as its profound rationale the 'new creation' of man in the likeness of God, sharing in the divine love and unity and glory; the likeness to God is understood in so far as it is received. Second, world-Creation is an impressive-expressive action which requires an affinity with the Agent if it is to be understood.

Where a *human* action is performative (Exercitive, Verdictive or Commissive) and impressive-expressive, utterances in response to it are often self-involving; and where a human action has a profound rationale and where it is impressive-expressive, utterances which refer to it are often rapportive. It is usually possible, however, to abstract from an action a 'core' which is not Exercitive (etc.), not impressive-expressive, and not profound in its rationale. If I say, 'Jones moved his arm', or 'Jones moved the stick', my utterance is neither self-involving nor rapportive. His action may have been a performative

---

[1] Cf. chapter 4, section 2.5.   [2] Cf. chapter 5, section 1.2.

command and an impressive-expressive gesture, and it may
have had a profound rationale, but I can abstract a causal
'core' of action and refer solely to it.[1] When I do so, my utterance is not Commissive, Behabitive or expressive, and no
special affinity or rapport with Jones is required for anyone to
understand what is meant.

At first sight it would seem that world-Creation can be
treated in the same way. Surely it is a causal action which *also*,
according to the Bible, is Exercitive, impressive-expressive and
profound in rationale. Jones 'moves' his arm or a stick; in
doing this, perhaps he *also* appoints me and impresses me and
baffles me. Similarly, it would seem, God 'makes' me, and in
doing so he *also* appoints me and impresses me and baffles
me. Thus, just as a man may at first recognize only Jones'
movement, not recognizing its additional meaning, so a man
may at first recognize only God's causal action in Creation,
and report this in an utterance which is neither self-involving
nor rapportive. Later on, he might come to look on world-
Creation as an action which is Exercitive, impressive-expressive
and profound in rationale; and only then would his references
to Creation become self-involving and rapportive.

If one examines biblical references to Creation, however, this
simple comparison between human actions and divine actions
breaks down. Indeed, I shall show how the 'causal' language
concerning Creation can be interpreted in terms of parabolic
onlooks,[2] so that this language too is self-involving and rapportive. Comparisons which seem at first to be straight-forward
analogies between human and divine causality turn out to be
comparisons of attitudes, expressed in parabolic onlooks.

(I do not claim that a parabolic interpretation *must* be given,
though I shall try to show that it is plausible and feasible. My
analysis is admittedly a reinterpretation: it involves an explicit
repudiation of various cosmological beliefs which biblical
writers held, and it does not rule out the possibility of alternative
reinterpretations. In this chapter, even more than chapters

---

[1] Constatives concerning the 'causal' aspect of actions seem to be connected with
Verdictives in which responsibility is ascribed, delimited or disclaimed. I have not
tried to elucidate this connection, which may be important in a study of world-
Creation as an action. For an analysis of the relation between causality and
responsibility in everyday references to human actions, see H. L. A. Hart and
A. M. Honoré, *Causation in the Law*, ch. III.

[2] Cf. chapter 3, section 2.2.

4 and 5, the 'descriptions' of philosophical analysis depend on 'prescriptions' of theological interpretation.)

1. The structure of biblical parables

If anyone wishes to apply the term 'parable' to biblical language generally, or to the biblical conception of Creation in particular,[1] he needs first to make it clear what he intends to mean by 'parable'; for the word was used in the Bible generically,[2] to refer to a host of comparative, figurative or non-literal uses of language: proverbs, metaphors, similes, symbols, allegories, illustrations, analogical arguments, and so on. Thus to a say of a passage of scripture, 'This is a parable', is to convey no more than, 'This involves some sort of comparison or figurative speech'—unless we select certain parables which have distinctive features in common, and use these as models. This is what I propose to do. Parables are open to many different types of classification;[3] but I should like to focus attention mainly on the New Testament parables, and to divide parables into three sorts, of which the third is the most relevant to biblical ideas of Creation: (i) *Exemplary* parables are stories or enactments of human behaviour which provides an example of what to imitate or to avoid: the publican and the pharisee,[4] the house on the rock,[5] the rich fool,[6] the good Samaritan,[7] the poor man's ewe lamb,[8] and Jesus' washing of the disciples' feet.[9] (ii) *Interpretative* parables are stories or enactments of human behaviour which provides an interpretation of specific events (for example, the Crucifixion) or persons (for example, Jesus) in terms of specific divine activity: the wicked husbandmen,[10] the marriage feast,[11] Israel the vine,[12] Jesus' entry into

---

[1] Various Christian thinkers have recently used the term 'parable' in discussions of Creation: A. Richardson, *Genesis I-XI, Introduction and Commentary*, pp. 17-42; T. R. Miles, *Religion and the Scientific Outlook*, London, 1959, pp. 165-79; W. A. Whitehouse, *The Six Days of Creation*, London, 1961, pp. 6-9; I. M. Crombie, 'The Possibility of Theological Statements', *Faith and Logic* (ed. B. Mitchell, London, 1957), pp. 67-81. Crombie also considers Creation in terms of a modified version of the traditional doctrine of the 'analogy of being' (pp. 62-5).

[2] Cf. J. Jeremias, *The Parables of Jesus*, tr. S. Hooke, London, 1954, p. 17.

[3] Contrast the systems of classification in W. O. E. Oesterley, *The Gospel Parables in the Light of their Jewish Background*, London, 1936, pp. 4-16, and B. T. D. Smith, *The Parables of the Synoptic Gospels*, Cambridge, 1937, pp. 16-25.

[4] Luke 18.9-14.   [5] Matt 7.24-7.   [6] Luke 12.13-21.
[7] Luke 10.25-37.   [8] II Sam. 12.1-6.   [9] John 13.1-16.
[10] Mark 12.1-12.   [11] Matt. 22.1-10.   [12] Ps. 80.8-14.

Jerusalem,[1] the miracle of the loaves.[2] (iii) *Relational* parables are stories which represent more generally the relation between God and any men at any time: the prodigal son,[3] the lost sheep,[4] the talents,[5] the visitor at midnight,[6] the unforgiving servant,[7] the labourers in the vineyard,[8] the dutiful servant,[9] the sheep and the goats,[10] and Hosea's forgiveness of Gomer.[11]

Note that, although Interpretative parables differ from other parables in that they are to be *applied* to specific historical events or persons, they resemble other parables in that the parable-story itself need not be historical. For example, the Interpretative parable of the wicked husbandmen is applied to a series of historical events, culminating in the Crucifixion. It does matter whether or not the Crucifixion occurred. But it does not matter whether there ever were some husbandmen who killed the son of a vineyard-owner. And similarly it does not matter whether there ever was a good Samaritan who helped a wretched man on the road to Jericho (Exemplary parable) or a prodigal son who looked after pigs and then decided to return home (Relational parable). (In section 5 we shall see that if a Creation-story is a parable, this does not automatically detach it from history, for it may be an *Interpretative* parable which is applied to the *first* event in history. So we shall ask the question, '*Is* it an Interpretative parable?'; that is, 'Does it matter whether the world had a beginning, a first event, to which the parable specially applies?')

The three-fold division of parables is far from being absolute. Indeed, one should realize that many modern exegetes would tend to expand the list of Interpretative parables so as to include nearly all those which I have classified as 'Exemplary' and 'Relational'. But it is useful to isolate the Relational parable, as a class which is specially relevant to biblical ideas of Creation.

1.1. *Relational parables*

These parables usually contain four distinct assertions or assumptions: (a) Such-and-such is the sort of thing that men often do, or might on occasion do. For example, a father welcomes home his penitent prodigal son. (b) It is obvious in

---

[1] Matt. 21.1-11; cf. Zech. 9.9.   [2] Mark 8.1-20; John 6.1-58.
[3] Luke 15.11-32.   [4] Luke 15.3-7.   [5] Matt. 25.14-30.
[6] Luke 11.5-13.   [7] Matt. 18.23-35.   [8] Matt. 20.1-16.
[9] Luke 17.7-10.   [10] Matt. 25.31-46.   [11] Hos. 3.1.

what way the recipient of such human action would or should respond. (The son should trust in his father's forgiveness.) (c) Of course, God is very different from man; He is transcendent.[1] (d) But He is related to men in a way which is similar to (a); so it is clear what my attitude ought to be towards Him. (God 'welcomes home' penitent sinners, so I should trust in His forgiveness.)

Each parable has one main point, a practical message concerning what attitude or conduct is appropriate in relation to God. This means that one is not justified in drawing additional conclusions from the details of the parable, as if it were an allegory.[2] For example, the householder is reluctant to help the midnight visitor,[3] and the unjust judge is reluctant to help the importunate widow,[4] but this does not mean that God is reluctant to help men; each parable is a way of saying that God is of such a nature that confident and persistent prayer is appropriate.

Furthermore, since each parable has a single practical point, it needs to be interpreted in relation to other parables. As Austin Farrer has said,

'Every parable needs to be balanced by a different parable with a contrasting bias. The art of balancing parables is acquired in use by believers, without their being conscious of it. That they use such an art becomes evident as soon as we attempt to fix upon them all the apparent logical consequences from any single parable. They will then begin to pick and choose, admitting some consequences and refusing others: and if we ask them why, they will draw in further parables supporting what they allow, and hostile to what they reject.'[5]

This mutual restriction of parables is obvious when we set the parable of the prodigal son[6] alongside that of the marriage feast:[7] 'Count on God's acceptance' but 'Don't presume upon it'.

Relational and Interpretative parables tell us little directly

---

[1] This element will be examined in section 1.2.

[2] This logical feature is stressed, though in different ways, by three outstanding modern experts on the parables: A. Julicher, C. H. Dodd and J. Jeremias; see C. H. Dodd, *The Parables of the Kingdom*, London, 1935, and J. Jeremias, *The Parables of Jesus*. Cf. also A. Richardson, *Genesis I-XI, Introduction and Commentary*, p. 28.

[3] Luke 11.5-13.   [4] Luke 18.1-8.

[5] 'A Starting-Point for the Philosophical Examination of Theological Beliefs', *Faith and Logic*, ed. B. Mitchell, pp. 10-11.

[6] Luke 15.11-32.   [7] Matt. 22.1-10.

concerning the nature of God. Rather, we learn that if we look on God as such-and-such, our attitude and our correlative conduct will be appropriate in relation to Him. A parable provides a *metaphysical parabolic onlook*,[1] 'Look on God as *y*', in which one cannot specify the similarity between God and *y* except in terms of the appropriateness of similar attitudes. I accept the parable largely[2] on the authority of the religious writer or teacher, though the onlook is to some extent self-verifying[3] and may lead to experiences which seem to me to be confirmations of it. For example, if I accept the authority of Jesus as a religious teacher and look on God as a forgiving Father who welcomes his penitent son, my penitence will probably lead to an assurance that I have been forgiven and accepted at the very depths of my personality. It is clear that in so far as biblical passages are parables, they are not theoretical, descriptive or analogical; they are not impersonal, flat Constatives. To accept a parable is to *adopt an attitude*, an attitude by which one lives so as to be in rapport with God and thus be enabled to *understand* the parable better in one's own experience. That is, the language of parables is self-involving and rapportive.

1.2. *Transcendental parables*

We recall that the third logical feature of Relational parables is the assertion or assumption that God is transcendent, that He is very different from men. This element of transcendence raises a crucial problem: Can the divine transcendence be understood by means of *analogies* with human nature? Or can it only be understood by means of a comparison between God and man which is indirect—a *parabolic* comparison in terms of human attitudes?

It would be difficult to establish conclusively that, of all the many ways in which the Bible indicates God's transcendence, none provide a genuine analogy and all are parabolic. I am inclined to think that this is so, but here I shall merely show that *some* of these ways are parabolic, so that there is a class of parables (or images)[4] which can be called 'Transcendental'. We will then be in a position to examine causal language

---

[1] Cf. chapter 3, section 2.2.   [2] Largely, but not entirely; see pp. 226-7.
[3] Cf. chapter 3, section 2.4.
[4] I shall not make any distinction between Transcendental parables and Transcendental images.

concerning world-Creation with three classes of parable in mind: Interpretative, Relational and Transcendental. (Exemplary parables are presumably irrelevant.)

First let us consider the comparison between human and divine glory. In chapter 5, we saw that this comparison cannot be made without a reference to human attitudes, and that the distinctiveness of God's glory is understood only to the extent that one's attitudes (and way of life) are transformed so that one is in rapport with God. The transcendence of God's glory is indicated in terms of the *unlimited glorification* which is appropriate:

> 'Where shall we find strength to praise him? For he is greater than all his works. Terrible is the Lord and very great, and marvellous is his power. When you praise the Lord, exalt him as much as you can; for he will surpass even that. When you exalt him, put forth all your strength, and do not grow weary, for you cannot praise him enough.'[1]

In chapter 4 we compared God and man in terms of authority and faithfulness: God is like a king or lord in His authority over men, but His authority is transcendent in that He requires *unlimited submission*. God is like a husband or friend in His faithfulness to men, but His faithfulness is transcendent in that an *unlimited trust* is appropriate. (It could also be argued that, in so far as God's eternity consists in His unchangeableness, it is an extension of the biblical idea of divine faithfulness.)[2] Here too the idea of divine transcendence is parabolic rather than analogical.

Biblical language concerning spatial transcendence[3] is also parabolic, at least for the modern interpreter. God is depicted as a being whose appearance resembles that of a man;[4] but His place of residence is in the immense and inaccessible sky, and His size is beyond human measure. However literally biblical men understood these ideas of divine transcendence, they character-

---

[1] Ecclus. 43.28-30.
[2] Biblical references to God's 'unchangeableness' are characteristically connected with His unchanging self-commitment or faithfulness to men: Mal. 3.6; Heb. 6.17-18; Ps. 102.25-7; Dan. 6.26-7; Deut. 33.27; cf. L. Koehler, *Old Testament Theology*, p. 21, concerning Isa. 31.3; Num. 23.19; Mal. 3.6. Cf. Isa. 26.3-4; 40.6-8, 28-31.
[3] *E.g.*, Ps. 2.4; 14.2; 113.5; 123; 145.3; Isa. 40.12; 57.15; 66.1-2; I Kings 8.27.
[4] Concerning biblical anthropomorphism, see W. Vischer, 'Words and the Word', *Interpretation*, 1949, pp. 1ff.; F. Michaeli, *Dieu à l'Image de l'Homme*.

istically occurred in the context of worship (praise[1] or supplication[2]) and their point was attitudinal. For modern believers, this 'greatness' of God is expressed in a parabolic onlook; if one imagines a human giant in the sky, one does not have an analogy for God; but one does have an image which, together with many other images, enables one to have an attitude to God which is appropriate: *unlimited awe*.

For a modern interpreter, the main biblical passages[3] which indicate divine *omnipresence* and *omniscience* would probably be parabolic rather than analogical; for these passages do not suggest a general theory or a straightforward analogy concerning divine attributes. Rather, their point is as follows: I cannot conceal myself or my thoughts from God; I ought to live as if He were a hidden man who constantly followed me, watching all that I do, overhearing even my secret thoughts. I cannot describe the transcendent way in which God is *present* or *knows*, but this imagery helps me to adopt an attitude towards Him which is appropriate: an *unlimited openness*.

These varied examples of transcendental imagery show that there is a class of parables which may be called 'Transcendental'. Thus parables can be distinguished into four classes:

(1) Exemplary (for example, the good Samaritan).
(2) Relational (for example, the prodigal son).
(3) Interpretative (for example, the wicked husbandmen).
(4) Transcendental (for example, the giant man in the sky).

Note that a parabolic interpretation of divine transcendence is very different from philosophical or mystical interpretations which oblige us to replace anthropomorphic religious language by non-personal language (for example, 'the ground of being') in order to express the difference between God and man. In a parabolic interpretation, I look on God as a *personal* being, and I speak of His 'glory', 'authority', 'faithfulness', 'greatness', 'presence', and 'knowledge'. God does differ from man in two ways, neither of which place him 'beyond' personality: (a) He is not identified by reference to a particular physical body; anthropomorphic talk about God's bodily parts and His spatial location is parabolic, not literal. (b) He is not only a metaphysical being, like the soul of man: He is a transcendent

---

[1] *E.g.*, Ps. 145.3.   [2] *E.g.*, Ps. 123.
[3] Ps. 139.1-12; Jer. 23.23-4; Prov. 15.3; I Sam. 2.3; Amos 9.2-3.

being. That is, He resembles the soul of man in that He can only be described indirectly in attitudinal terms; but He differs from the soul of man in that the attitude which is appropriate to Him is worship, which is an *unlimited* acknowledgment of personal qualities (glory, authority, faithfulness, etc.). The differences between God and man do not make God impersonal. Divine transcendence can be expressed in anthropomorphic language, provided that this language is interpreted parabolically, attitudinally.[1]

It is important to realize that both God and the human soul are metaphysical entities; that is, they are beings that can only be described in terms of human attitudes which are believed to be appropriate. The appropriate attitude towards God is worship, which is unlimited glorification, submission, trust, awe and openness. It is inappropriate—indeed it is idolatrous—to worship a man (unless he is divine); in relation to men, one's glorification, submission, trust, awe and openness must be limited. A Christian would claim that the appropriate metaphysical attitude towards men is '*agapē*', since men are 'persons' who have 'souls'.[2]

In short, God, like the soul of man, is a metaphysical entity; and, unlike the soul of man, He is also a transcendental entity. All biblical parables concerning God, whether these be Transcendental, Relational or Interpretative, express metaphysical parabolic onlooks; but some—that is, Transcendental parables —express onlooks which are also transcendental, unlimited.

We have been considering Transcendental parables and divine transcendence. Let us digress for a moment so as to clarify one important feature of all biblical parables concerning God, in so far as they are *metaphysical*: the reference to *observables*. For, on the one hand, when I look on God, as y, I can only specify the similarity between God and y attitudinally; I believe or hope that God is *such that* the attitude which is appropriate towards Him is similar to the attitude which is appropriate

---

[1] For a philosophical defence of biblical anthropomorphism, see E. LaB. Cherbonnier, 'The Logic of Biblical Anthropomorphism', *The Harvard Theological Review*, July, 1962. Cherbonnier, however, does not seem to see any need for a non-literal interpretation of the anthropomorphic language. Perhaps some Transcendental parables were once literal comparisons as well as parables (for example, 'God is great'); but the modern interpreter needs to discard the literal comparison so that he retains only the attitudinal, parabolic meaning. Cf. pp. 229, 232, n. 1, 241.

[2] Cf. pp. 134-5.

towards *y*. On the other hand, parables concerning God are also connected with *observables*: natural phenomena, historical events, people. Each biblical onlook can usually be expressed in two alternative ways:

(a) I look on the hidden, metaphysical God as such-and-such, in relation to these observables.
(b) I look on these observables as such-and-such, in relation to the hidden, metaphysical God.

For example:

(a) 'I look on God as a self-involving "speaker" and a self-revealing "artist" in relation to the stars.'
(b) 'I look on the stars as the "pledge" and "self-expression" of God.'

The observables may provide a minimal *basis* for the particular biblical onlook, though a different onlook is quite reasonable. For example, we have seen that the regularity and beauty of the stars make it plausible, though not obviously necessary, to look on the stars as God's pledge and self-expression, and to look on God as a self-involving 'speaker' and a self-revealing 'artist'. The onlook includes a Verdictive judgment: certain observables (the stars) are similar to the observables which human beings use for communication (utterances, paintings). No direct similarity between God and man is alleged in the onlook, but a similarity of observables in divine and human actions is alleged. That is, even though a biblical onlook is purely metaphysical in its reference to God, this does not rule out an appeal to observables as a minimal rational basis for the onlook. An appeal to the authority of a religious teacher or writer is primary, however. There are two reasons for this: (i) The metaphysical reference cannot be checked by me. I am not in a position to make a direct comparison between God and anything else; but someone else may be. (ii) The Verdictive judgment in the onlook is at best plausible; other judgments and onlooks are reasonable. If there is a divine onlook, I am not in a position to claim knowledge of it myself; but someone else may be.

In the concluding sections of the book[1] we shall again consider the relation between religious onlooks and religious authority. Here, however, let us set aside such questions. Our

---

[1] *Some Further Problems*, sections 1 and 3.

immediate task is to consider various sorts of causal language which are applied to Creation in the Bible.

2. *'Causal' parables of Creation*

Some of this causal language is *obviously* parabolic.

2.1. *The parable of the potter*

In the Bible, the relation between God the Creator and individual men is compared to the relation between a potter and a pot (or the potter's clay). It is assumed that these relations are in some way similar, and various aspects of the relation between potter and pot are then pointed out so as to suggest that an attitude of humility is appropriate towards the Creator: the potter has the right to decide the shape and the use of the earthen vessel which he is making: so men should submit to God's dealings with them as He shapes and uses them.[1] The potter knows every detail of the pot as he makes it, whereas it knows nothing; so men should not foolishly attempt to keep secrets from God or presumptuously set their paltry wisdom against His.[2] The potter knows what is best for the pot; so men should seek to understand God's will for them.[3]

This comparison between God-and-man and potter-and-pot indicates a relation between God and man, alongside the relation of father to prodigal son, master to servant, or householder to steward. But the parable is not only Relational; it is also Transcendental. For usually in the story of a Relational parable the recipient of activity is a human being—a son, a servant or a steward. But here the recipient is a pot, and it is the imagined 'attitude' of a pot to its potter which provides the model for a proper human attitude to God. The parable thus indicates divine transcendence as it also indicates a relation between God and man. Both the transcendence and the relation are indicated in terms of appropriateness of attitudes.

The parable of the potter has given rise to serious difficulties. For a pot has no freedom and no rights; it would seem to follow from this that a man has no freedom and no rights. But these difficulties disappear if we interpret the potter-idea as a parable rather than an analogy or an allegory. For then we will refuse

---

[1] Isa. 45.9-12; Rom. 9.19-22; Ecclus. 33.10ff; Wis. Sol. 15.7-8.
[2] Isa. 29.15-16; Jer. 18.1-12 (R.S.V.); Ps. 94.9; Ps. 139.1-18; Heb. 4.13.
[3] Ps. 119.73.

to go beyond the practical message of the parable: humility is the appropriate attitude to the Creator. And we will balance this parable with other parables which counteract the unwelcome implications which it apparently has. For example, we will point out the parable in which man is created with a right to rule over the rest of nature as God's steward, so that man is *responsible* to God; and we will also refer to the parable in which man is created with the *free* choice of obeying or disobeying God's command not to eat from the sacred tree, so that man should not presume to attain divinity except by divine grace.

Was the parable of the potter ever a literal comparison? It is probable that, at an early time, the story in Genesis 2 of the 'forming' of the first man was understood literally, and also as a parable concerning the Creation of later men. For many modern Christians, however, this Genesis story is purely a parable, which depicts the relation of any man to God at any time.

Thus the utterances, 'Jones forms pots' and 'God forms men' may seem to be logically parallel, but they are not. The first utterance describes an action without including any performative or impressive-expressive element which might make it self-involving or any profound-rationale elements which might make it rapportive. In the biblical context, however, the second utterance is an expression of a parabolic onlook, and so it is self-involving; also, one comes to understand it as one lives according to it, and thus grows in rapport with God. The causal language seems to indicate a flat Constative which does not involve the speaker in any way; and it looks like an utterance which anyone can understand, regardless of personal attitude or mode of life; but it is actually both self-involving and rapportive.

In the Bible, the imagery of human handiwork is applied not only to the Creation of man but also to the Creation of the earth,[1] the firmament[2] and the heavens.[3] God is like a human architect-builder,[4] who surveys the land, works out the dimensions and number of parts for a house, and builds it on firm foundations; but God's 'house' is the whole universe.[5] Here we

---

[1] Ps. 95.5.　　[2] Ps. 19.1.　　[3] Ps. 8.3; 102.25; Isa. 45.11-12.
[4] Job. 38.4-7; Isa. 40.12-14; Prov. 8.22-30; cf. Ps. 24.1-2; 119.90; cf. E. Jacob, *Theology of the Old Testament*, p. 136.
[5] Heb. 3.4.

have a Transcendental parable, which expresses a humble and worshipful way of looking on the vastness of the natural world.

'Who has measured the waters in the hollow of his hand and marked off the heavens with a span?'[1]

Like the talk about a potter and his pot, this is imagery, but not *mere* imagery; it is part of a parabolic onlook which is seriously adopted and lived.

2.2. *The parable of the victor*

In Old Testament thought, the idea of world-Creation, like the idea of Israel's creation, was connected with an alleged historical event which involved a *victory*.[2]

The Israelite had cosmological beliefs which he shared with his pagan contemporaries.[3] For him, the sky was a solid firmament, holding back a vast deep of waters which, like the earthly seas, menaced human life unless they remained in their place. He also believed that there was an underworld of darkness, Sheol, the gloomy abode of departed spirits; this too was a threat to human life. In Old Testament references to world-Creation we find this cosmology read back to the beginning of the world, as a cosmogony.[4] It is questionable whether any culture understood the cosmology except in relation to a cosmogony of some sort; the Israelites, however, gave the cosmology-cosmogony a distinctive theological interpretation. God had created the protective firmament and had divided the earthly waters into seas which are separated from the dry land; the firmament and sea-shore are God's barriers against the menace of the waters.[5] And God had created light, separating it from the darkness which might otherwise have merged chaotically with it.[6] (Darkness was not thought to be the mere absence of light.[7]) Just as the Exodus-victory over Pharaoh initiated Israel's history, so world-Creation was God's initial victory in world

---

[1] Isa. 40.12.

[2] Concerning Creation as victory, see G. A. F. Knight, *A Christian Theology of the Old Testament*, ch. 10; G. von Rad, *Genesis, A Commentary*, pp. 48-52; B. S. Childs, *Myth and Reality in the Old Testament*, London, 1960, pp. 30-42; K. Barth, *Church Dogmatics*, III, 1, pp. 95-150; G. C. Berkouwer, *The Triumph of Grace in the Theology of Karl Barth*, London, 1956, ch. III; L. Koehler, *Old Testament Theology*, pp. 88-90.

[3] Cf. E. Jacob, *op. cit.*, pp. 144-6; cf. E. C. Rust, *Nature and Man in Biblical Thought*, London, 1953, pp. 45-7.

[4] Gen. 1.1-9; Ps. 104.5-9; Ps. 24.1-2; Ps. 136.6; cf. Gen. 49.25; Exod. 20.4.

[5] Ps. 104.6-9; Jer. 5.22; Job 38.8-11; cf. Job 7.12; 9.8.

[6] Gen. 1.3-4.   [7] Cf. B. S. Childs, *op. cit.*, p. 33.

history. And just as Pharaoh and the Reed Sea came to be interpreted as symbols of a hidden cosmic power which threatened
Israel,[1] so the cosmic sea and darkness were not only physical
realities, but also symbols of hidden forces which threaten
mankind. The *sea* was associated with a mythological sea-
monster (the Babylonian 'Tiamat') against whom God fought
in the act of world-Creation, which was a battle between the
power of order and the power of chaos.[2] The protective firmament was not only a physical reality but also a symbol of God's
continued protection against the chaos which menaces mankind. The *darkness* represented death, disaster and evil in
general;[3] unless darkness is kept clearly separate from light—
in reality and in the mind—spiritual chaos results.[4] God had
separated light from darkness, but Sheol remained an enemy to
be overcome,[5] and the New Testament refers to a 'power of
darkness'[6] which opposes God's purposes for man. Darkness
and light, like the sea and the firmament, are thus not only
physical realities but also symbols of chaos.

The waters and the darkness, and the chaos which these
symbolize, were not annihilated by God. According to the
Bible, they continue to exist, menacing human existence.[7]
Indeed, it is probable that the existence of chaos 'in the
beginning' was read back from the Israelites' contemporary
experience of spiritual threat or danger.[8] God would not win
completely over chaos until the end of the world, when He
will annihilate the sea[9] and the darkness.[10]

[1] Isa. 51.9 ('Rahab' is Egypt, see Isa. 30.7); Job. 26.12-13; Ps. 89.8-10; Ps.
74.12-14.
[2] Job 26.12-13; Ps. 74.12-17; Ps. 89.9-11; cf. Isa. 27.1; cf. Job 7.12; 9.8; cf. the
'deep' in Gen. 1.2. In Rev. 12.9, the Devil is identified with the sea-monster and
also with the serpent of Gen. 3.
[3] Job 18.18; 38.17; Ps. 49.19; 88.3-12; Isa. 45.7; 59.9; Amos 5.18-20; Matt. 8.12;
22.13; 25.30. For a study of 'darkness' as a symbol in relation to the sea and to
Creation, see K. Grayston, 'The Darkness of the Cosmic Sea', *Theology*, April, 1952.
[4] Job 17.12; Isa. 5.20; Job 10.22; Matt. 6.23; II Cor. 6.14-15; cf. K. Barth,
Church Dogmatics, III, 1, p. 127.
[5] Cf. G. B. Caird, *Principalities and Powers*, Oxford, 1956, p. 63.
[6] Col. 1.13; Luke 22.53; cf. Eph. 6.12; II Cor. 4.4; 6.14-15.
[7] Cf. G. A. F. Knight, *op. cit.*, pp. 114-16, 163; E. Jacob, *Theology of the Old
Testament*, p. 140; G. von Rad, *op. cit.*, p. 49; B. S. Childs, *op. cit.*, p. 42; L. Koehler,
Hebrew Man, tr. P. R. Ackroyd, London, 1956, pp. 127-8.
[8] The waters symbolize a spiritual threat to the individual (Ps. 69.1, 2, 14; 18.16;
46.3; 130.1) or men who are enemies (Ps. 88.17; 124.2-5; 144.7) or nations which
threaten Israel (Isa. 5.30; 8.6-8; 17.12-13; Jer. 6.23) and which come to be associated with the primal chaos (Jer. 4.23-9).
[9] Rev. 21.1; cf. the sea-monster in Isa. 27.1 and perhaps in Dan. 7.1-9.
[10] Isa. 60.19; Rev. 21.25; 22.5.

Here we have a literal story about darkness, light, sea, and perhaps a sea-monster, a story which indicates that man should have an attitude of confident optimism as he meets the threat of spiritual chaos: God has banished chaos to the outskirts of human life and He continues to protect man against it. In relation to modern science, the literal cosmology of the story is archaic and false: there is no inverted bell in the sky, holding back cosmic waters; there is no Sheol under the earth, and darkness is not a power or substance. But the story of Creation as victory need not be abandoned. It can be reinterpreted as a parable concerning the relation between God and man, like the parable of the prodigal son. Such a reinterpretation cannot purport to be a presentation of all that the biblical writers meant when they wrote about Creation as victory; it can only be an attempt to preserve the attitudinal significance of their story.[1] The factual story which suggests a religious attitude becomes a non-factual parable which expresses much the same attitude.

There are two main ways in which this story may be reinterpreted as a parable. On the one hand, I may combine it with a non-literal but serious belief in the *Devil*, that is, with the parable of the Devil: I look on the evil within myself as a manifestation of a hidden, evil person. Then the story of Creation as victory can be combined with the story of a Devil so as to form a complex parable: The Devil has not been annihilated, but he has been excluded from the possibility of any ultimate triumph; so if I trust in God's protective power, I need not fear the power of the Devil.

On the other hand, I may interpret the story of Creation as victory in relation to the parable of Creation by the *performative* divine *word*. For if the 'threat' to human existence is not a hostile personal power but the absence of *meaning*—divinely-authorized meaning—for human existence, it is God's word

---

[1] Cf. G. Pidoux, 'Creation', *Vocabulary of the Bible*, ed., J.-J. von Allmen, p. 72: 'The significance of the Genesis creation-stories is to be seen not so much in the view of the world which lies behind them and which is peculiar to their own age . . . as in the religious attitude to which they bear witness.' This detachment of the religious from the cosmological produces a gap between biblical exegesis (what the Israelite writer meant at the time) and modern theology; consider, for example, D. W. Hay: 'If we desire to understand the Old Testament, we must not too quickly abstract the "theological concept" from its "cosmological vesture". For our own theology we shall in some degree have to turn this language into symbol, but in Scripture it is intended realistically.' ('Christianity and Cosmology', *The Canadian Journal of Theology*, October, 1959, p. 233.)

which overcomes this threat. On such an 'existential' interpretation of Creation, God rescues me from an existence which would be fundamentally meaningless: in such an existence my actions would have only an arbitrary, self-imposed meaning, my ultimate status and role would depend solely on my arbitrary choice, and my appraisal of human existence would have no authority except my own opinion. When God creates me, He has an authoritative onlook in which human actions have meaning,[1] He authoritatively prescribes my ultimate status[2] and role,[3] and He gives an authoritative verdict concerning the goodness of human existence.[4] Thus two ideas of Creation—as performative word and as victorious conflict—are combined: When God creates man, the performative force of His word overcomes the threat of meaninglessness which is represented by the sea and darkness. The stories of Creation by the performative word and by victorious conflict join to form a parable which expresses a way of looking on one's own existence. If I accept this parabolic onlook, it makes sense to try to *discover* the ultimate meaning of my actions and the ultimate status and role which have been in some way 'assigned' to me; and I can maintain a positive appraisal of human existence, in spite of all its ambiguity and evil. God protects me from the chaos of a meaningless life.

These two interpretations of Creation as victory are not incompatible; God may protect me against both the Devil and the chaos of a meaningless life. The second interpretation, however, is likely to find most favour with those for whom the idea of a Devil—even a parabolic Devil—is unacceptable. But in either case (and this is the main point), the story of Creation as victory has become part of a total complex parable. I accept the parable by adopting an attitude, and I understand it in so far as I live in accordance with it and thus grow in rapport with God. Though Creation is here described in 'causal' terms, as a successful battle, the language is self-involving and rapportive.

3. *The causal power of the Creative word*

In chapter 4 we saw that God's word of Creation has both performative force and causal power. We examined the

---

[1] Cf. chapter 3, section 2.4.   [2] Cf. chapter 4, section 2.1.
[3] Cf. chapter 4, section 2.2.   [4] Cf. chapter 4, section 2.3.

performative or institutional element and found that, in so far as the Creator is Lord, Appointer, Evaluator and Guarantor, human language concerning Him is self-involving—in the biblical context. We set aside the causal element for consideration in this chapter. Our first step is to show how it is related to the ideas of 'creatio ex nihilo' and 'dependence-for-existence'

According to Gen. 2.7 God moulded man out of dust; but when He said, (Gen. 1.3), 'Let there be light' and there was light, there is no indication that He created light out of anything. Creation by the word is not merely a way of causing something to exist in a new way; there need not be any pre-existing matter on which a form is imposed, or in which a change is produced. Creation by the word is a way of causing something to exist which otherwise would not exist at all.[1] Thus when the idea of Creation by the word was combined with the biblical insistence on God as the Creator of all[2] things, the theological slogan creatio ex nihilo eventually[3] arose. This is best interpreted as, 'Creation of everything, but not out of anything'.

This slogan has had various uses in Christian writings. It has been used in attacks on world-views which are radically dualistic—views in which God is opposed by something uncreated and recalcitrant (matter, flesh or devil) out of which, or in spite of which, He creates the cosmos. (This anti-dualistic implication raises difficulties for the parable of Creation as victory; we shall consider this later.) Creatio ex nihilo has also been used so as to rule out monistic theories in which the world is created out of God Himself—theories which make the world a part of God, or make it ontologically continuous with Him.[4]

---

[1] An exception to this is Heb. 11.3, as it appears in a typical modern translation (R.S.V.): 'By faith we understand that the world was created by the word of God, so that what is seen was made out of things which do not appear.' For two contrasting interpretations of this passage, see Th. H. Robinson, Commentary on Hebrews, pp. 155-6, and J. Moffatt, Commentary on Hebrews, Edinburgh, 1924, p. 162. Usually, however, when the Bible refers to Creation by the word, there is no hint of Creation out of anything; and my point is that there need not be, logically.

[2] Heb. 3.4; cf. Exod. 20.11; Neh. 9.6; Ps. 146.6; Jer. 10.16; Acts 4.24; 14.15; Rev. 10.6; 14.7.

[3] It is not clear just when this happened. The phrase, 'creation out of nothing' appears in II Macc. 7.28, but A. Ehrhardt argues that its meaning here is derived, not from Jewish theology of Creation, but from a tradition in Greek philosophy which stressed the unreality and transience of the observable world ('Creatio ex nihilo', Studia Theologica, Vol. IV, Fasc. I-II, 1951-2, pp. 22-8).

[4] The use of creatio ex nihilo to combat both dualism and monism is discussed by E. L. Mascall, Via Media, London, 1956, ch. 1, and L. Gilkey, Maker of Heaven and Earth, New York, 1959, chs. I, II.

What I wish to stress here, however, is the intimate connection between *creatio ex nihilo*, the causal aspect of Creation by the word, and ideas of *dependence for existence*. Creation by the word is not the source of the world's structure (except, of course, the institutional structure brought about by performative force rather than causal power), and it is not the source of changes within the world; Creation by the word is connected with the sheer *existence* of anything and everything. Even Karl Barth admits[1] that some such ideas are included or implied in the biblical conception of Creation; his protest against non-biblical conceptions of Creation is directed mainly[2] against their failure to link dependence-for-existence with Creation-by-the-word, so as to include what I have called the 'performative' aspects of the biblical conception.

We should realize that the notion of sheer existence is an abstraction from biblical thought. If we strip from the idea of 'existence' all institutional elements (existence with a status and role) and impressive-expressive elements (existence as a revelation of God's glory) and mysterious elements (existence having a meaning in terms of God's mysterious purpose), we have made a distinction which was not explicit in the Bible when it was written. Moreover, the causal element in Creation-by-the-word is not introduced in the Bible in isolation from the institutional elements. The Bible does not separate man's dependence on God's word of magic *power* for his sheer existence from man's dependence on God's word of *command* for his ultimate role in the world,[3] or from man's dependence on God's word of *promise* for his ultimate security in the world.[4] Nevertheless the notions of *creatio ex nihilo* and dependence-for-existence provide an essential element in the biblical conception of Creation as we understand it today.

Divine *creatio ex nihilo* involves bringing things into existence. Is there any imaginable human analogy to this? Imagine a vacuum in a bottle, in which a bird suddenly appears when Jones says, 'One bird, please'. Let us suppose that we can prove that the bird, and the matter of which it consists, did not exist before, so that there has been an increase in the total

---

[1] *Church Dogmatics*, III, 1, p. 44.
[2] Mainly, but not entirely: he also wishes to maintain that Creation was an event *in* time, at the beginning (*Church Dogmatics*, III, 1, pp. 14-15, 42-9, 59-94).
[3] Gen. 1.26.   [4] Ps. 33.4-9; 119.88-91.

amount of matter (or energy) in the universe. Let us suppose that Jones demonstrates his ability to create birds by repeating his feat again and again. Surely we would say, 'Jones creates birds out of nothing'. The phrase 'out of' would be used merely to signify *temporal* order; if this seems too odd a use, we could say, 'Jones creates birds, and does not create them out of anything'. Of course, we would not know how Jones could do this, and all this is in the realm of fantasy rather than fact. But the idea of *creatio ex nihilo* is intelligible. Indeed, it is not non-sensical to say that modern science might one day discover a way of verifying the serious hypothesis that hydrogen atoms continually come into existence in the universe (according to a 'continuous creation' theory). Moreover, we would be sur-prised, but not conceptually bewildered, if a scientist claimed that he had developed a laboratory method for bringing additional matter-or-energy into existence. Finally, there is the fanciful hypothesis that some men have powers of psycho-kinesis which go beyond the mere control of dice: they can create atoms at will! If someone suggested that we try to test this hypothesis, his proposal would be dismissed by everyone. But this would be because human creation *ex nihilo* by psychic power is so improbable; it would not be because it is an unintell-igible notion. Similarly the suggestion that some men can annihilate atoms by psychic power is fantastic rather than incomprehensible. I am not suggesting that any human beings actually possess such powers. This is irrelevant. All that I wish to maintain is that such powers are conceivable, and that we thus seem to have an analogy with divine Creation *ex nihilo*.

The analogy breaks down, however, when we examine it further. We must remember that divine Creation *ex nihilo* is Creation of *all* things; for this produces conceptual difficulties which do not arise for imaginary human acts of creation or annihilation. Since divine Creation *ex nihilo* is Creation of all things, there *was* nothing at all except God before world-Creation, and there *would be* nothing at all except God if God annihilated the world. If we imagine human acts of creation or annihilation, we assume the prior existence of an observable context in which the change (more atoms or less atoms) takes place; we assume the existence of a human observer of this change; and we assume a temporal succession: first there is one state of affairs, and then there is another. But the idea of divine Creation or annihilation of all things allows no such observable context and no such observer; and it raises classical problems concerning Creation and temporal succession: Can we speak intelligibly of a time 'before' the world began? Does it make sense to speak of God existing 'before' or 'after' the world?

Some theologians deny that we can speak of temporal succession unless there already *is* a world, since God is 'outside' time. According to a traditional interpretation of divine 'eternity', God created (or creates) the world *with* time, but He Himself is *outside* time; hence temporal predicates apply to God only metaphorically. If the world had a beginning in time this was also a beginning *of* time; God did not exist 'before' this beginning, for the begining of the world was the beginning of time. If, on the other hand, the world has always existed, this infinite duration of the world's existence in time does not in any way rival God's eternity, for God is categorically 'outside' time, like a mathematical entity.

Such an interpretation of divine eternity assumes that whereas it makes no literal sense to speak of God existing 'before' the world, since temporal predicates cannot be applied to God, it does make literal sense to speak of God existing 'outside' time (or in the so-called 'standing now'). It seems to me that this assumption is untenable, though I cannot provide an adequate criticism here. Any attempt to give positive content to the assertion that temporal predicates are inapplicable to God must involve picture-language which is just as anthropomorphic as talk about God existing 'before' the world: we imagine (or try to imagine) a man-like being who never changes, and who sees the past, present and future of the world spread out before him. This is a picture rather than an analogy, but it is not merely a picture: it is a parable with an attitudinal point, suggesting the supreme reliability and wisdom of Him in whom men put their trust. (This parable is connected with various ideas of *continuous* dependence-for-existence which we shall soon consider, in section 4.) But the main point here is that *creatio ex nihilo* also depends on a picture which is a parable: we imagine a man-like being who is all by himself; he utters a word of magic power and *then* he is surrounded by various creatures. The temporal *succession* is not meant literally.

What about the temporal *beginning* of the world? Is this a literal, factual core for the parable of *creatio ex nihilo*? Is the parable Interpretative rather than Relational: is it an interpretation of a first *event* in world-history? Does it matter, in the biblical conception of Creation, whether or not the world actually had a beginning? This will be the issue, later on, in section 5. Here we should note that the idea of Creation as a bare bringing-into-existence has only a limited religious relevance, except in so far as it does suggest a beginning of world-history. For let us imagine an invisible agent who could bring atoms into existence and who could also annihilate them; let us extend the agent's power so that it covers stones and people and all things. Would this be a divine being, inherently worthy of worship? Only, it seems to me, if this Creator differs from His creatures in some additional ways. In particular, He must differ in that He does not depend on any other agent for His own existence. Nowhere is it explicitly affirmed in the Bible that God differs from creatures in this way, but the absence of any theogony suggests that it was assumed to be obvious, so obvious that it need not even be mentioned.[1]

But let us turn to consider creaturely dependence-for-existence, not in terms of God's *bringing* creatures into existence, but in terms of His *sustaining* them in existence.

4. *Continuous Creation*

When a Christian says that he depends on God for his very existence ('In him we exist')[2] he does not mean that new matter or energy came into existence at the moment of his conception; no verifiable (and miraculous) event is being reported. He wants to say that he depends on God for his existence continuously, so that his creation is not a temporal change from nothing into something, but a continuous relation. He may also believe that God could annihilate him at any time. But we should not make the mistake of thinking that this power to annihilate is the same thing as a continuous causing-to-exist. Consider a

---

[1] Cf. Th. C. Vriezen, *An Outline of Old Testament Theology*, p. 181; F. Michaeli, *Dieu à l'Image de l'Homme*, p. 137; E. Jacob, *Theology of the Old Testament*, pp. 38, 138.
[2] Acts 17.27 (N.E.B.); cf. B. Gärtner, *The Areopagus Speech and Natural Revelation*, pp. 188, 196.

fanciful example: Suppose I say, 'The Queen created a man *ex nihilo*, bringing new matter into existence, and she has the power to annihilate him'. This statement would not entail the statement, 'The Queen continuously sustains him in existence'. Nor would it show what is meant by 'sustaining in existence'. Indeed, what *can* this mean, and what can 'continual dependence' or 'continual causing-to-exist' mean, when we are not referring to a change from nothing into something or from something into nothing? The same problem arises if we consider, not the existence of a particular man, but the existence of the world. Suppose that we consider the idea that only God existed 'before' world-Creation and that nothing at all except God would exist if He were to annihilate the world. This idea by itself does not provide a meaning for the notion that the world is 'continuously sustained in existence' by God.

Indeed, the idea of continuous dependence-for-existence does not arise from analogies between divine and human *creation* at all; for creation is a change, not a relation. What we have instead are parables; we have images of continuous dependence which indicate appropriate human attitudes towards God. In Thomist philosophy, we have the image of the earth being continually illuminated by the sun.[1] In the Bible, there is the image of a man being held up continuously by someone who supports him from below: 'Underneath are the everlasting arms'.[2] Most important of all is the biblical idea that, just as man's life is continuously dependent on the presence of air, so it is continuously dependent on the presence of God's Spirit.[3] In the Bible, however, this is no mere comparison. There, either the breath or wind which sustains life *is* God's Spirit, or it is imparted and withdrawn by the *power* of God's Spirit. We should realize that breath or wind is also an image of non-physical action, an image of spiritual transformation.[4] But men believed, quite literally, that the breath which distinguishes a man from a stone or a corpse comes continually from a hidden divine power. Such dependence on God is not the same thing as the dependence of both animate and *in*animate creatures on God for their very existence. So at best we have

---

[1] *E.g.*, A. D. Sertillanges, *L'Idée de Création et ses retentissements en philosophie*, Paris, 1945, p. 70.
[2] Deut. 33.27.   [3] Cf. chapter 4, section 3.2.   [4] *E.g.*, John 3.8.

here only an analogy to dependence-for-existence: as men depend on God's breath for their life, so men depend on God's Creative action for their very existence. Moreover, it seems to me that modern believers should reinterpret the 'breath of God' as a parable. If it is interpreted in terms of an intervening hidden power which is the special cause of life, one would have to maintain that science will never be able to explain biological life and death without having to postulate the literal 'action' of a hidden divine power. Such a 'God of the gaps'[1] in scientific explanation shrinks as science continually falsifies the claims which are made on His behalf.

What then would a parabolic interpretation be? On such an interpretation God is compared to an imaginary person from whom comes the air which I must breathe in order to live. Even when I am not aware of any divine presence, I depend on Him for my very existence. This sustaining power of God is to be interpreted in attitudinal terms: the appropriate attitude towards God is an unlimited adherence and reliance. To accept this parable (or the parable of the sun's illumination or the parable of the everlasting arms) is to take up an attitude, a parabolic onlook. The parable is both Relational (God and man in continuous relation) and Transcendental (*unlimited* adherence and reliance is appropriate). As one lives by the parable, one gains understanding of its meaning, for one is in rapport with God.

Man is not alone in being dependent on God, according to the Bible. *Animals* depend on God's breath[2] and His provision of food[3] for their animate existence. God is the hidden rain-maker,[4] without whom there would be no *plant life*. He also has stabilized the *earth* by building it on strong foundations.[5] In Nehemiah 9.6 God's preservation of *all things* is even described as a giving of *life*. (This may reflect a primitive view of nature in which life is attributed to inanimate objects.)[6] All these ideas of dependence on God were probably understood quite literally,

---

[1] C. A. Coulson, *Science and Christian Belief*, London (Fontana), 1958, p. 32.
[2] Ps. 104.29-30.   [3] Ps. 104.14, 27; 136.25; 145.15-16; 147.9; Job 38.39-41.
[4] Gen. 2.5-6; Deut. 11.11-15; Ps. 147.8; Jer. 5.24; 10.13; Acts 14.17; Jubilees 12.4; cf. Luke 12.22-31.
[5] Ps. 104.5; 119.90; cf. Isa. 48.13; Ps. 24.2; 102.25; Job 38.4-6.
[6] Concerning this view of nature, see H. Wh. Robinson, *Inspiration and Revelation in the Old Testament*, pp. 12-16. Robinson, however, seems to advocate a return to this primitive view.

though sometimes they were given a symbolic meaning as well. Some modern Christians may attempt to reinterpret these ideas in a quasi-literal way by claiming that (a) only God provides the answers to the gaps in scientific explanation which remain for biology, meteorology, and physics, and (b) the existence of a continuum from inanimate to animate nature confirms the animistic outlook of the ancient Hebrews. This seems to me to be a desperate expedient. It seems much more reasonable to reinterpret these ideas concerning animals, plant life and the earth as *parables* of continuous dependence-for-existence.

Note that the idea of continuous Creation, like the idea of *creatio ex nihilo*, is parabolic in so far as we talk about the divine *action*. The *result* of the action is describable in non-parabolic terms, for it is the sheer *existence* of anything and everything.

One important biblical idea should be mentioned in any discussion of continuous Creation: the idea that all *events* are God's *actions*.[1] This idea may seem to us to be very different from the idea that all things and persons are 'sustained' in existence, but the two ideas were very closely related in biblical thought. We have already seen in chapter 5[2] that God's glory and holiness are revealed in a continuous 'Creative' action through 'observables' which are *either* events or entities (things or persons). Consider also the words of Isa. 45.7:

'I form light and create darkness,
I make weal and create woe.'

The second clause seems to refer to events, like the passage in Amos 3.6:

'Does evil befall a city,
unless the Lord has done it?'

It is not possible here to discuss the theoretical and practical difficulties which arise if the utterance, 'All events are God's actions' is interpreted as a flat Constative—difficulties concerning human freedom and independence, divine responsibility for evil, the relation between theological and scientific explanations of natural events, etc. Here I shall merely state, dogmatically, that these difficulties can be overcome if we interpret the

[1] Concerning this idea in the Bible see H. Wheeler Robinson, *op. cit.*, pp. 1-47, 159; H. Knight, 'The Old Testament Conception of Miracle', *Scottish Journal of Theology*, December, 1952. W. Temple expounds the idea philosophically in *Nature, Man and God*, London, 1934, Lectures XI, XII.
[2] See especially section 2.1; also sections 1.1; 1.3; 2.3.2.

utterance as the expression of a parabolic onlook: A man *looks on* every event (whether it is scientifically explicable or not) *as* a divine action through which God may reveal Himself to him.[1] God reveals Himself more fully in some events than in others; for, according to the parable, He is like a man who reveals himself in all that he does, but who reveals himself more fully in some actions than in others.

To summarize: The idea of continuous Creation may be interpreted in two ways. First, there are various parables concerning the continuous dependence of all things and people on God for their very existence. Second, there is a parable concerning the continuous divine self-revelation in all events.

In section 3 we considered Creation as a bringing-into-existence, and we set aside questions concerning the beginning of the world. I tried to show that imaginary *human* acts of bringing-into-existence do provide an intelligible picture, but do not provide an analogy to divine *creatio ex nihilo* because they require a temporal sequence; the story of God existing 'prior' to the existence of all things and 'then' bringing them into existence is a parable. But this conclusion did not rule out the possibility of a world-beginning, and it raises the question: Does it matter, in the biblical conception of Creation, whether or not the world had a beginning?

5. *Creation as an event 'in the beginning'*

There is very little agreement among modern Christian theologians concerning the relation between world-beginning and world-Creation.[2] Indeed, there is so much disagreement that a philosophical analyst is likely to despair of saying anything definite or acceptable. The issue cannot be ignored here, however. There are two reasons for this.

---

[1] My interpretation here is fairly similar to that of R. Bultmann, *Jesus Christ and Mythology*, London, 1960, ch. 5; but here, as elsewhere, I would differ from his theological individualism and say, '*We* look on every event . . .'; see pp. 139, 159, n. 2, 196, n. 2.

[2] See, for example, A. D. Sertillanges, *L'Idée de Création et ses retentissements en philosophie*; K. Barth, *Church Dogmatics*, III, 1, pp. 14-15, 42-94; B. S. Childs, *Myth and Reality in the Old Testament*, London, 1960, pp. 72-82; L. Gilkey, *Maker of Heaven and Earth*, New York, 1959, ch. 9; E. L. Mascall, *Christian Theology and Natural Science*, London, 1956, chs. 3, 4; A. Richardson, *Genesis I-XI, Introduction and Commentary*, p. 45. Biblical theologians differ concerning the relation between time and eternity; contrast J. Marsh, *The Fulness of Time*, London, 1952, with O. Cullmann, *Christ and Time*, tr. F. V. Filson, London, 1951.

In the first place, we seem at last to have a striking exception to my parabolic account of world-Creation. If belief in world-Creation involves a belief that the world came into existence by divine agency at some time in the past, we seem at last to have isolated a hard core of alleged fact, an element in the biblical idea of world-Creation which is neither self-involving nor rapportive. Indeed, the alternative physical cosmologies of modern science seem to become highly relevant, for they differ concerning an alleged beginning of this universe. Also, we should admit that the average Christian layman and the average unbeliever both tend to think that someone who speaks about the Creation of the world is referring to a world-beginning: an event in the very distant past, it is true, but nevertheless an event. Belief in world-Creation seems to commit one to taking sides in the current scientific controversy about physical cosmologies:[1] If scientists go back far enough they will find a state of affairs which is 'preceded', not by a primal atom which exploded, but by *nothing at all*—nothing at all, that is, except a hidden spiritual power who is beyond the reach of scientific investigation but whose existence is thus indicated by such investigation. Science will thus force us to infer the existence of a divine Creator who brought the world into existence.

Such a scientific 'discovery', however, is extremely unlikely. Two objections may be made. On the one hand, it is doubtful[2] whether there could be scientific evidence which showed that the universe had a beginning, though there might be scientific evidence which showed that some process *within* the universe had a beginning (for example, the expansion of this universe from a primal atom). On the other hand, even if such evidence were possible, and scientists came to believe that the universe began to exist at time t^1, the inference to a hidden Creator-God would not have become scientifically obligatory. The non-believer could look on the origin of the world at time t^1 as a brute fact which requires no supernatural explanation; the cosmological argument for the existence of a Creator-God would not suddenly have become irrefutable. As E. L. Mascall

[1] The controversy is clearly outlined by E. L. Mascall, *Christian Theology and Natural Science*, ch. 4; Mascall does not think it is relevant to belief in God the Creator.

[2] See Michael Scriven, 'The Age of the Universe', *British Journal for the Philosophy of Science*, November, 1954, p. 182.

says, 'If we are *not* already convinced of God's perpetual activity, why is the first moment of the world's existence a sign of his activity *then*?'.[1]

Let us admit the force of Mascall's objection; a world-beginning *is* irrelevant to the cosmological argument for the existence of God. What is of interest to us, however, is the relevance of a world-beginning to those who already have a biblical faith in God the Creator. So let us suppose that the first objection can be met; that is, let us suppose that some scientist provides evidence which shows that there was indeed a world-beginning 'before' which there was nothing at all. Would such a discovery be relevant to a biblical conception of world-Creation?

This question brings me to my second reason for investigating the relation between world-beginning and world-Creation: *the relation is obviously important in the Bible*. Biblical writers repeatedly describe Creation as an event which happened 'in the beginning';[2] world-history began with the divine action of Creation. 'Before' this first event in world-history, God had decided what would be the intention or purpose of His action; according to the New Testament, He planned to reveal and to bestow His glory on men through Jesus Christ.[3] After the first divine action, there occurred a series of divine actions, each one involving both a repetition and a genuinely-novel fulfilment of the previous actions.[4] In the End, the series will culminate in a divine action which will be both the complete revelation and the complete achievement of God's purpose for the whole series; thus the series will have an overall unity as a total divine action. The purpose of the first action, Creation, has gradually been revealed as it has been increasingly realized in the subsequent actions—in the Exodus, and in Jesus of Nazareth.[5] In the

---

[1] *Op. cit.*, p. 148 (his italics).

[2] Gen. 1.1; John 1.1; cf. Prov. 8.22-3; Matt. 13.35; 19.4, 8; Mark 13.19; Rom. 1.20; II Peter 3.4.

[3] Cf. chapter 5, section 4; cf. Matt. 25.34; John 17.5, 22, 24; I Cor. 2.7; Eph. 1.4; II Thess. 2.13; II Tim. 1.9; I Peter 1.20; Rev. 13.8; 17.8; cf. Rom. 8.19, 28-30.

[4] B. S. Childs (*op. cit.*, pp. 72-82), rejects the common claim that the Israelite view of history differed from other views in having a Beginning and an End and in lacking an element of cyclical repetition. He maintains that the real difference lies in the genuine *novelty* of God's actions in creating Israel and in eventually bringing an End which fulfils everything.

[5] The series was actually much more complex than Creation-Exodus-Jesus. In the Old Testament, the central event is the Exodus (including the Sinai Covenant and the Conquest), but before it, came the Creation and the covenant with

End, the purpose will be fully achieved, and thus it will be fully revealed. Yet the first action provided a typological 'preview' of what was going to happen later. The *institutional* elements of world-Creation (for example, God's self-commitment to man and His appointment of man to have authority over nature) and the *impressive-expressive* elements (for example, the glory revealed in the stars) and the element of *victory over evil*—all these foreshadow or prefigure the Exodus, the Cross-and-Resurrection and the Last Day.

In the Bible, the basic beliefs concerning God arose primarily as interpretations of historical events, especially the Exodus and the life of Jesus;[1] if Israel did not actually become a nation during an Exodus from Egypt, or if the man Jesus never actually lived and died, Israelite faith and Christian faith become empty shells. Similarly, it would seem, the historicity of Creation as the first event in the series of divinely initiated events must be crucial to biblical faith. Moreover, one must take seriously the whole view of world-history as a divine action with a beginning, a middle (a cumulative succession of events) and a culminating end; for this view has had profound personal relevance to believers; it has given to the life and actions of individual people a religious dimension of meaning which is typically and distinctively biblical. There thus seem to be many good reasons for thinking that an idea of world-Creation as a *beginning* of world-history is an essential part of biblical faith.

For some modern Thomists, however, it matters little whether or not the world had a beginning.[2] On this view, Creation is essentially a relation of dependence-for-existence. This relation would have been the same at any alleged 'beginning' of the world as it is now, or will be in the future; and it is a relation which involves no change, no succession. But such a view does not take seriously the intimate connection between

---

Abraham, and after it, the Davidic covenant and the Exile-and-Return (Deut. 6.20-4; 26.1-9; Josh. 24.2-14; Ps. 78; 105; 106; 135, 136; Ps. 89.3-4; Isa. 43.14-21). The New Testament added to this series the ministry, death and resurrection of Jesus, and the coming of the Spirit to the Christian fellowship (Acts 13.17-41; I Cor. 15.1-7; Acts 2.14-39; 7.2-49; 10.36-43).

[1] Cf. G. E. Wright, *God Who Acts*, chs. 2, 3; and C. H. Dodd, *The Apostolic Preaching and its Developments*, London, 1936, Lecture 1.

[2] See E. L. Mascall, *Christian Theology and Natural Science*, ch. 4, espec. pp. 132-3 and 149; cf. A. D. Sertillanges, *L'Idée de Création et ses retentissements en Philosophie*, p. 16.

Creation as world-beginning and the rest of biblical theology; it leaves out most of the 'practical import' (Barth)[1] of the biblical conception of Creation.

Thomists are not alone in minimizing the importance of a world-beginning. Existentialism provides another objection: Any scientific discovery would be irrelevant to religious faith for the very reason that it would be a *scientific* discovery. The religious irrelevance of the utterance, 'The world had a beginning' might be claimed on the basis of a test which I should like to call 'the existentialist *a priori* test for religious utterances':[2]

> *If* utterance A is open to scientific investigation so that (i) it can be undermined or falsified by scientific evidence and so its truth can only be asserted tentatively,
> and (ii) it can be accepted and understood by anyone regardless of his fundamental attitudes,
> *then* utterance A is not itself a religious utterance and it cannot form an essential part of a genuine religion.

If this test is used to exclude, 'The world had a beginning' it must also exclude, 'Jesus of Nazareth was crucified'; but the latter obviously forms an essential part of the Christian faith. The Christian faith does not depend on the historicity of all the details in the Gospels, but it does depend on a hard core of fact which includes the crucifixion. Similarly (one may argue) the Christian religion does not depend on the historicity of all the details in Gen. 1-2, but it does depend on the fact that the world had a beginning. The *a priori* test does not provide a simple way of settling the question of whether 'The world had a beginning' is important to the Christian faith. We must try a different approach.

Let us suppose that the world had no beginning, that it has always existed in some form or another. What difference would this make to the biblical view of history? We recall that, according to this view, history is a unified divine action which extends over a succession of events towards a final culmination in the future. As W. A. Whitehouse has said,

---

[1] K. Barth, *Church Dogmatics*, III, 1, p. 11.

[2] I have never seen the test formulated in exactly this way, but arguments which depend on something very similar to this test (or to parts of this test) can be found in L. Gilkey, *Maker of Heaven and Earth*, p. 285 (concerning Creation as a beginning), E. Brunner, *The Mediator*, tr. O. Wyon, London, 1934, pp. 575-8 (concerning the empty tomb of Jesus), and R. Bultmann, *Jesus Christ and Mythology*, ch. 5.

'It is a presupposition of Biblical thinking that there is a line of salvation-history which runs forward to the consummation and also backward to *the* creation of all things—that is, to an event where God established a theatre for the historical enactment of the covenant of grace.'[1]

The final culmination has already been foreshadowed or pre-figured in the first event, world-Creation; it has been more completely anticipated in the Exodus; and its essence has been achieved and revealed in Jesus. The life and actions of individual men are interpreted in relation to the divine purpose which is gradually being worked out in human history.

What happens to this biblical view of history if the world had no beginning? It seems to me that most of it can be retained. One can still believe that *human* history had a beginning and that human history and cosmic history will culminate together in an End; thus the history which men and nature have in common has a 'direction' which comes from God, and an individual man can interpret his life and actions in relation to God's purpose for humanity and the cosmos. (As St Paul said, 'The creation waits with eager longing for the revealing of the sons of God . . . because the creation itself will be set free from its bondage to decay and obtain the glorious liberty of the children of God'.)[2] One can also believe that the cosmos is continuously created by God in an action which has an intrinsic unity with His actions in human history. That is, continuous world-Creation is an action which includes the institutional, impressive-expressive and profound-rationale elements which are revealed more fully in the Jesus of history and of Christian experience. And the picture of God deciding on the purpose of world-Creation before He began to create can be replaced by another picture: God acting at any time with this purpose in mind. *Temporal* priority of intentions is not conceptually necessary even when we are thinking about *human* actions. It would be unwise to claim that a scientific discovery of a world-beginning would be totally irrelevant to someone who has a

---

[1] 'Christ and Creation', *Essays in Christology for Karl Barth*, ed. T. H. L. Parker, London, 1956, p. 125. Cf. G. Miegge: 'Myth is the poetical expression of a timeless truth . . . (but) the biblical account of creation is the imaginative record of something which really happened. . . . The centre of interest in this account is not the origin of the world but the beginning of history' (*Visible and Invisible*, tr. S. Neill, London, 1958, pp. 110-11).

[2] Rom. 8.19, 21.

biblical view of history; the idea of a cosmos which has always existed does not fit happily with the idea of a cosmos which is bound up with mankind in a common history. Nevertheless the idea of a world-beginning does not seem to be indispensable for a biblical view of history. *World-Creation need not be a first event in world history.*

We may sympathize with Karl Barth's concern to go beyond Thomist ideas of dependence-for-existence so as to connect world-Creation with God's redemptive actions in human history. But we need not accept his interpretation of Creation as a 'pre-historical history', which is linked historically and causally with ordinary history, but which is not open to historical or scientific investigation.[1] We should retain the biblical account of Creation 'in the beginning' as a parable which is Relational and Transcendental. Whether or not the parable is also Interpretative—an interpretation of a particular event—can be left as an open but non-essential question. In any case, the parable will need to be combined and 'balanced' with other parables: parables of Creation as a continuous sustaining-in-existence and a victorious conflict against chaos, and Interpretative parables which are applied to historical events of redemption—Exodus, Crucifixion-Resurrection, and the End. All together, the parables form a complex parabolic onlook concerning the world, human history and one's personal existence.

It is obvious that these parables require considerable 'balancing'. Perhaps the most serious difficulties arise when the parable of Creation as victory is set alongside the parables in which Creation is the originating or sustaining of *all* things in existence. We may ask, 'Did (or does) God create the chaos—the sea and darkness—against which He fought (or fights) in creating everything else?' Some theologians give, or imply, a positive answer to this question.[2] They have ample biblical evidence for

---

[1] *Church Dogmatics*, III, 1, pp. 63-94. According to Barth, 'We have to accept both the fact that Paradise was planted and existed somewhere and not just everywhere or nowhere but also the fact that there can be no actual investigation of this somewhere. . . . There all the rivers of the earth have their common origin in a single river' (*ibid.*, pp. 252-3). Barth wants both to have his cake (his apple of empirical knowledge!) and to eat it.

[2] *E.g.*, E. Brunner, *Dogmatics*, II, pp. 10-11; W. Foerster, '*Ktizo*', *Theologisches Wörterbuch zum Neuen Testament*, ed. G. Kittel, Band III, p. 1,009; Th. C. Vriezen, *An Outline of Old Testament Theology*, p. 181.

their views: not only do some passages refer to the Creation of *all* things,[1] but others explicitly affirm the Creation of both the darkness[2] and the sea.[3] Yet there is scriptural support for those theologians who disagree;[4] in section 2.2, we noted various passages which presuppose the existence of the darkness and the sea as God's opponents in the battle of world-Creation. We can only do justice to the variety of the biblical witness if we interpret Creation-of-all-things and Creation-as-victory parabolically: The believer should look on all things, even the hidden power of evil, as creatures who are 'sustained' in existence by God; but he is not to look on the power of evil as something which has the *positive* institutional, impressive-expressive or purposive aspects of existence which God has given to everything else; on the contrary, he is to look on the power of evil as something to which God has said, 'No',[5] something which does not reveal His nature and which has no positive part in His purposes, something which thus lacks 'reality' in comparison with other creatures.

6. *Parables and the reality of divine action*

I have shown that 'causal' language concerning Creation can be interpreted as an expression of various parabolic onlooks. Appropriate onlook-attitudes are indicated by various interrelated images: potter,[6] builder,[7] victor,[8] magic word,[9] breath of life,[10] self-revealer,[11] and directive purpose.[12] To accept each parable is to adopt an onlook-attitude; the language is self-involving. Also, a non-superficial understanding of each parable requires a life lived in accordance with the onlook; the language is rapportive. (One may accept each parable as a lone individual, but in the biblical context the acceptance is likely to

---

[1] See p. 234, n. 2.

[2] Isa. 45.7. (Even Barth finds this verse 'intransigent'; see *Church Dogmatics*, III, 1, p. 106.)

[3] Ps. 95.5; 146.6.

[4] *E.g.*, B. S. Childs, *Myth and Reality in the Old Testament*, p. 42; G. von Rad, *Genesis, A Commentary*, pp. 48-9; K. Barth, *Church Dogmatics*, III, 1, pp. 101-9. Barth's view is elaborated by G. C. Berkouwer, *The Triumph of Grace in the Theology of Karl Barth*, ch. III. Von Rad says that Gen. 1.2 preserves a 'special concern of faith' (*op. cit.*, p. 48); then he gives his own version of what I have called the 'parable of Creation as victory'.

[5] Cf. K. Barth, *Church Dogmatics*, III, 1, pp. 366ff., and G. C. Berkouwer, *op. cit.*, ch. III.

[6] Section 2.1.   [7] Section 2.1.   [8] Section 2.2.   [9] Section 3.
[10] Section 4.   [11] Section 4.   [12] Section 5.

involve a self-identification with a group:[1] '*We* look on *ourselves* as pots, formed by a Potter'.)

At the beginning of this chapter I said that, even if a *human* action is performative (Exercitive, Verdictive or Commissive), impressive-expressive and profound in rationale, it has a causal 'core' which we can abstract. If we say, simply, 'Jones moves his arm' or 'Jones makes pots', our language is neither self-involving nor rapportive. What then is the causal 'core' of the divine action which is called 'Creation'? In this chapter, I have argued that when the causal element in Creation is abstracted from the elements which are obviously performative, impressive-expressive or profound in rationale, we can only talk about it in parables, in language which is both self-involving and rapportive. Does this mean that Creation is not really an action at all?

No. It does mean, however, that Creation differs from human actions in two important ways. In the first place, human actions are related to particular observables as these are distinguished from other observables: *This* arm would not have moved, *this* pot would still be clay, if Jones had not acted. World-Creation, however, has to do with *any* and *all* observables. If we ask, 'What difference would it make if there were no such action?' the answer is, 'There would be no events and no entities; there would be nothing at all (except God)'. If we ask, further, 'What human action is analogous to this action of "sustaining" everything in existence?', the answer is, 'No human action is genuinely analogous; human actions provide only images for parables, and these parables indicate appropriate onlook-attitudes to God.'

The first way in which world-Creation differs from human actions is thus its (parabolical) all-inclusiveness. The second way is closely connected with the first. A human action is related to an event or an entity which can be (or could have been) reported *neutrally*—regardless of one's onlooks or other attitudes. A human action may also include elements which cannot be observed and reported neutrally, but there must be this 'core'. World-Creation, however, has no such 'core' which can be observed and reported neutrally—except *everything* (the result of the action); and this 'core' does not serve to distinguish

[1] Cf. pp. 139, 159, n. 2, 196, n. 2, 242, n. 1.

the action. World-Creation is distinguished only in terms of onlook-attitudes; world-Creation is an action *such that* various onlook-attitudes are appropriate, various metaphysical parabolic onlooks.[1] Onlooks are not mere metaphors. The expression of an onlook commits me to a way of behaving and thinking, a mode of life.[2] Moreover, such an onlook is not a case of 'Let's pretend'. I do not merely *act as if* I believed that there is a God who is like a potter (or a victor, etc.). I act in accordance with a positive belief that God *is* like a potter; but I cannot describe this likeness except by referring to human attitudes. The *reality* of God, or of God's action, is not being denied; but what is *meant* by 'God the Creator' cannot be abstracted from human attitudes. Indeed, if 'reality' is not merely a question of sheer existence but of *importance* to men, then surely the 'reality' of God is being strenuously affirmed by anyone who expresses the various parabolic onlooks concerning God the Creator.

In the biblical context there are various parabolic onlooks concerning God the Creator. Some are expressed in 'causal' language which *becomes* self-involving when it is used as part of a parable: I look on God as a potter who forms me, a victor over chaos, a man breathing life into me, and so on. Other parabolic onlooks are expressed in language which already *is* self-involving when it is used as part of a parable: I look on myself as God's servant and steward, I look on my own existence as a gift, I look on nature's beneficial regularities as God's pledge, and I look on nature's impressive features as expressions of God's glory. All biblical language concerning God as Creator is parabolic; but this does not detract from the 'reality' of the Creator or His action. It does mean that the power, authority and glory of the Creator are recognized or discerned only in so far as we respond to them, and that we respond to them by taking up a group of onlook-attitudes which together form part of a whole religious way of life.

What does this account of Creation indicate concerning other Christian affirmations of faith? I cannot give an adequate answer to this question here, but I shall close this chapter by forestalling one possible misinterpretation: No minimizing of the factual element is *inherent* in my philosophical analysis. Even if the only 'matter of fact' which is directly connected

[1] See pp. 131-5.   [2] See pp. 130-1.

with the idea of Creation is the sheer existence of anything and everything, many Christian affirmations (concerning atonement, providence or miracles) may have an inherent connection with particular matters of fact. My analysis does not rule out the possibility of such a connection. On the contrary, it provides a logical framework which may be very useful to theologians who discuss the connection or lack of connection. In chapter 1, I noted several ways in which matters of fact may be connected with Behabitive, Commissive or Verdictive utterances:

(1) Any such utterance may have factual *presuppositions*: When I thank you, or pledge you my support, or find you guilty of assault, I presuppose your existence. Similarly, whatever self-involving elements there may be in the utterance, 'Jesus died for my sins', it does presuppose the death of Jesus.

(2) A Behabitive utterance may have a factual *content*: 'I thank thee that I am not as other men are'. Similarly the Behabitive element in 'I thank thee for helping me through life's journey' does not rule out the possibility that divine help may be 'factual' in the sense that it is an observable supernatural intrusion into particular situations, an intrusion which is detectable by scientists. On the other hand, it is possible that Christian utterances concerning providence or miracle are pure expressions of onlook which involve no supernaturalist factual claims. My analysis leaves the issue open.

(3) A Verdictive utterance is usually *based*, in some way, on matters of fact: 'I think that Jones is more handsome than Brown *because* . . .' Similarly, the Christian can base his belief that God is good (loving, holy, etc.) on matters of fact—historical facts concerning Jesus of Nazareth.

Obviously these issues require a more thorough investigation than is possible here. The issues are tangential, so we shall leave them. But three problems do arise directly and inescapably from the main arguments and conclusions of the book as a whole: (1) the difference between religious and secular onlooks, (2) the relation between linguistic and existential self-involvement and (3) the modern Christian basis for belief in world-Creation. I should examine these problems carefully, even if I can only deal with them briefly.

7

SOME FURTHER PROBLEMS

1. *The difference between religious and secular onlooks*

THIS PROBLEM is closely related to the problem which we considered at the end of chapter 6, where I claimed that the 'reality' of God's action in Creation is not minimized when this action is understood entirely in terms of parables. My account of biblical language concerning Creation may be criticized on the score that I have not maintained a clear distinction between religious parabolic onlooks and secular (non-religious) ones. The emphasis on parabolic onlooks may seem to reduce religious belief in God to a mere world-view alongside non-religious world-views.

Let us approach the problem by recalling the 'autonomy of value',[1] which reminds us that a man is under no *logical* compulsion to accept the complex system of biblical parables concerning Creation. For example, a man may decide to describe the stars only in non-'evaluative' terms, using flat (and impersonal) Constatives. If he does, his utterance does not entail any 'evaluative' utterances concerning the stars as God's pledges to man, as God's revelations of glory, or as God's victory over darkness. Similarly a man may describe a human being in neutral terms which do not logically-commit him to saying, 'I look on Jones as a brother for whom Christ died'. Because of the 'autonomy of value', we are *logically free* to refrain from expressing any religious onlooks. (We recall[2] that this freedom has no inherent connection with psychological 'freedom' or with moral 'freedom'.)

But the 'autonomy of value' also provides a logical freedom

---

[1] See ch. 1, section 7.3; ch. 2, section 4.2.; ch. 3, section 2.3.
[2] See ch. 1, section 7.3; ch. 2, section 4.2.

from expressing various *secular* onlooks. If I describe death or sex in biological terms, I do not logically-commit myself to looking on death as the mockery of human hopes, or to looking on sex as a sordid animal urge. I do not logically-commit myself to *any* onlook. It is true that the decision to restrict one's language to flat non-expressive Constatives (plus 'I'm for it' or 'It's important') looks like a queer sort of 'onlook' itself: I decide to look on each thing as it is and not as anything else. This 'onlook which rejects onlooks' is perhaps part of what some people have called 'the scientific attitude'. If a positivist claims universal application for this view, he is likely to provoke a counter-claim which is equally extreme: the claim that *no* language is 'literal' or 'non-symbolic'. A less extreme positivistic position would be one which restricts onlooks to analogical onlooks,[1] eliminating only the parabolic ones.

What I want to point out here, however, is that religious onlooks are not the only alternative to a flat-Constative view of the world. There are various secular onlooks which may be adopted. I may look on my life as a pilgrimage to heaven; but I may look on my life as a game or a dream. I may look on Jones as a brother for whom Christ died; but I may look on Jones as a comrade in the class-struggle. I may look on the State as the servant of God; but I may look on the State as the servant of the people. What makes religious onlooks different from secular ones?

The occurrence or non-occurrence of the word 'God' provides no more than a clue, a clue which may be misleading in some instances. Indeed, the question opens up a vast and complex area for investigation; another book would be required for even an initial exploration.[2] It is possible, however, to point out four ways in which religious onlooks may be distinguished from secular onlooks.

In the first place, a secular onlook approaches religious onlooks in so far as it is parabolic and *metaphysical*. This is a matter of degree: a parabolic onlook is metaphysical in so far as we not only *do* not but also *can* not specify the similarity between x and y except in terms of a similarity of appropriate

---

[1] See chapter 3, section 2.2.

[2] For example, what is the difference between the 'agnostic' parabolic vision of R. W. Hepburn (*Christianity and Paradox*, ch. 11) and the 'theistic' outlook of R. Bultmann, whose religion seems to be primarily a new way of looking on one's self?

attitudes. A religious onlook includes references to unobservable entities which are recognizable and describable only in relation to particular human attitudes. Hence the word 'person' may form a bridge between the realm of the secular and the realm of the religious.[1]

In the second place, a man's religious onlook is not only metaphysical but also *transcendental*; it involves him in worship, which is an acknowledgment of a transcendent authority, faithfulness, glory and power. I have analysed 'transcendence' in terms of the *unlimited* element in the human acknowledgment:[2] unlimited submission, trust, glorification and humility. In so far as secular onlooks include this unlimited element and thus verge on worship, they become religious.

In the third place, a man's religious onlook includes the conviction that there exists a hidden being who has an *authoritative onlook*.[3] He believes or hopes that his own onlook conforms to this divine onlook. He believes or hopes that he is not merely imposing or concocting an onlook; he believes or hopes that he is discovering an onlook which is being revealed to him. Here too we have an element in onlooks which varies in degree. At one extreme there is the theological dogmatist who equates his own onlook in every detail with the divine onlook. In the middle there is the cautious religious liberal who is sure that there is a divine onlook and who tries to discover it, but who is not ready to give any of his onlooks the authority of the divine onlook. At the other extreme of religion there is the agnostic who hopes that there is a divine onlook and who goes on searching; his very search implies a faith.[4] Beyond this is the man who regards his own onlooks simply as his own creations.

Finally, in so far as a man's religious onlook is focused on his own personal life and actions, he believes that the onlook is self-verifying not merely because he himself makes it true as he lives in accordance with it,[5] but primarily because a *hidden*

[1] See pp. 134-5 and 225-6.
[2] See chapter 6, section 1.2, and chapter 4, section 4.
[3] See chapter 3, section 2.4, and chapter 6, section 2.2.
[4] Cf. P. Tillich: 'Something remains, namely, the seriousness of that doubt in which meaning within meaninglessness is affirmed. The source of this affirmation of meaning within meaninglessness, of certitude within doubt, is not the God of traditional theism but the "God above God", the power of being, which works through those who have no name for it, not even the name of God' (*Systematic Theology*, II, London, 1957, p. 14).
[5] See p. 139.

influence enables him to act in accordance with it. Hence he not only *resolves* to look on himself as (say) a steward of talents and property; he also *prays* for help in living according to his self-commitment, and he believes or hopes that this prayer will be answered. That is, not only does his onlook claim some divine authority for its Verdictive aspect (my third point); it also relies on some divine influence in relation to its Commissive aspect.

These four points concerning religious onlooks suggest that there is no sharp dividing-line between religious onlooks and onlooks which many believers would call 'secular'. Nevertheless this lack of a sharp boundary-line does not detract from the important distinction between most 'secular' onlooks and those religious onlooks which are strongly and distinctively 'religious'. The former may have *no* metaphysical element, *no* transcendental (worshipful) element, *no* notion of an authoritative onlook, *no* belief in a helpful hidden influence. Obviously such secular onlooks are different from the religious onlook of the biblical writers. I have not reduced religious belief to a secular world-view.

Indeed, I have made it feasible for a religious dogmatist to dismiss all secular onlooks—and everyone else's religious onlooks! Someone can meaningfully claim (though I would not) that his own religious onlook is the one true onlook since it alone conforms to the divine onlook, and that all other onlooks, both secular and religious, are false. On the other hand, a religious liberal could accept the authoritarian[1] theory of religious truth which my onlook-analysis indicates:

> The true onlook is true because it is God's, rather than being God's because it is, independently of divine authority, true.

For the religious liberal need not commit himself to any authoritarian claims concerning his *own* religious onlook; and he can meaningfully grant a measure of truth to many onlooks, both religious and secular.

Incidentally, we should note that my account of 'religious' onlooks is obviously derived from an examination of the *Christian* religion; my account may not be very satisfactory as

---

[1] My theory is also *personalistic*: a religious onlook is true in so far as it facilitates an acknowledgment of God's personal self-revelation which brings a knowledge of God which is 'acquaintance' or 'encounter' (cf. p. 199).

an interpretation of the language or conceptions of other religions. The differences between Christian onlooks and the onlooks (or other conceptions) of various non-Christian religions have not been considered in this book. For example, I have not emphasized the peculiar concentration of Christian onlooks on particular *matters of fact*, that is, the 'Jesus of history'. Perhaps scholars in the field of comparative religion may find that the technical apparatus which has been developed and applied in this book is useful in their studies. But I do not wish to make any advance claims concerning this.

Let us turn to another issue which arises directly from the main arguments in the book. A religious critic might object strenuously to the preoccupation with *words*: 'You have reduced religion to mere words. You have talked about *linguistic* self-involvement, which is obviously not trivial; but you have left out the core of religion, which is personal or *existential* self-involvement.'

2. *The relation between linguistic and existential self-involvement*

This objection deserves very careful consideration. First, however, we should distinguish it from a very different objection against my alleged verbalism, an objection which can easily be answered. Someone might say, 'Surely you have replaced religion by trivialities. Religion is concerned, not with words, but with realities—with people and things as creatures of God, and with God's transcendence and His actions in the world.' To this I can reply, 'Surely I have shown that words are deeds, words commit men, words express attitudes. Surely I have shown that words are inseparable from a biblical understanding of people and things, of God's transcendence and actions.'

Such a hypothetical critic is a straw man, easily demolished. A more formidable adversary, however, will agree with my reply to the straw man, agree with my claim that linguistic self-involvement is important, but insist that personal or existential self-involvement is what really matters in religion. Sometimes an utterance is non-trivial in that it does commit a man linguistically; but, according to this critic, it may be 'merely verbal' in that the speaker is *insincere*. What matters in religion is the speaker's sincerity, the genuineness and depth of his personal self-involvement. Even a solemn pledge of loyalty to Christ may be 'merely verbal' if the speaker is insincere, not meaning what he says.

In order to deal with this objection, I must first review some features of linguistic self-involvement:

(a) If my utterance is Commissive, I imply that I intend to do such-and-such.
(b) If my utterance is Behabitive, I imply that I have such-and-such an attitude.
(c) If my utterance expresses a feeling, I imply that I have this feeling.

In each case I may be *insincere*:[1]

(a) When I imply that I intend to do such-and-such, I may not *mean what I say*. (Similarly, when my utterance is Verdictive, and I imply that I think such-and-such, I may not mean what I say.)
(b) When I imply that I have such-and-such an attitude, I may not have this attitude.
(c) When I imply that I have such-and-such a feeling, I may not have the feeling.

Moreover, such insincerity is a matter of degree:

(a) I may mean what I say half-heartedly or without any 'private backing' whatsoever.
(b) and (c) The attitude or feeling which I actually have may differ in various ways and various degrees from that which I imply.

When a man expresses religious faith by saying, in the biblical context, 'God is my Creator', he is expressing a complex parabolic onlook which includes Commissive, Behabitive and expressive elements. (The Commissive element is connected to a Verdictive element as well.)[2] But when a man involves himself linguistically, he may not be involving himself existentially, for he may be utterly insincere. Moreover, there are degrees of sincerity or insincerity: one man may involve himself to the very depths of his personal being, whereas another man's personal involvement may be superficial. Thus a critic of this book may well protest that what matters is the depth of a man's existential self-involvement, not his verbal behaviour. Existential depth is what makes for genuine, authentic religion; such

---

[1] See pp. 81-3.   [2] Cf. pp. 128, 194-5.

religion may be present even when a man gives no public verbal expression to it.

With all this I would agree. But the *religious* importance of existential self-involvement does not show that linguistic self-involvement is irrelevant in a *philosophical* study of religion. Indeed, it still seems to me that a linguistic study is an indispensable prerequisite for any philosophy of religion, whatever else may be added later. For let us consider the man of genuine, authentic religion, who has involved himself existentially. What has he committed himself to with such whole-hearted zeal? What views does he hold with such fervent conviction? What attitudes and feelings does he have with such integrity and intensity? In order to answer such questions we *must* investigate his self-involvement in *linguistic* terms.

Consider, for example, an outstanding exponent and exemplar of 'existential' religion, Martin Buber. In his classic work, *I and Thou*,[1] Buber commends a religious attitude which has for him an intrinsic connection with what he calls a 'primary word': the combination 'I-Thou'.[2] This primary word is clearly a linguistic act, a Behabitive and Commissive utterance: in some contexts, when I address someone as 'Thou', I acknowledge his presence and his claim upon my exclusive attention and concern. The 'I-It' attitude which Buber contrasts with an 'I-Thou' attitude is similarly connected with a linguistic act: in some contexts, when I refer to 'it' or 'he', I am describing something without involving myself. Buber rightly indicates that sometimes a man may have an 'I-Thou' attitude though he does not *say* 'Thou';[3] and, conversely, he rightly points out[4] that a man may sometimes say 'Thou' insincerely, not with his 'whole being', not expressing an actual 'I-Thou' attitude. Nevertheless when Buber tries to explain what he means by an 'I-Thou' attitude, he has to refer to paradigm cases where someone both *says* 'Thou' and *means* it; that is, cases where one man sincerely acknowledges another man's personal presence and claim. It is true that Buber is more interested in religious sincerity, the wholeness of a man's existential self-involvement, than the linguistic act as such; but he does not ignore the linguistic aspect, for he can not—he can not make his basic

[1] Tr. R. G. Smith, Edinburgh, 1937.
[2] *Ibid.*, p. 3.   [3] *I and Thou*, p. 39.   [4] *Ibid.*, p. 34, cf. p. 3.

'I-Thou'/'I-It' contrast without reference to linguistic acts. It is true that Buber does not confine himself to a philosophical analysis of linguistic acts, since his work is mainly a poetic exploration of fleeting moments in the religious consciousness; but his distinctive phenomenology depends on his initial doctrine of 'primary words'.

Any adequate philosophical study of existential self-involvement in religion requires a thorough (and prior) examination of linguistic self-involvement. This examination may leave various questions open, to be explored in some other way—existential questions concerning religious sincerity, and phenomenological questions concerning religious states of mind. The analysis of linguistic acts, nevertheless, needs to come first. An existentialist theologian needs to refer to linguistic acts in order to explain what he means. This is illustrated in the following passage from Rudolf Bultmann (a passage which also illustrates Bultmann's need for a more refined and detailed account of linguistic self-involvement):

> 'Only such statements about God are legitimate as express the existential relation between God and man. Statements which speak of God's actions as cosmic events are illegitimate. The affirmation that God is creator cannot be a theoretical statement about God as *creator mundi* in a general sense. The affirmation can only be a personal confession that I understand myself to be a creature which owes its existence to God. It cannot be made as a neutral statement, but only as thanksgiving and surrender.'[1]

A philosophical study of religious self-involvement should include an analysis of linguistic self-involvement. Linguistic analysis is necessary; but it may nevertheless be *inadequate*, not only religiously but philosophically. My own account of 'sincerity'[2] or 'meaning what one says' was inadequate. The main point was a negative one, a rejection of introspective psychology or phenomenology as a solution; I said that there need not be any special mental event or activity concomitant

---

[1] *Jesus Christ and Mythology*, London, 1960, p. 69; cf. pp. 48 and 76-7, concerning 'indicative' and 'imperative'. Cf. his rhetorical questions in *Kerygma und Mythos*, II Hamburg-Volksdorf, 1952, p. 187: 'Is there no other language than the language of myth and science? Are sentences like "I love you" or "I ask for your forgiveness" spoken in the language of science? And, if not, is their language mythological?' (quoted and translated by D. S. Cairns, *A Gospel Without Myth?*, London, 1960, p. 97).
[2] Ch. 2, section 1.

with, and in addition to, the utterance of the words in which I express my intention or opinion. No positive account was offered, however, and we seemed to be left with an ultimate mystery concerning private meaning. It is true that a framework of public meaning is required if one is to say X and mean it; and it is true that where sincerity is in question, subsequent public behaviour may be relevant not only to the observer but also to the speaker. Nevertheless there is an inherently private element which is extremely puzzling. If Jones said, 'I'll return this book to-morrow', in most cases he knew at the time whether or not he meant what he said. How did he know? What is it to mean what one says? A linguistic philosopher may object: 'Jones did not *know* whether he meant what he said; he merely was in a position to *say* whether he meant what he said'. Very well then, let us ask, 'How was he in this position?'. Surely it was not *merely* by virtue of a convention of language, similar to a rule in a game ('Umpires are in a position to say whether a play is offside'). Another linguistic philosopher may object: 'You have missed the point; you are asking a question which ought not to be asked, for there is no possibility of an answer.' But if that is the 'point', it may merely indicate a limitation of the particular philosophical method which has been employed.

Another problem concerning private meaning arises when we consider cases where the meaning of an utterance is, to some extent, speaker-dependent.[1] On what basis does one say, afterward, 'That's what I meant'? Indeed, what is it, at the time, to say such-and-such, *intending* the words to have one meaning rather than another meaning? Here too we presuppose the existence of a framework of public meaning; here too the speaker as well as the observer may find that his subsequent public behaviour is relevant; but here too there is an inherently private element which cannot be dismissed by reference to a convention of a language, or by a dogmatic claim that one has asked an unanswerable question.

Both 'meaning what one says' and 'intending one's words to have this meaning rather than that' are matters of great importance in religion. Indeed, they are both crucial in my attempt to analyse the biblical conception of Creation. If

[1] Ch. 1, section 6; cf. ch. 4, section 2.6.

someone says, in the biblical context, 'God is my Creator', the mere utterance has religious value only if he means what he says. What is it to 'mean what one says'? And what is it to intend that the utterance have its meaning in the biblical context rather than some other context? These are questions which I have not answered.

In this section I have tried to indicate both the necessary connection between linguistic and existential self-involvement and the possible limitations of a study which confines its attention to the former. This issue concerning self-involvement arose because of the basic *method* employed in the book. Now I wish to consider an issue which arises from the main *conclusions* of the book: I have given a modern account of the *meaning* of the biblical conception of Creation. What light does this shed on the problem of the modern *basis* for a biblical belief in Creation?

3. *The modern Christian basis for belief in world-Creation*

The existence of a Creator-God was not questioned by those Jews and God-fearing Gentiles who became Christians in the early years of the Christian Church. The authority and glory and power of Jesus were grounds for belief in his divinity, grounds for identifying him in some way with the world-Creator in whom they already believed; Jesus did not provide the one ground for belief that there *is* a world-Creator. But if, today, a man who does not believe in the existence of a world-Creator looks for a rational basis for such a belief, where should he look? Some Christians would say that it is possible, indeed desirable, to base one's belief in a Creator-God on something other than Jesus; then one can go on to identify Jesus as the divine agent or instrument in world-Creation. E. L. Mascall, for example, accepts a form of cosmological argument as his reason for believing '(1) that God exists, and (2) that God causes the existence of finite beings'.[1] Other Christians, however would say that the only adequate basis for belief in a world-Creator is to be found in Jesus. W. A. Whitehouse, for example, argues that we do not *know* that God is the Creator unless we derive this conviction from a 'new existence in filial

---

[1] *Existence and Analogy*, London, 1949, p. 87.

relationship'[1] with God, an existence which Jesus (or rather, God in Jesus) has made possible through the Crucifixion and Resurrection.

Thus there seem to be two main alternatives.[2] Either one begins by inferring a Creator-God from nature and then one identifies Jesus (the Jesus of history and of Christian experience) with this Creator; or one begins with the transforming divine power of Jesus and then one infers world-Creation.

3.1. *Nature as the basis*

Let us consider the first alternative. One sort of inference from nature to a Creator-God is the teleological argument. We look at nature and see orderly patterns which resemble the results of human design, and which go far beyond these results in their scale and their intricacy. So we infer a hidden designer, an intelligent agent who is commensurate with these effects.

Such a conclusion does not have any intrinsic relevance to religion. The utterance, 'An intelligent designer made the world' lacks any inherent connection with religion, especially biblical religion, because it is not religiously self-involving. In the biblical context, to say 'God is my Creator' is to involve oneself, for Creation is an action which is institutional (performative) and impressive-expressive. I acknowledge the Creator as Lord, Appointer, Evaluator and Guarantor, and I express an attitude as I respond to the Creator's glory and acknowledge it in worship. Even the causal 'core' of His Creative action is interpreted parabolically, so that my acknowledgment is attitudinal in this respect as well. In the biblical context, to say 'God is the Creator' is to involve oneself in a complex religious way of life.

The conclusion to a quasi-scientific teleological argument, however, is a flat Constative (non-Commissive and non-Behavitive) which is impersonal (non-expressive); no act of worship is performed in the utterance, no religious feeling-Response is expressed, and no religious way of life is adopted. Unless particular onlooks are presupposed in the teleological argument, or imposed on its conclusion, the action of the

---

[1] *Christian Faith and Scientific Attitude*, Edinburgh, 1952, p. 58; see also pp. 55-8. Cf. D. Bonhoeffer, *Creation and Fall*, p. 16: 'It is because we know of the resurrection that we know of God's creation in the beginning.'

[2] A similar issue is being debated in relation to the Israelite basis for belief in world-Creation: was it nature or was it the Exodus? See p. 146, nn. 1, 2.

'intelligent agent' is not looked on as a definite performative and impressive-expressive action. The starry heavens show God's Exercitive, Verdictive and Commissive 'word', or His benevolent glory, or His victory over evil darkness, only if I adopt a particular way of looking on them; other onlooks are possible. In so far as the teleological argument is quasi-scientific and does not depend on any particular attitude or onlook, we surely cannot go beyond the conclusion in Hume's *Dialogues*, that 'the cause or causes of order in the universe probably bear some remote analogy to human intelligence'.[1] Such a conclusion lacks both positive religious relevance and psychological certainty.

We should realize, nevertheless, that the teleological argument must be able to go this far, if there is to be any rational basis in nature for a biblical Creation-onlook. If there is *no* reason at all for inferring a Designer from the order of the universe, there is no reason apart from sheer biblical authority[2] for looking on natural phenomena as God's pledge or self-expression to man.

In so far as the teleological argument goes beyond a Humean conclusion, it depends on attitudinal elements which resemble, to some extent, the *biblical* onlook towards nature.[3] Let us suppose that, one evening, John Jones contemplates the heavens. He does this in a very special frame of mind: he does not merely notice order or design, he looks on the moon and the stars as things which have a 'role' in human life; he values them highly —for him it is good that they should exist; he is reassured by their stability and regularity, which seems 'friendly'; he is awesomely impressed by their beauty; and he rejoices in their light, which has overcome the dark depression of his own mind. For John Jones, the conclusion of a teleological argument is likely to have both religious relevance and subjective certainty. Tomorrow night, however, he may be in a different frame of mind when he gazes at the heavenly bodies; he may feel that he has been confirmed in his fear that he lives in an indifferent universe. Next week the universe may seem even hostile. Indeed,

---

[1] *Dialogues Concerning Natural Religion*, part 12 (*The English Philosophers from Bacon to Mill*, ed. E. A. Burtt, New York, 1939, p. 763).

[2] Or an appeal to Jesus; see the next section.

[3] Cf. H. H. Farmer's claim that natural theology depends on natural religion (*Revelation and Religion*, London, 1954, ch. 1).

if he should turn his attention away from the heavens towards a smashed and suffering child, the victim of an earthquake, even the bare Humean 'analogy' may seem difficult to accept. Moreover, in a more positivist frame of mind, he might one day decide to renounce all imaginative and parabolic onlooks, so that he views the heavens with a 'neutral' eye. It is surely obvious that the positive religious relevance and the psychological certainty of the teleological argument depend on the adoption of particular onlook-attitudes and the focusing of one's attention on particular aspects of the world.

Why should a man adopt such onlooks? Why should a man focus his attention on one feature of the world rather than another? What reason has a man for putting himself in a frame of mind such that, for him, the conclusion of the teleological argument is a self-involving utterance? Here the Christian will point to the Jesus of history and of Christian experience.

In the next section we shall consider this appeal to Jesus—the Exercitive, Verdictive and Commissive Word of God, the expression of God's glory, the victor over sin and darkness. But first let us note the other main way in which the conclusion of a quasi-scientific teleological argument lacks an inherent connection with religion, especially biblical religion: the conclusion is not rapportive. In the biblical context, the utterance, 'God is the Creator of the world' is understood only to the extent that one's way of life is Christ-like and one is transformed by the Spirit into the likeness of God; for the rationale of Creation is a mystery which involves divine glory as an impressive and expressive quality. What about the conclusion of the teleological argument? This can be understood regardless of one's way of life or one's inner nature. The meaning of 'An intelligent agent designed the world' may well be obscure, but it is no clearer to those who are spiritually mature than it is to those who are completely irreligious. If I think that the action of the intelligent agent has a rationale which provides a profound and mysterious meaning for human life, this sense of mystery does not come from the quasi-scientific teleological argument as such. Here too a reference to the Jesus of history and of Christian experience may be made, to provide what is lacking.

We have considered some of the defects of the teleological

argument. I shall not examine the *cosmological* argument here, though quasi-scientific versions of this argument seem to me to be similarly defective; that is, if one argues from a series of mundane causes to a world-cause, the conclusion will lack intrinsic religious relevance (since it will be neither self-involving nor rapportive) and it will lack psychological certainty. On the other hand, the cosmological argument, like the teleological argument, can lose these defects if it pays the price of becoming attitude-dependent; that is, if the argument is reinterpreted so that one does not expect an inquirer either to *understand* it fully or to give his *assent* to it unless he adopts an attitude which resembles the biblical Creation-onlook, then the conclusion *will* be religiously relevant and psychologically certain—once one adopts the required attitude.

3.2. *Jesus as the basis*

In chapter 4 (section 3) we saw that for the early Christians the Jesus of history and of religious experience was the vehicle for a divine action by which they received a new status and role and self-evaluation, and a new covenantal assurance of divine self-commitment. In chapter 5 (section 3) we saw that Jesus is *the* impressive-expressive revelation of divine glory. In both chapters we saw that Jesus was the vehicle for a transforming divine action which occurs, and which is accepted and understood, in so far as men respond. This 'new creation' of man by divine influence is similar to 'causal' aspects of Creation which we considered in chapter 6: Jesus is the victor over the sea and darkness and Satan; from him come words of spiritual power and breath of spiritual life.

It is obvious that we have here the primary basis for the self-involving and rapportive elements in the Christian faith as a whole, and the primary basis for its subjective certainty. If this basis is combined with an inference from nature to a Creator-God, it supports those attitudes which give the conclusions of such an inference religious relevance and psychological certainty. (For example, if a man has been impressed by the glory of Christ, this will confirm his view of the impressive stars as expressions of divine glory.)[1] But can we *start* with the

---

[1] Cf. L. Gilkey concerning the conviction that nature is good: 'Because God is known to be "good" in Christ, the world He made is known to be "good" in creation' (*Maker of Heaven and Earth*, p. 227).

action of a hidden divine being in Jesus, and from this legitimately infer the *existence* of a world-Creator? That is, if we
respond to the authority, glory and transforming personal
influence of the Jesus of history and of Christian experience,
does this by itself warrant our looking on nature as God's
Creation? Surely the answer must be, 'No'. Consider, for
example, a man's awareness or conviction that he depends on
Christ for whatever profundity there is in his own personal
existence; surely this is not an adequate basis for saying that
the moon depends on a Creator for its existence. Moreover,
many of the ways in which one interprets the authority, glory
and spiritual power of Jesus are not possible unless one already
assumes a world-Creator with whom this historical man or
spiritual presence is being identified.

Some people may propose a simple solution: the basis for
belief in world-Creation is the Bible as a whole. Such a claim
cannot be ignored, even if one does not believe in an inerrant
inspiration of the scriptures; for neither nature nor Jesus provide
an adequate basis for a self-involving confession of faith in God
the Creator unless they are interpreted *biblically*—that is,
interpreted in terms of a complex pattern of biblical onlooks.
Without the biblical interpretation—or something akin to it—
nature provides at best only a Humean conclusion to a teleological argument and Jesus provides at best only a man whom
critical historians may investigate. It is true that the biblical
onlooks include Verdictive judgments which need the Humean
conclusion and the Jesus of history as minimal rational bases.
But this does not affect what has been said about Creation and
self-involvement: Neither nature nor Jesus provide an adequate
basis for a *self-involving* confession of faith in God the Creator
unless they are interpreted in terms of a complex pattern of
biblical or quasi-biblical onlooks.

In this book, we have seen that for a Christian, there is an
intimate connection between faith in Jesus Christ as the divine
word, divine glory and divine saviour, and faith in the biblical
Creator-God; these are bound up together in a complex biblical
onlook which is accepted and adopted in a decision of faith. A
Christian acknowledges Jesus Christ as the Lord, Appointer,
Evaluator and Guarantor of human life, the unique revelation
of divine glory, and the victor over darkness and chaos who

transforms men by his Spirit. These self-involving elements in the biblical conception of Christ combine with the self-involving elements in the biblical conception of Creation. The Creator-God whom Christians acknowledge is the God revealed in Jesus Christ.

BIBLIOGRAPHY

I · MODERN ANALYTIC PHILOSOPHY OF RELIGION

(In order to amplify reference 1 on page 17, several important works have been included which were not mentioned in the book; they are marked with an asterisk.)

* Braithwaite, R. B., *An Empiricist's View of the Nature of Religious Belief*, London, 1955.

Crombie, I. M., 'The Possibility of Theological Statements', *Faith and Logic*, ed. B. Mitchell, London, 1957.

Evans, D. D., 'Three Philosophers Discuss Christianity', *Scottish Journal of Theology*, June, 1960.

Farrer, Austin, 'A Starting-Point for the Philosophical Examination of Theological Belief', *Faith and Logic*, ed. B. Mitchell, London, 1957.

Ferré, Frederick, *Language, Logic and God*, New York, 1961.

* Flew, A. (and A. MacIntyre), eds., *New Essays in Philosophical Theology*, London, 1955.

—— (and R. W. Hepburn) 'Problems of Perspective', *The Plain View*, Winter, 1955.

Foster, M., *Mystery and Philosophy*, London, 1957.

Hepburn, R. W., *Christianity and Paradox*, London, 1958.

—— (and A. Flew), 'Problems of Perspective', *The Plain View*, Winter, 1955.

* Hick, John, *Faith and Knowledge*, Cornell University Press, Ithaca, New York, 1957.

Jones, O. R., *The Concept of Holiness*, London, 1961.

* MacIntyre, A. (ed.), *Metaphysical Beliefs*, London, 1957.

* —— (and A. Flew), eds., *New Essays in Philosophical Theology*, London, 1955.

* Martin, C. B., *Religious Belief*, Cornell University Press, Ithaca, New York, 1959.

Miles, T. R., *Religion and the Scientific Outlook*, London, 1959.

* Munz, Peter, *Problems of Religious Knowledge*, London, 1959.

* Ramsey, Ian T., *Religious Language*, London, 1957.
—— *Freedom and Immortality*, London, 1960.
Smart, Ninian, *Reasons and Faiths*, London, 1958.
* Wilson, John, *Language and Christian Belief*, London, 1958.

II · OTHER PHILOSOPHY OF RELIGION OR PHILOSOPHICAL
THEOLOGY

Anderson, James F., *The Bond of Being*, Herder Press, St Louis, 1949.
Baillie, John, *Our Knowledge of God*, Oxford, 1939.
Bevan, E., *Symbolism and Belief*, London, 1938.
Buber, Martin, *I and Thou*, tr. R. G. Smith, Edinburgh, 1937.
Butterfield, H., *Christianity and History*, London, 1949.
Coulson, C. A., *Science and Christian Belief*, London (Fontana paper-back), 1958.
Farmer, H. H., *Revelation and Religion*, London, 1954.
Gilkey, L., *Maker of Heaven and Earth*, New York, 1959.
Hume, David, *Dialogues Concerning Natural Religion* (*The English Philosophers from Bacon to Mill*, ed. E. A. Burtt, New York, 1939).
McLelland, J. C., *The Visible Words of God*, Edinburgh, 1957.
Malcolm, Norman, 'Anselm's Ontological Arguments', *The Philosophical Review*, January, 1960.
Mascall, E. L., *Christian Theology and Natural Science*, London, 1956.
—— *Existence and Analogy*, London, 1949.
—— *Via Media*, London, 1956.
Otto, R., *The Idea of the Holy*, tr. J. Harvey, 2nd ed., Oxford, 1923.
Schleiermacher, F., *The Christian Faith*, 2nd ed., tr. H. R. Mackintosh, Edinburgh, 1928.
—— *On Religion*, tr. J. Oman, New York (Harper paper-back), 1958.
Sertillanges, A. D., *L'Idée de Création et ses retentissements en philosophie*, Paris, 1945.
Temple, William, *Nature, Man and God*, London, 1934.
Tillich, Paul, *Systematic Theology*, I, London, 1953.
—— *Systematic Theology*, II, London, 1957.
Whitehouse, W. A., *Christian Faith and Scientific Attitude*, Edinburgh, 1952.
—— *Order, Goodness and Glory*, Oxford, 1960.

III · PHILOSOPHY

Anscombe, G. E. M., *Intention*, Oxford, 1957.
Austin, J. L., *Philosophical Papers*, ed., J. O. Urmson and G. J. Warnock, Oxford, 1961.
—— *How to do Things with Words*, ed., J. O. Urmson, Oxford, 1962.
Dray, William, *Laws and Explanation in History*, Oxford, 1957.
Emmet, Dorothy, *Function, Purpose and Powers*, London, 1958.

Farrer, Austin, *The Freedom of the Will*, London, 1958.

Grice, H. P., 'Meaning', *The Philosophical Review*, July, 1957.

Hampshire, Stuart, *Thought and Action*, London, 1959.

Hare, R. M., 'Freedom of the Will', *Aristotelian Society Supplementary Volume 25*, 1951.

—— *The Language of Morals*, Oxford, 1952.

Hart, H. L. A. (and A. M. Honoré), *Causation in the Law*, Oxford, 1959.

Nowell-Smith, P., 'Contextual Implication and Ethical Theory', *Aristotelian Society Supplementary Volume*, 1962.

—— *Ethics* (Penguin), 1954.

Ryle, Gilbert, *Dilemmas*, Cambridge, 1954.

Strawson, P. F., *Individuals*, London, 1959.

Whitehead, A. N., *Science and the Modern World*, New York, 1927.

Wittgenstein, L., *Philosophical Investigations*, tr. G. E. M. Anscombe, Oxford, 1953.

IV · BIBLICAL THEOLOGY AND BIBLICAL EXEGESIS

Anderson, B. W., 'The Earth is the Lord's', *Interpretation*, Vol. IX., 1955.

Baillie, John, *The Idea of Revelation in Recent Thought*, London, 1956.

Barr, James, *Biblical Words for Time*, London, 1962.

—— *The Semantics of Biblical Language*, Oxford, 1961.

Barth, Karl, *Church Dogmatics* (Eng. tr. of *Die Kirchliche Dogmatik*), Edinburgh, I, 1 (1936); I, 2 (1956); II, 1 (1957); III, 1 (1958).

—— *A Shorter Commentary on Romans*, tr. D. H. von Daalen, London, 1959.

Berkouwer, G. C., *The Triumph of Grace in the Theology of Karl Barth*, London, 1956.

Bonhoeffer, D., *Creation and Fall*, London, 1959.

Bonnard, P., 'Holy', *Vocabulary of the Bible*, ed. J.-J. von Allmen, London, 1958.

Bouyer, L., '*Mysterion*', *Mystery and Mysticism, A Symposium*, Blackfriars (no editor), London, 1956.

Brockington, L. H., 'The Presence of God, a Study of the Use of the Term "Glory of Yahweh" ', *Expository Times*, October, 1945.

—— 'Glory', *A Theological Word Book of the Bible*, ed. A. Richardson, 1950.

Brown, R. E., 'The Pre-Christian Conception of Mystery', *The Catholic Biblical Quarterly*, Vol. XX, No. 4, October, 1958.

—— 'The Semitic Background of the New Testament *Mysterion*', *Biblica*, Vol. 39, Fasc. 4 (1958); Vol. 40, Fasc. 1 (1959).

Brunner, Emil, *The Divine-Human Encounter*, tr. A. W. Loos, London, 1944.

Brunner, Emil, *Dogmatics*, tr. O. Wyon, London, Vol. I (1949) and
Vol. II (1952).
—— *The Letter to the Romans, A Commentary*, tr. H. A. Kennedy,
London, 1959.
—— *The Mediator*, tr. O. Wyon, London, 1934.
Bultmann, R., *Gnosis*, tr. from *Theologisches Wörterbuch zum Neuen
Testament* (ed. G. Kittel) by J. R. Coates, London, 1952.
—— *Jesus Christ and Mythology*, London, 1960.
Caird, G. B., 'The Biblical Doctrine of the Word', unpublished
paper.
—— *The New Testament Conception of Doxa*, unpublished Oxford
doctoral thesis.
—— *Principalities and Powers*, Oxford, 1956.
Cairns, D. S., *A Gospel without Myth?*, London, 1960.
Campbell, J. Y., 'Authority', and 'Word', *A Theological Word Book
of the Bible*, ed. A. Richardson, London, 1950.
Cherbonnier, E. La B., 'The Logic of Biblical Anthropomorphism',
The Harvard Theological Review, July, 1962.
Childs, B. S., *Myth and Reality in the Old Testament*, London, 1960.
Cobham, J. O., 'Covenant', *A Theological Word Book of the Bible*, ed.
A. Richardson, London, 1950.
Cullmann, O., *Christ and Time*, tr. F. V. Filson, London, 1951.
Dahl, N. A., 'Christ, Creation and the Church', *The Background of
the New Testament and its Eschatology*, ed. W. D. Davies and
D. Daube, Cambridge, 1956.
Danell, G. A., 'The Idea of God's People in the Bible', *The Root of
the Vine*, ed. A. Fridrichsen, London, 1953.
Davies, W. D., *Paul and Rabbinic Judaism*, London, 1948.
Deden, D., 'Le "mystère" Paulinien', *Ephemerides Theologicae Lovani-
enses*, Vol. XIII, 1936.
Dodd, C. H., *The Apostolic Preaching and its Developments*, London,
1936.
—— *The Epistle to the Romans*, London, 1932.
—— *The Interpretation of the Fourth Gospel*, Cambridge, 1953.
—— *The Johannine Epistles*, London, 1946.
—— *The Parables of the Kingdom*, London, 1935.
Ebeling, G., 'The Meaning of "Biblical Theology"', *Journal of
Theological Studies*, VI, 1955.
Ehrhardt, A., '*Creatio ex nihilo*', *Studia Theologica*, Vol. IV, Fasc. I-II,
1951-2.
Eichrodt, W., *Theology of the Old Testament*, Vol. I, tr. J. A. Baker,
London, 1961.
Farrer, Austin, *The Glass of Vision*, London, 1948.
Fisch, H., 'The Analogy of Nature', *Journal of Theological Studies*,
1955.
Foerster, W., '*Ktizo*', *Theologisches Wörterbuch zum Neuen Testament*,
ed. G. Kittel, Band III, Stuttgart, 1938.

Foerster, W., *Lord*, tr. from *Theologisches Wörterbuch zum Neuen Testament* by H. P. Kingdon, London, 1958.

Fuller, R. H., *The Mission and Achievement of Jesus*, London, 1954.

Gärtner, B., *The Areopagus Speech and Natural Revelation*, tr. C. H. King, Uppsala, 1955.

Grayston, K., 'The Darkness of the Cosmic Sea', *Theology*, April, 1952.

Hay, D. W., 'Christianity and Cosmology', *The Canadian Journal of Theology*, October, 1959.

Hebert, A. G., *The Throne of David*, London, 1941.

Hendry, G. S., *God the Creator*, London, 1937.

—— 'Mystery', *A Theological Word Book of the Bible*, ed. A. Richardson, London, 1950.

Horst, F., 'Face to Face, the Biblical Doctrine of the Image of God', tr. J. Bright, *Interpretation*, July, 1950.

Hoskyns, E. (and N. Davey), *The Riddle of the New Testament*, London, 1931.

—— *The Fourth Gospel*, London, 1940.

Jacob, E., *Theology of the Old Testament*, tr. A. W. Heathcote and P. J. Allcock, London, 1958.

Jeremias, J., *The Parables of Jesus*, tr. S. Hooke, London, 1954.

Johnston, George, 'Spirit', *A Theological Word Book of the Bible*, ed. A. Richardson, London, 1950.

Kirkpatrick, A. F., *Commentary on Psalms*, Cambridge, 1902.

Kittel, G., '*Doxa*', *Theologisches Wörterbuch zum Neuen Testament*, ed. G. Kittel, Band II, Stuttgart, 1935.

Knight, G. A. F., *A Christian Theology of the Old Testament*, London, 1959.

Knight, H., 'The Old Testament Conception of Miracle', *Scottish Journal of Theology*, December, 1952.

Knox, J., *Exegesis of Romans*, *The Interpreter's Bible*, Vol. 9, New York, 1954.

Koehler, L., *Hebrew Man*, tr. P. R. Ackroyd, London, 1956.

—— *Old Testament Theology*, tr. A. Todd, London, 1957.

Leuba, J.-L., 'Know', *Vocabulary of the Bible*, ed. J.-J. von Allmen, London, 1958.

Lindeskog, G., 'The Theology of Creation in the Old and New Testaments', *The Root of the Vine*, ed. A. Fridrichsen, London, 1953.

Marsh, John, *The Fulness of Time*, London, 1952.

Martin, A. D., *The Holiness of Jesus*, London, 1934.

Martin-Achard, R., 'Glory', *Vocabulary of the Bible*, ed. J.-J. von Allmen, London, 1958.

Michaeli, F., *Dieu à l'Image de l'Homme*, Paris, 1950.

—— *Le Livre de la Genèse*, Vol. I, Neuchâtel, 1960.

Miegge, G., *Visible and Invisible*, tr. S. Neill, London, 1958.

Moffatt, J., *Commentary on Hebrews*, Edinburgh, 1924.

s

Moule, C. F. D., *The Epistles of Paul the Apostle to the Colossians and to Philemon*, Cambridge, 1957.

North, C. R., *The Old Testament Interpretation of History*, London, 1946.

Nygren, A., *Commentary on Romans*, tr. C. C. Rasmussen, London, 1952.

Östborn, G., *Yahweh's Words and Deeds*, Uppsala Universitets Arsskrift, 1951.

Oesterley, W. O. E., *The Gospel Parables in the Light of their Jewish Background*, London, 1936.

Pedersen, J., *Israel*, London, Vols. I-II (1926) and Vols. III-IV (1940).

Pidoux, G., 'Creation', *Vocabulary of the Bible*, ed. J.-J. von Allmen, London, 1958.

Plummer, A., *A Critical and Exegetical Commentary on the Second Epistle of St Paul to the Corinthians*, Edinburgh, 1915.

—— *Exegetical Commentary on St Matthew's Gospel*, London, 1917.

Rad, G. von, *Genesis, A Commentary*, tr. J. H. Marks, London, 1961.

Ramsey, A. M., *The Glory of God and the Transfiguration of Christ*, London, 1949.

Rankin, O. S., 'Saint', *A Theological Word Book of the Bible*, ed. A. Richardson, London, 1950.

Reid, J. K. S., 'Sanctify', *A Theological Word Book of the Bible*, ed. A. Richardson, London, 1950.

Richardson, A., *The Bible in the Age of Science*, London, 1961.

—— *The Biblical Doctrine of Work*, London, 1952.

—— *Genesis I-XI, Introduction and Commentary*, London, 1953.

—— *An Introduction to the Theology of the New Testament*, London, 1958.

——' The Biblical Knowledge of God', *A Theological Word Book of the Bible*, ed. A. Richardson, London, 1950.

Robinson, H. Wheeler, *Inspiration and Revelation in the Old Testament*, Oxford, 1946.

Robinson, J. Armitage, *St Paul's Epistle to the Ephesians*, 2nd ed. (Macmillan), London, 1922.

Robinson, James M., *A New Quest of the Historical Jesus*, London, 1959.

Robinson, John A. T., *The Body*, London, 1952.

Robinson, Th. H., *The Epistle to the Hebrews*, London, 1933.

Rowley, H. H., *The Biblical Doctrine of Election*, London, 1950.

Rust, E. C., *Nature and Man in Biblical Thought*, London, 1953.

Sanday, W. (and Headlam, A. C.), *A Critical and Exegetical Commentary on the Epistle to the Romans*, 5th ed., Edinburgh, 1902.

Scott, E. F., *The New Testament Idea of Revelation*, London, 1935.

Selwyn, E. G., *The First Epistle of Peter*, London, 2nd ed., 1947.

Smart, James D., *The Interpretation of Scripture*, London, 1961.

Smith, B. T. D., *The Parables of the Synoptic Gospels*, Cambridge, 1937.

Snaith, N. H., *The Distinctive Ideas of the Old Testament*, London, 1945.

Stählin, W., *The Mystery of God*, tr. R. B. Hoyle, London, 1937.

Stauffer, E., *New Testament Theology*, tr. J. Marsh, London, 1955.
Strachan, R. H., *The Second Epistle of Paul to the Corinthians*, London, 1935.
Taylor, V., *The Names of Jesus*, London, 1953.
Thornton, L. S., *Revelation and the Modern World*, London, 1950.
Tresmontant, C., *Essai sur la Connaissance de Dieu*, Paris, 1959.
Vischer, W., 'Words and the Word', tr. J. Bright, *Interpretation*, January, 1949.
Vriezen, Th. C., *An Outline of Old Testament Theology*, Oxford, 1958.
Whitehouse, W. A., 'Christ and Creation', *Essays in Christology for Karl Barth*, ed. T. H. L. Parker, London, 1956.
—— *The Six Days of Creation*, London, 1961.
Wingren, G., *Creation and Law*, tr. R. Mackenzie, Edinburgh, 1961.
Wright, G. E., *God Who Acts*, London, 1952.
—— *The Old Testament against Its Environment*, London, 1950.

V · Miscellaneous

Cooke, D., *The Language of Music*, Oxford, 1959.
Farrer, Austin, *Lord I Believe*, 2nd ed., London, 1958.
Frye, Northrop, *Anatomy of Criticism*, Princeton, 1957.
Izutsu, Toshihiko, *Language and Magic*, Studies in the Humanities and Social Relations, Vol. I, Keio University, Tokyo, 1946.
Scriven, Michael, 'The Age of the Universe', *British Journal for the Philosophy of Science*, November, 1954.

INDEX OF REFERENCES

OLD TESTAMENT

T

OTHER SOURCES

INDEX OF SUBJECTS

INDEX OF AUTHORS